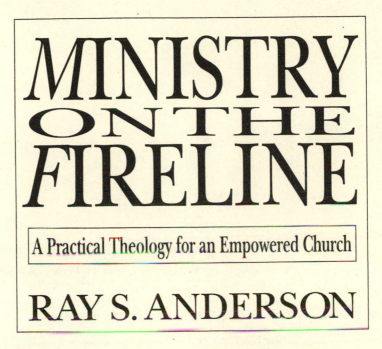

MINISTRY ON THE FIRELINE

A Practical Theology for an Empowered Church

RAY S. ANDERSON

INTERVARSITY PRESS
DOWNERS GROVE, ILLINOIS 60515

InterVarsity Press® is the book-publishing division of InterVarsity Christian Fellowship®, a student movement active on campus at hundreds of universities, colleges and schools of nursing in the United States of America, and a member movement of the International Fellowship of Evangelical Students. For information about local and regional activities, write Public Relations Dept., InterVarsity Christian Fellowship, 6400 Schroeder Rd., P.O. Box 7895, Madison, WI 53707-7895.

Scripture quotations, unless otherwise noted, are from the New Revised Standard Version of the Bible, copyright 1989 by the Division of Christian Education of the National Council of the Churches of Christ in the U.S.A., and are used by permission.

Cover photograph: Paul Steel

ISBN 0-8308-1850-2

Printed in the United States of America ∞

Library of Congress Cataloging-in-Publication Data
Anderson, Ray Sherman.
    Ministry on the fireline: a practical theology for an empowered
  church/Ray S. Anderson.
      p.   cm.
    Includes bibliographical references.
    ISBN 0-8308-1850-2
    1. Mission of the church. 2. Theology, Practical.
  3. Pentecostalism.   I. Title.
  BV601.8.A53   1993
  253—dc20

93-13686

CIP

15	14	13	12	11	10	9	8	7	6	5	4	3	2	1
04	03	02	01	00	99	98	97	96	95	94	93			

To the Fuller Seminary
Doctor of Ministry students and graduates—
my companions and partners
in the praxis of ministry and theology.

Preface

There is a fire burning in my bones as I write. Partly stimulated by a hunger for a theology of the Spirit that is creative and contemporary, and partly stirred up by a growing impatience with a theology that is captive to the cult of the professional scholar.

For seventeen years I have been directly involved with more than fifteen hundred pastors through a doctor of ministry program in theological reflection seminars. Simultaneously I have been teaching theological students at the master's degree level who are being prepared for ministry as pastors, counselors and missionaries. Increasingly I have become aware of the growing discontent among both students and church leaders with the curriculum of theological education. I am troubled by the cynicism toward theological study that I find among Christians at every level of leadership and service.

I think that I have discovered the growing edge of a new vision that will be the beginning of repentance and renewal, both theologically and institutionally. It is not too late. But the time is fast approaching when organized Christianity will have to open its doors and windows to Pentecost and follow the Holy Spirit where it leads—or else sit among the ruins of its own dry wineskins.

Earlier in this century, when the mainline theological schools became preoccupied with questions of biblical criticism and theological speculation, a network of Bible schools sprang up to serve the church in a growing concern for evangelical and biblically astute pastors and leaders. This is already beginning to be repeated in our generation. A significant number of larger churches are creating Bible academies and, in some cases, theological seminaries as a means of preparing men and women for ministry suited more to the needs of the church and its ministry through the members. The church will not wait for the theological seminaries and colleges to discover too late that the tide has turned, the momentum has shifted, and people of God have looked to other sources for help.

This book is an attempt to set an agenda for discussion that will call the church and theological institutions back to a task centered in a mission theology, with critical questions and scholarly discipline once more made the servant rather than the master. This is a call for theological and institutional repentance, with a positive and creative alternative as the church prepares to move into the third millennium, and ever closer to the day in which the Lord will return and conduct his own examination!

Second, this book is an attempt to heal the breach between pentecostal and mainline church theology by providing the contours of a mission theology that is centered in the Pentecost event as a continuing praxis of the Holy Spirit in the encounter between Christ and the world for the sake of liberation and reconciliation. The contemporary resurgence of charismatic and pentecostal events and experiences, accompanied by excitement over "signs and wonders" that sometimes appear to overrun all boundaries, suggests that it is time for a theology of Pentecost that is biblical, ecclesial and oriented to the mission of God in and for the world.

In presenting this book I wish to acknowledge the valuable and significant contribution of my faculty colleague Charles Van Engen, who produced copious notes and suggestions on reading the first draft, and also to David Allan Hubbard, president of Fuller Theological Seminary, for his helpful comments and encouragement upon reading the first draft.

Others who have made contributions to my thinking and the writing of this book will find their suggestions incorporated and sprinkled throughout the pages. I take final and full responsibility, of course, for all that is written, especially for the shortcomings and flaws. My hope is that where my purpose is obscure and my perspective skewed, my passion will burn through, and your hearts will burn too in this walk on the Emmaus road!

Ray S. Anderson
Easter 1993

Firefighters and Theologians: A Parable

Driven by fierce winds and fed by drought-stricken brush and trees, the fire storm moved down the canyons and into the residential areas of Santa Barbara, California, on a hot June evening in 1990. In less than two hours, more than five hundred homes were destroyed. Firefighting units from nearby towns were summoned and dispersed to the areas where flames were leaping from roof to roof. One unit parked on the street immediately in front of a house that was already on fire. The homeowner rushed over and frantically pled for the firefighters to attack the flames destroying his home.

"We cannot move until we receive our orders," the captain responded. "We were instructed not to freelance but to follow the firefighting plan being developed by those at the mobile command post."

To the homeowner, such inaction at a critical time was an outrage. For the firefighters, waiting for orders while watching this one home burn was agonizing and frustrating. Those who are on the fireline where the flames are searing and the smoke stifling know the urgency of immediate action. This is where their training and experience are measured for effectiveness. They are firefighters, and in the midst of flames and smoke they fulfill their calling.

Back at the command post, the larger picture begins to emerge. Some homes must be abandoned so that fire-fighting equipment and personnel can be deployed more strategically in order to save the entire city. This is why individual units are given the order: "No freelancing! Don't try to save the nearest house. You are to go where you are deployed, not where you see the flames."

The firefighter who talked with me about this situation expressed his personal frustration at being placed in this terrible dilemma. But he also expressed confidence in the overall strategy. "As long as those in the command post have themselves felt the flames and inhaled the smoke, I trust their judgment," he said. "But if they are only theorists and not firefighters, I have little confidence in their strategy."

After the fire is under control, while the embers are still smoldering, a debriefing is held, where the captains who were on the fireline meet with the strategists in the command post. Here the wisdom and strategy for fighting the next fire emerge, I was told. Where the strategy did not work as well as expected, those who created it listened to those who were actually fighting the fire and learned from them. The best theory for fighting fires comes from actually engaging in the battle against the flames. Fire-fighting science, I am told, is most effective when done by those whose teacher is the fire.

If Jesus were to address the contemporary leaders and theologians of the church I believe that he might begin this way: "A firefighter went out to fight a fire . . ." And he might well end the parable with this question, "What do you say? Which is the source of truth, the fire that burns or the manuals that firefighters read?"

The metaphor of fire and burning is not unknown in the witness of Scripture to God's manifestation of his Word and Spirit of truth. Moses discovered his mission through an encounter with God in the phenomenon of the "burning bush" (Ex 3:2). Elisha was confirmed in his calling to succeed Elijah when he saw the "chariot of fire and horses of fire" that separated him from Elijah (2 Kings 2:11). Isaiah received his prophetic commission when his mouth was touched by the "live coal" from the altar of fire (Is 6:6-7). Jesus described John the Baptizer as a "burning and shining lamp" (Jn 5:35). John himself said of Jesus, "I baptize you with water; but . . . he will baptize you with the Holy Spirit and fire" (Lk 3:16). And at Pentecost, the Spirit of God descended upon those gathered in the upper room in "tongues as of fire" (Acts 2:3).

Which then is the source of truth for us, the blazing fire or the manuals that we read?

Let us think beyond the parable and expand the metaphor. God's Word of truth has always been a demonstration of God's power and presence before it has become an inspired and infallible writing. The scriptures that make up our biblical canon of the Old and New Testaments are Holy Scripture only because they emerged out of and continue to relate us to God as the One who alone is holy, and to Jesus Christ who is the Holy One (Lk 1:35). The Holy Spirit is the power and presence of God as sanctifier so that the people filled with the Spirit become a "holy people," a dwelling place of God (1 Cor 3:16-17). The same Holy Spirit who sanctifies is also the "Spirit of truth" and the One who will "guide you into all the truth," said Jesus (Jn 16:13).

Saul of Tarsus was arrested by the risen Christ on the road to Damascus, filled with the Holy Spirit and transformed from one who fanatically defended the truth as he had received it in the teaching of the Pharisees to one who learned the truth from the Spirit of Christ. As Jesus promised, the Holy Spirit led him into all truth and he became Paul the apostle of Christ. This same Holy Spirit spoke through the gathered Christians in Antioch and said, "Set apart for me Barnabas and Saul for the work to which I have called them" (Acts 13:2). Paul understood that he and Barnabas were "sent out by the Holy Spirit" (Acts 13:4) and performed signs and wonders through the power of the Holy Spirit (1 Thess 1:5).

Paul also came to see that the manifestation of the Spirit of God in the lives of those to whom he preached was a theological criterion for the development of his theology. The core of his argument to the church in Galatia is based on the fact that the Spirit of Christ has come and produced freedom from an attempt to gain righteousness through the law. This freedom in the Spirit is more than an ethical principle; it offers a new criterion for interpreting the law as fulfilled in Christ's death and resurrection (Gal 5). Saul the Pharisee became Paul the Christian theologian through the truth revealed by the Spirit of Jesus Christ.

Paul's letters to the exploding new churches came into existence through the power of the Holy Spirit as the gospel of Jesus was preached. They became the "manual" for others who were to follow in the mission of proclaiming the gospel of Christ and the ministry of building up the church as the body of Christ. Even so, the source of truth for these inspired writings is always Jesus Christ, who is the "way and the truth and the life" (Jn 14:6). This Jesus Christ is not only a historical person who lived, died and was resurrected, but also the Lord who is present through the Spirit, who has the "mind of Christ" (1 Cor 2:10-16). Those who undertake the mission of God in the world through the anointing of the Spirit are those who are building on this foundation in Jesus Christ.

The truth of all mission and ministry will be disclosed through the revelation of Jesus Christ and his judgment upon that ministry. So be careful, advises Paul, "because it will be revealed with fire, and the fire will test what sort of work each has done" (1 Cor 3:10-13). Even as the manual for the fighting of fires is constantly under review with respect to the reality of the fire, so the theological manuals written by those responsible for the mission of the people of God in the world must be subject to review by the reality of the presence and work of the Spirit through those engaged in "frontline" mission and ministry.

Paul does not even dare to claim absolute authority for the truth of his own writing, though he writes with apostolic authority and with full assurance of having the "mind of Christ." "It is the Lord who judges me," writes Paul. "Therefore do not pronounce judgment before the time, before the Lord comes, who will bring to light the things now hidden in darkness and will disclose the purposes of the heart. Then each one will receive commendation from God" (1 Cor 4:4-5). The authority of Scripture as the Word of God is rooted in its source as inspired of the Holy Spirit through the human authors. The authority of Scripture is also ongoing in its effect as taught, preached and applied through the wisdom and power of the Holy Spirit. "So shall my word be that goes out from my mouth," says the Lord; "it shall not return to me empty, but . . . succeed in the thing for which I sent it" (Is 55:11).

Those who study Scripture as the Word of God without being instructed by the effect of the Word as the Holy Spirit applies it to human lives are like unto those who write dissertations on the nature of fire but have never experienced the flames and smoke! Those who claim to be theologians and teachers of pastors in the church but do not allow their theology to be reviewed and corrected by those who experience God in burning bush and tongues of fire are like unto those who train firefighters to polish the truck but never to fight a fire!

My aim is to set forth a new vision for a Christian mission theology that is biblically based and is singed by the flames of a burning bush and touched by the tongues of fire lighted at Pentecost. This book is written for those who are hungry for a theology that is sweet and digestible as honey and who are sick to death of a fiber-filled oatbran where the kernel is gone and the husks pounded into indigestible wafers.

For the thousands of pastors and church leaders who are on the "firelines" of God's mission in the world, we need a theology that sings, even as it stings, igniting the mind and stirring the heart. I want all to experience burning hearts within by hearing again the living Christ who is the theologian of the Emmaus road (Lk 24). I appeal to every member of the body of Christ, because every member is a minister of Christ, to become an enlightened theologian in life and deed. I seek to write a theology that warms us from the back by the flames from the burning bush and moves before us in the light of the flaming tongues of Pentecost.

I want to fan the fires of renewal already burning and light new ones among the underbrush of the church's institutional bureaucracy. I want the fire to burn back into the theological faculties and to reinvigorate weary and disheartened academicians, opening windows and throwing open doors through which men and women of the Spirit can learn from each other. I want our theological manuals and mission strategies to be opened for audit by those who have stories to tell of God's power and presence and who themselves have been transformed, healed and empowered by the reality of Christ who comes where the two or three are gathered in his name.

We need to begin again with Pentecost; the waiting is over. The Jesus who has ascended comes again through his Holy Spirit to lead us back into the mystery and miracle of God's mission, and forward into the glorious dawn of the reconciliation of the world.

PART 1

CHRISTOPRAXIS

1

THE CHRIST OF PENTECOST

Jesus started a fire and ran away. Most people who do this are called arsonists! The fire, of course, was ignited at the event called Pentecost, when the Holy Spirit descended in "tongues as of fire" upon those gathered in the upper room (Acts 2:3). Jesus promised that he would come to them, but then left when the fire broke out. He ascended into heaven before their very eyes, on the Mount of Olives (Acts 1:9).

Did Jesus really start the fire on earth and vanish into heaven? Having received the Spirit and so becoming the Christ (Messiah) of God, did Jesus leave and send the Spirit as his replacement? Hardly! A world without Jesus but with the Spirit would be one filled with power but not with presence.

Rather, Jesus himself is the flame of the Spirit that warms cold hearts, inspires weary souls and ignites the cheering fire of hope on the darkened hearth of a lost and frightened world. He promised that he would return, and at the Pentecost event he fulfilled that promise in the coming of the Holy Spirit upon the assembled believers. He is the

Christ of Pentecost. The fire of Pentecost reveals his face, as the power of Pentecost ignites the true character of his person.

If our vision of Pentecost is only one of a fire without a face and a power without a presence, then we will be left cold when the fire goes out and weary and weak when the power is gone.

This book is about a revisioning of Pentecost through the Christ of Pentecost. It is a new look at Christ through the glow of Pentecost and a new look at Pentecost through the glory of the risen and present Christ. This allows us to walk with Christ on the Emmaus road (Lk 24) and to experience his power with Paul on the Damascus road (Acts 9).

Many spirits are at work in the world today, just as many were during the New Testament period. The question for the contemporary church is not only, Is the Spirit's presence and power the source of the church's life and ministry? but also, Whence did this Spirit come and whither will it take the church? This chapter lays the foundation for an answer to this question by showing that the Spirit of Pentecost is the reality of the Christ of Pentecost.

The Inner Logic of Pentecost
Pentecost, as a festival in the Jewish religious calendar, received its New Testament significance as the event in which the Holy Spirit came upon those gathered in the upper room following the ascension of the resurrected Christ (Acts 2). From the beginning the early church recognized the significance of Pentecost as marking the birth, or the rebirth, of the church after the resurrection of Christ. Following the celebration of the resurrection and ascension, Pentecost Sunday has an important place in the liturgical calendar of the church.

In more recent church history Pentecost has become associated with a particular form of Christian experience marked by visible manifestations of the Holy Spirit. Those who expect and experience the phenomena of the Spirit in the form of "speaking in tongues" as a form of worship and the exercising of the gifts of the Spirit came to be known as "Pentecostal Christians." The Pentecostal tradition sees the coming of the Spirit as liberating the church from bondage to institutional and formal structures of worship and ministry. This emphasis on the contemporary presence and power of the Spirit tends to diminish the importance of the historical continuity of the church and the transmission of the authority of Christ through the office.

Other traditions, such as the Anglican, link the church more directly to the historical event of the birth, life, death and resurrection of Jesus Christ. This event, theologically known as the Incarnation of God, is seen by some to establish a strong line of continuity with the people of Israel as the earlier form of God's presence in the world. Following the resurrection and ascension of Jesus, the apostles continued this link with the historical Jesus through their own witness as empowered by the Holy Spirit given at Pentecost. The Reformed tradition, following Luther and Calvin, views Pentecost as instrumental to the apostolic mission of extending the church into the world. Pentecost, in this way of thinking, fulfilled its purpose in multiplying the witness of the apostles to Christ, equipping and empowering them to "make disciples of all nations" (Mt 28:19).

In this book I use the term *Pentecost* both in its historical sense as the occasion on which the Spirit came upon the early believers, and to represent the church as the formation of the Spirit of Christ disclosed and manifest in ways that are often experienced in discontinuity with historical and institutional antecedents. My attempt will be to create a bridge between the various traditions, maintaining the continuity that the incarnational emphasis seeks to preserve with the historical expressions of God's salvation history. At the same time my approach will take seriously the reality of the Spirit of God as creating and revealing to us that essential link between mission and church, between experience and faith, and between revelation and history.

I view Pentecost as the pivotal point of faith from which we can look back to the incarnation of God in Jesus of Nazareth and look forward into our contemporary life and witness to Jesus Christ in the world. It is my belief that Pentecost is more than a mere historical and instrumental link between a theology of the Incarnation and a theology of the institutional church.

If this approach at first glance seems novel, it is because Christian theology has generally begun with the revelation of God in Jesus Christ. Christology then is developed by examining the person and work of Christ as foundational for a doctrine of atonement, justification and

sanctification through the indwelling of the Holy Spirit. This theological tradition has served the church well through the centuries, and has
preserved the core of orthodox faith in the face of competing theories
and theologies.

I do not wish to supplant the formal dogmas of Christology, but
rather to approach the historical Christ in his power as the risen Christ.
This, as I will develop more fully in later chapters, is the situation for
the apostle Paul. Following Pentecost, Saul of Tarsus encounters the
risen Christ on the Damascus road and through that experience views
the event of the death and resurrection of Jesus Christ as the "end of
the law" and the beginning of the new humanity in which hostility and
divisions are overcome (Eph 2). The reality of the Spirit of Jesus Christ
became normative for Paul, and yet it was Paul, more than any other
apostle, who bridged the old with the new, and linked Jesus with Adam.

Pentecost can serve as a compass that performs two functions:
theologically it orients us to the inner logic of God's incarnational
manifestation in the world through Jesus Christ, and *experientially* it
orients us to the eschatological vision of redemption for the world
through Christ's presence and coming.

Theologically Pentecost is the beginning point for a theology of
Jesus Christ because the Holy Spirit reveals to us the inner life of God
as the Father of Jesus and of Jesus as the Son of the Father. To receive
the Spirit of God, wrote the apostle Paul, is to "have the mind of Christ"
(1 Cor 2:10, 16). Jesus said, "All things have been handed over to me
by my Father; and no one knows the Son except the Father, and no
one knows the Father except the Son and anyone to whom the Son
chooses to reveal him" (Mt 11:27). The Holy Spirit is the revelation to
us of the inner being of God as constituted by the relations between
Father and Son.

Experientially Pentecost is the beginning point for our own relationship with God through Christ, for apart from the Spirit we are alienated
from the life of God. Paul wrote, "Anyone who does not have the Spirit
of Christ does not belong to him" (Rom 8:9). Pentecost is thus both a
theological and an experiential compass. Without true knowledge of
God (theology) our experience can slip into delusion and even become
demonic. Without authentic experience of Christ (faith) our theology

can become vain and empty speculation.

Pentecost thus serves as a compass that orients both our theology and our experience to the inner logic of God's incarnational and eschatological vision of redemption for the world. Through God's embodiment in Jesus of Nazareth (incarnation) the reality of humanity as created by God is grasped by God and retrieved from its fatal plunge into the abyss of eternal separation from God. But in becoming human God also died and "descended into hell," as the Apostles' Creed tells us. In the resurrection from the dead Jesus Christ puts an end to the power of death and hell. This is the eschatological vision of the redemption of humanity, for the *eschatos,* or "final event," has now already occurred in Christ. In Pentecost we view the inner logic of incarnation and resurrection as the beginning and end of God's vision for humanity. This is true because the Spirit which descended at Pentecost is the Spirit of the resurrected Christ as well as of the incarnate Son, Jesus of Nazareth.

Without the incarnation of the divine Logos who is the eternally begotten Son of God, Pentecost becomes "glossolalia without logos." It becomes a profusion of spirits without the unity of the Spirit. Jesus charged his opponents with failing to understand his speech *(lalia)* because they did not perceive his word *(logos)* (Jn 8:43). It is the incarnate Logos of God, as John clearly saw (1:11, 14), who maintains the unity of Spirit in its diversity.

Without the light of Pentecost as the empowerment of Spirit, the resurrection recedes into mere historical memory. The eschatological reality of the risen Christ as the parousia (the presence empowering each contemporary event of faith and ministry) is replaced by historical theology on the one hand and pragmatic principles for institutional life and growth on the other.

Pentecostal experience without incarnational theology is like a sailboat with neither oars nor rudder—it can only move when there is a wind, though it cannot steer when it is moving. Incarnational theology without pentecostal experience is like a barge of coal anchored to shore. It has fuel but no fire, and even if it should burn it has no engine so as to turn water into steam and steam into power. And so, not being able to transport people, it takes on more coal!

Peter's sermon on that first Christian Pentecost argued that Jesus of Nazareth was attested by God through "deeds of power, wonders, and signs" to be the Christ. This is the Messiah they crucified, but whom God raised up to be exalted with him at his right hand. This Jesus received the promise of the Holy Spirit from the Father, and this Jesus has "poured out this that you both see and hear" (Acts 2:22-23, 33). The early apostles understood very clearly that Pentecost is grounded in the person of Jesus Christ, that is, in incarnation. They remembered his promise of the Spirit by which those who were obedient in love to him and to one another would receive the power of the Spirit and do "greater works than these" (Jn 14:12).

Pentecost is the manifestation of incarnational mission, not merely an infusion of spiritual enthusiasm. For the church to be both incarnational and pentecostal in its theology and praxis, it must recover the dynamic relation between its nature and its mission.

The Inner Logic of the Church's Nature and Mission

When I speak of the nature as well as the mission of the church, I am making a somewhat artificial distinction between what the church is and what it does. In a sense the church becomes what it is (nature) by virtue of its existence as a witness to Christ's continued ministry of reconciliation in the world (mission). Mission and nature thus cannot be separated as though the church could exist without mission, or as though mission could take place without the existence of the church as the presence and power of Christ.

Nature and mission are connected as constitutive parts of the church by the reality of the Holy Spirit as the Spirit of the historical Jesus as well as the Spirit of the resurrected Jesus Christ. The Spirit of the resurrected Christ directs the church toward its future. The Spirit of the historical Jesus calls the church back to its apostolic foundation and grounding in the mission of God through the Abrahamic covenant for the sake of all humanity.

The Holy Spirit is thus the creative power and presence of Jesus Christ as the "inner logos" or inner logic of God's mission of redemption. Thus the experience of the Holy Spirit at Pentecost was not only an event that Christ promised but an event in which the same Christ continues to be present as the goal, or *telos,* of history.

The inner logic of the Holy Spirit, which connects the mission of the church with its nature, can be expressed through the concept of *praxis.* I have chosen this word carefully in order to capture the extraordinary relation between the *person* of Jesus Christ as the ascended Lord and the *presence* of Christ as disclosed through the manifestation of the Holy Spirit.

Before his crucifixion and resurrection Jesus demonstrated in both his person and presence the power of God. As the anointed one (the Messiah), Jesus manifested the power of the kingdom of God to forgive sin, banish demons, heal the sick and raise the dead. Jesus constantly pointed to the work which God performed through him and which testified to the power of God. Even if they did not believe in him, Jesus counseled his contemporaries to "believe the works" so that they might know that "the Father is in me and I am in the Father" (Jn 10:37-38). The kingdom of God that was to come into the present out of the future was already present in a provisional form through the person and work of Jesus Christ as the *praxis* of the Spirit.

Praxis is quite different from the mere application of truth or theory. The word *practice* ordinarily refers to the methods and means by which we apply a skill or theory. This tends to separate truth from method or action so that one assumes that what is true can be deduced or discovered apart from the action or activity which applies it in practice. In this way of thinking, truth is viewed as existing apart from its manifestation in an event or an act.

I mean by *praxis* something of what Aristotle meant when he distinguished between *poiesis* as an act of making something where the *telos* lay outside of the act of making, and *praxis* as an act that includes the *telos* within the action itself. The *telos* of something is its final purpose, meaning or character.[1]

Praxis is an action that includes the telos, or final meaning, and the character of truth. It is an action in which the truth is discovered through action, not merely applied or "practiced." In praxis one is not only guided in one's actions by the intention of realizing the telos, or purpose, but one discovers and grasps this telos through the action itself.

For example, a builder might be asked to build a house in accordance with a specific design and blueprint. When the house is finished he is paid in full if the building has been constructed according to the design. If, after several years, persons living in the house commit illegal or immoral acts, the builder of the house cannot be held liable for these actions. In other words, the ultimate use of the house, its telos, was not part of the builder's responsibility. This is poiesis, not praxis. In praxis the telos of the action includes the ultimate purpose or goal of the action, so that not only is one held accountable for the final purpose, but through the action the truth of the action becomes revealed.

Let us consider the task of constructing a sermon from the Bible. If the sermon manuscript is the goal, based upon exegetical methods that are faithful to the text, then the preacher has fulfilled her or his responsibility when the manuscript is completed and the sermon is read. This is poiesis. And if, when the sermon is preached, no one's heart is convicted of sin and turned to God, then the telos of the sermon as an event of the Word of God preached is not reached. The sermon manuscript by itself is not the praxis of God's Word. Praxis includes the effect of the Word as well as a presentation of it.

The homiletics professor in seminary might award an A grade to the sermon manuscript, but from the standpoint of the purpose of the Word of God, the sermon has not realized its telos until the Word of God has had an effect. "So shall my word be that goes out from my mouth," says God through the prophet Isaiah, "it shall not return to me empty, but it shall accomplish that which I purpose, and succeed in the thing for which I sent it" (Is 55:11). The preparing and preaching of a sermon from the Word of God ought to be praxis, not poiesis. It follows then that the *effect* of the Word of God is bound to the authority and power of the Word in the same way as its source is inspired by the Spirit of God. What the Word of God creates in its proclamation belongs to the truth and authority of the Word, and not to the human act of proclaiming.

When Jesus taught he identified his words with the very truth of God (Jn 8:46). Jesus also said that to believe these words and to live by them was the very work of God: "This is the work of God, that you believe in him whom he has sent" (Jn 6:29). The transformation of the human heart in response to the Word of God is a work of God. This work of God is bound to the truth and authority of the Word of God as a praxis of Word and Spirit. "The words that I have spoken to you are spirit and life" (Jn 6:63).

In the case of a sermon, the truth of the Word of God resides in the Scripture text as originally inspired by the Holy Spirit through the human author. The praxis of the preaching event, however, goes beyond the preparation of a sermon manuscript and includes the power of the inspired Word to accomplish God's purpose in the human heart. The truth and authority of the inspired text thus finds its completion (telos) in producing a truthful response. This is what I mean by praxis as the "inner logic" of the relation of the written Word to the preached Word.

A theology of preaching thus emerges from within the context of the preached Word and not in abstraction from it. This means that the inspired Word of Scripture contains truths that are only discovered and revealed through the praxis of teaching and preaching. This does not mean that we can disregard careful exegetical methods of determining what the biblical text says. On the contrary, we must take up the biblical text with full commitment to its intrinsic character as the Word of God written. At the same time, by the authority of the Scripture itself, we must take with the same seriousness the praxis of the Holy Spirit by which our preaching and teaching reaches God's purpose in the transformation of human hearts and lives.

In praxis God's truth is revealed through the structures of reality by which God's actions and presence are disclosed to us through our own actions. Our human actions do not constitute the praxis of God. Rather, God acts through our human actions to reveal the truth. The truth of God's Word, for example, is not something which can be extracted from the Bible by the mind so that one can possess this truth as a formula or doctrine without regard to its purpose of bringing us "into the truth." There is also true doctrine as opposed to false doctrine. But God's truth does not end with our concept of truth, nor is the human mind the absolute criterion for God's truth. God is the authority for what is true of God. How could it be otherwise? "Although everyone is a liar," wrote Paul, "let God be proved true" (Rom 3:4).

When Jesus experienced the work of God through a miraculous healing on the sabbath (Jn 9), he argued that the truth of the sabbath was to be found in the restoration of humanity, not in keeping the law of sabbath. When the Pharisees challenged his view of the sabbath, he responded, "The sabbath was made for humankind, not humankind for the sabbath; so the Son of Man is lord even of the sabbath" (Mk 2:27). This is what I mean by praxis. The work of God in our midst discloses to us the Word of God, even as the Word of God reveals its truth in producing God's work. God's Word of truth reaches its telos in healing, making whole and restoring God's created purpose. This is the praxis of God's Word as truth.

The praxis of Pentecost is revealed in the story of Peter's preaching in the house of Cornelius, a Roman centurion and a Gentile. Peter acknowledges that what he is doing is unlawful according to the Mosaic law, but says that he has been persuaded by a vision from God that he must preach the gospel to Cornelius (Acts 10:28). While Peter was still telling the story of Jesus, the Holy Spirit came upon "all who heard the words" and, as a result, Peter said, "Can any one withhold the water for baptizing these people who have received the Holy Spirit just as we have?" (Acts 10:47). Peter did not come to the conclusion that circumcision was no longer necessary through reflection upon the Old Testament Scriptures, but through the praxis of the Spirit operating through the witness to Jesus Christ.

The continued presence and work of the Holy Spirit constitute the praxis of Christ's resurrection. This means that the truth of resurrection is not only the fact of a historical event but the presence and power of a resurrected person, Jesus Christ. Christ's work of making peace between humans and God does not take place through the application of methods, ideologies or even theories derived from Scripture. Rather, Christ himself "makes peace" through the praxis of his Spirit in a dialogical relationship with our truth and methods.[2]

Pentecost places us into the praxis of Christ's reconciling death and resurrection, and carries out its theological task by informing the church of its nature and mission from the perspective of the world as loved and reconciled to God through Christ (2 Cor 5:18-20).

It became clear to the apostles that in receiving the Spirit as a praxis of ministry through which thousands came to saving knowledge of Christ, the mission and ministry of God through incarnation were being revealed. As nature and mission are both necessary to define the reality of Jesus Christ, so nature and mission are necessary to the reality of the church. The church can become the church only through the mission of the Spirit as the continued reality of the incarnate Word of God, Jesus Christ, raised from the dead.

The church is a continuing witness to the presence and power of the crucified and resurrected Messiah, Jesus Christ our Lord. The church is not an "extension of the Incarnation" through its historical and institutional life alone. Jesus Christ himself is the continuing mission of God in the world and thus the reality that constitutes the church as the body of Christ. Mission, thus understood, precedes and creates the church. In other words, the nature of the church is revealed through its existence in the world as the mission of the people of God who receive the Spirit of Pentecost as their point of origin and means of empowerment.

The nature of the church as the continuing mission of God through Jesus Christ is determined by its relation to Pentecost, not only to the Great Commission given by Jesus prior to his crucifixion and resurrection. The command "Go and make disciples of all nations" (Mt 28:19) anticipates the promise "You will receive power when the Holy Spirit has come upon you; and you will be my witnesses" (Acts 1:8).

If the Great Commission gives the church its instructions, Pentecost provides its initiation and power. "At the beginning of the history of the New Testament Church stands the Pentecost event," writes Harry Boer. "It does not stand *approximately* at the beginning, or as a first among several significant factors, but it stands *absolutely* at the beginning. . . . It does not, however, stand in *isolation* from preceding and succeeding redemptive history."[3]

Boer argues persuasively that Pentecost, not the Great Commission, was a conscious ingredient in the mission thinking of the early church. This is set in contrast to much of the modern mission emphasis, which attempts to locate the mission imperative of the church on obedience to the Great Commission rather than to Pentecost. This tendency has sometimes led to a dichotomy between the church and its mission program. If we view the nature of the church as a continuation of the mission of Christ through the power of the Spirit, then the Great Commission becomes a command that is to be heard by a church already empowered by the Holy Spirit to fulfill that command as its very nature. The missionary thrust and program of the church thus issues out of its own nature and not as an addendum or appendage.

Karl Barth points to the same priority of Pentecost when he says, "As the quickening power which accomplishes sanctification [the Holy Spirit] comes down with utter novelty and strangeness from above (as described in the story of Pentecost) and thus constitutes an absolute basis and starting point."[4] It is in this sense that one must speak of the nature of the church as revealed in its participation in the mission of God as empowered and directed by the Holy Spirit.

In suggesting that Pentecost determines the nature of the church, I am attempting to recover an essential Hebraic concept of history as oriented toward the future rather than rooted deterministically in the past. The nature of the people of God as promised in the Abrahamic covenant and as constituted by the Exodus covenant under the leadership of Moses can never be explained by historical and sociological criteria alone. The kingdom of God was experienced in history and as history, but not determined finally by worldly history. The author of Hebrews sees the community of faith correctly as always moving from the present into the future, from the known to the unknown, from the temporal to the eternal. So it was that Abraham "looked forward to the city that has foundations, whose builder and maker is God" (Heb 11:10 RSV).

In the same way, the author of Hebrews reminds us, Jesus is the "pioneer and perfecter of our faith, who for the sake of the joy that was set before him endured the cross, disregarding its shame, and has taken his seat at the right hand of the throne of God" (Heb 12:2). Pentecost calls us to be a people of God whose nature it is to be moving toward the goal already determined for it through the resurrection of Jesus Christ from the dead. To say that the church is the body of Christ, or the community of Christ, is to speak of the nature of the church as grounded in a relationship with Christ as the Lord who is present and who is coming. When the church prays "Thy kingdom come," it reveals that its nature is open to the coming of the kingdom and thus is a witness to the reality of the kingdom already manifest through the Holy Spirit.

This accords with more recent views of nature as open, relational and vital as opposed to closed, static and lifeless. The Greek concept of nature was abstract and identified it more as a metaphysical substance than a physical process. The early theologians in the first few centuries tended to rely upon this Greek concept of nature, so that the language of the christological creeds that emerged from this period speaks of the natures of Christ in static, abstract terms. Once this was done, it became virtually impossible to define the relations between the human and divine natures, except in somewhat paradoxical language. This view of nature led to mechanistic views of the world, which dominated the Cartesian and Newtonian periods following the Enlightenment. In contemporary physics, for example, the nature of the physical world is now held to be open to contingency and change rather than closed in on itself.[5]

When the Spirit poured out at Pentecost is directly related to the Spirit of the resurrected Jesus of Nazareth, the Christ, the Pentecost event forms the basis for the nature of the church. Pentecost could not have occurred as it did without the resurrection of Jesus of Nazareth. It is important to know that the Spirit which came upon the disciples at Pentecost is the Spirit of the resurrected and incarnate Son of God, Jesus Christ. In this way we avoid thinking that we can receive the Spirit in the same manner that Jesus did. It is not the Spirit which provides continuity between the mission of God in Jesus and in the church; rather, it is Jesus Christ himself, through the coming of the Holy Spirit.

The nature of the church created and sustained by the Spirit of Pentecost is grounded in the mission of God through Israel, which resulted in the incarnation and continued through the power of the resurrection and the giving of the Holy Spirit. It was not only that the Messiah (Christ) was crucified and raised again. It was Jesus of Nazareth who was raised from the dead and who, as Paul writes, was sent forth by God as his "Son, born of woman, born under the law, in order to redeem those who were under the law" (Gal 4:4-5). Born of woman, wrote Paul, not "born of the Spirit." So it is Jesus of Nazareth who fulfilled the divine mission, not simply the Spirit that anointed him.

There is a sense in which we approach the incarnation more directly through mission (Pentecost) than we would by attempting to define the church first of all in its nature as a continuation of incarnation. This is because when we speak of incarnation we must speak of the incarnate One. The presence and power of the Holy Spirit mediates our relation to the historical Jesus Christ and thus to the incarnation of God.

One cannot avoid the praxis of the Holy Spirit in creating a theology of the church. One cannot set aside Pentecost as marginal and resurrection as unnecessary in order to link the church directly to the concept of "Emmanuel"—God with us in the form of the person and teaching of Christ. Any attempt to do this tends to confuse the humanity of the church in its ideal form with the humanity of God in Christ as the real form of the church.

A theology of the church as the continuing mission of the resurrected Christ, on the other hand, enables us to view the church as the form of the resurrected Christ present in his "new nature," the church as the dwelling place of the Spirit. When we begin theological reflection upon the nature of the church in its pentecostal form, we are led to a clearer understanding of the church in its incarnational form as the continued mission and ministry of God in Christ. Without Pentecost as the beginning, the church can lose its connection with the mission and ministry of God. The church then becomes the incarnation of a human ideal rather than the continuing mission of the incarnate One, Jesus Christ.

When the nature of the church becomes the object of theological reflection in such a way that it is separated from the context of the life of the church in its praxis of the Spirit, the doctrine of the church becomes more of an academic enterprise than a praxis event. This leaves the life and ministry of the church to be determined by pragmatic and often nontheological methods. When students who are preparing for ministry within the church leave seminary, they are often well-prepared academically for their theological examinations, but ill-equipped to examine critically the tactics and methods that they must use to be successful in ministry. As I have often suggested to my students, the moment you graduate from seminary, all of your theology becomes historical theology! Only when one demonstrates competence in theological reflection from the context and praxis of ministry can theology be kept relevant to the church and ministry be protected from capitulation to sheer pragmatism. This creates a gap between the factual existence of the church in its ministry praxis and the theological reflection on the origin and nature of the church.

Christoph Schwöbel has spoken insightfully to this situation, and his comments are worth quoting in full:

> This essential interconnection between the practical questions of the life of the Church and the theoretical problems of the theological understanding of the Church, and their relation to the focal point of the nature of Christian faith and its constitution, is so important because we are today painfully aware of the gap between the factual existence of the Church in society and the theological fomulae in which its nature is expressed. This leads to a situation in which the practical questions of day-to-day living in the Church are often decided on the basis of pragmatic and wholly untheological considerations, while the ecclesiology of academic theology, operating, as it seems, at one remove from the social reality of the Church, seems often unable to relate to the practical questions which face the Church in its struggle for survival in a society more and more shaped by a plurality of religious and quasi-religious world views. The challenge of the ecclesiology of the Reformers is the challenge of a theological reflection on the Church which is closely related to the practical problems of Christian life in the Church, and which is at the same time theoretically rigorous.[6]

The situation that Schwöbel describes, and the one that I am attempting to overcome in this chapter, results from a failure to understand the inner logic of the church's nature and mission as grounded in the relation of Pentecost to resurrection and incarnation.

Christian theology must be a contextual theology because it is a theology of the living God who continues to be present to the world in the context of its historical reality. In his timely book *Thinking the Faith*, Douglas Hall says:

> It is particularly the Holy Spirit who provides the dogmatic basis for

the insistence that theological reflection necessarily means engagement with the historical context. The corrective to a theology which has neglected or dismissed the context by means of a rationalized and doctrinaire concentration on the second person of the Trinity is a theology which is goaded into engagement with the worldly reality by a fresh apprehension of the Holy Spirit. For the Spirit will permit us to rest neither in the church nor in doctrinal formulations that know everything ahead of time. The Spirit will drive us, as it drove Jesus, to the wilderness of worldly temptation and the garden of worldly suffering.[7]

The church is not only Spirit-filled, it is raised with Christ and through Christ has access to the Father in the one Spirit (Eph 2:17-18). As the inner life of Jesus in his relation to the Father is constitutive of Christology, so the inner life of the church in its experience of Jesus Christ by the presence of the Holy Spirit is constitutive of ecclesiology. The Spirit which creates the church through the renewal of life and faith is the Spirit of the resurrected Jesus Christ. As Jesus Christ was raised from the dead by God, the Father of glory, and so designated Son of God, we too have been made alive, argues the apostle Paul, as a dwelling place of God in the Spirit and so become children of God (Rom 1:3; Eph 1:5, 20; 2:2, 22).

This is the theological axis on which the church turns in its mission and ministry to the world. Jesus' mission and ministry were carried out in the power of the Spirit, though he is not an "incarnation" of the Spirit. He is the incarnation of the divine Logos, not the divine Spirit. The Spirit of God dwells fully in Jesus, but does not assume the flesh of Jesus in the same way that the divine Logos became flesh. This is why we say that the Spirit has no incarnation of its own.

Neither is the church an incarnation of the Spirit, as though our own flesh and blood could replace that of Jesus. The church is a human institution, but its humanity cannot replace that of Jesus. Nor is the church an incarnation of Christ, as though his deity could assume the form of our humanity so that the church could become the one mediator between all persons and God. Yet the church is an incarnational presence of Jesus Christ in the world through its inner life grounded by the Spirit in Christ and in solidarity with all men and women in a common humanity.

On the one hand, the nature and mission of the church are dependent upon the vital life that it shares with Christ. For this, the church receives and celebrates its life in the Spirit, for without the Spirit it cannot have its life rooted in Christ. On the other hand, the nature and mission of the church are dependent upon its bearing the continuing ministry of Christ to the Father on behalf of the world. For this, the church receives and exercises the gifts of the Spirit through its members as the ministry of Christ.

If the church were to abandon the mission and ministry of Christ which now take place in the humanity of the church's solidarity with the world, the church would forsake its share in the reconciliation of the world to God through Christ (2 Cor 5:18-21). If the church were to lose the presence and life of the Spirit as the source of its own existence and life, the church would sever its vital connection to Christ so that its worship would become worthless and its religion mere ritual.

The church's nature and mission are bound together in the same way that incarnation and Pentecost are linked, with death and resurrection being the inner logic of atonement for sin and reconciliation to God. This led Paul to say that the church is the mystery *(mystērion)* of God now revealed through Christ, that "through the church" the manifold wisdom of God would become known throughout the entire cosmos (Eph 3:9-10). Because Jesus Christ himself is this mystery (Eph 3:4), Paul can say that there is "one body and one Spirit, just as you were called to the one hope of your calling, one Lord, one faith, one baptism, one God and Father of all" (Eph 4:4-6).

The mission and ministry of the church are grounded in its conception and birth as the community of those who are children of God, whose lives are personally drawn into the very life and being of Christ. Those who are born anew by the Spirit of God are not merely Christians or followers of Christ, but have been adopted into the filial relationship between the Son and the Father as children of God and "fellow heirs with Christ" (Rom 8:17).

When I refer to the mission of the church, I mean the mission and ministry of the entire people of God spilling out into the world in fulfillment of the apostolic commission to "go into the world." The church's mission is not to build up an empire or kingdom that it controls, but to disperse the mission of God through the lives of its members as well as the various groups and organizations that they form. The church finds its being in its mission, under the guidance and power of the Spirit. Its intention and direction is oriented to the world which God loves and to which it is sent.

By the ministry of the church I mean its life, activities and programs by which it carries out this mission. Jesus had both a mission to fulfill as the apostle who was faithful to his calling (Heb 3:2-3), and a ministry by which he carried out this mission. The church carries out ministries and so participates in God's mission. In this book the ministry of the church should always be understood as grounded in the mission of God in Christ to reconcile the world to himself (2 Cor 5:19). In this way the ministries and programs of the church are informed by the praxis of the Spirit in the life of the members of the community.

Before there is a mandate of mission given to the church, there is the mandate of God's love, which issues in his own mission to the world. The church does not exist otherwise than in its life given to its members as the visible and corporate manifestation of God's mission to the world. The church has no doctrine of God except its understanding of God as revealed in his mission to the world. The church has no theology of mission except that it articulates the theology of God's mission originating in the creative will of the Father, accomplished through the reconciling life, death and resurrection of Jesus Christ, his Son, and continuing in the world through the redemptive power and presence of the Holy Spirit, of which the church is the servant and sign of this kingdom power.

The Christ of Pentecost
We cannot have a Pentecost without Christ. He did not cast the firebrand of the Spirit into the world and then withdraw. Pentecost is Christ's parousia, his manifestation in the world, empowering his disciples with his presence as they bear witness to him to the ends of the earth. This is the fulfillment of his promise before his crucifixion: "I will not leave you orphaned; I am coming to you" (Jn 14:18).

Nor can we have a Christ without Jesus of Nazareth. The anointing of Jesus by the Spirit to be the Messiah (the Christ) was preceded by his conception and birth as the very incarnation of the Logos of God existing with God before the world began (Jn 1:1-4). The divine Son of God came into the world through the historical and human birth of Jesus of Nazareth. The early Christians, of course, discovered his divine sonship only in retrospect. His mission revealed to them his origin as the "only begotten" Son of the Father, conceived by the Holy Spirit. Following his baptism, this trinitarian reality was secured in the tradition by the witness of John: "the Father loves the Son and has placed all things in his hands" (Jn 3:35), and by the descent of the Spirit upon him and the voice from heaven, "This is my beloved Son" (Mt 3:16-17 RSV).

From this we might conclude that the growing awareness of his anointing to be the Messiah led Jesus deeper into his self-consciousness as the Son of Man, the one spoken of by Daniel (7:13), with a mission on earth that has its origin in heaven. His understanding of his messianic mission led Jesus to discover his unique origin as one "born from above" (Jn 6:38). Or, to put it another way, in his personal development as a young man Jesus came to know himself as having a special relationship with God that later came to be expressed in filial terms as being the Son of the Father.

In fulfilling the office of Messiah by demonstrating the power and work of God, Jesus exemplified his obedience and faithfulness as the Son of the Father. He did not become a Son of God through obedience, but because he was the Son of God, he "learned obedience" and thus became the source of salvation for others (Heb 5:8-9). Already in the Old Testament obedience is the primary characteristic of those who have a relationship to God. With Jesus this obedience has its source in his very being as the one begotten of God from all eternity, as later Christology was to affirm. Using less technical language, Jesus spoke of his life as the bread of heaven which comes from above and gives eternal life, in contrast to the bread which the people of Israel ate in the wilderness "and they died" (Jn 6).

Jesus' messianic mission under the anointing of the Spirit disclosed the original source of his obedience as issuing out of the filial love of the Son for the Father and the Father for the Son. The power of God manifest in the form of the Spirit that came upon Jesus is not what made him the divine Son of God. Rather, Jesus has the source of his being in a unique relation with God that can only be spoken of in terms of being the eternal Son of the eternal Father.

In this one person, born of God, loved of God, the Spirit of God formed an indissoluble union with the Spirit of Jesus. Jesus forever became the Christ of God. Henceforth, as the apostle Paul clearly shows, the Spirit of God and the Spirit of Jesus Christ are experienced as one and the same Holy Spirit. In his letter to the Roman Christians, Paul freely uses the phrases "Spirit of God," "Spirit of Christ" and "Holy Spirit" interchangeably (see Rom 8:9-11; 9:1). Paul's emphasis is on the experience of the Spirit of Christ as Holy Spirit. Hence he does not stress the essential differentiation between the Holy Spirit and Jesus as Son of God in this context. It is the union of Jesus as Son with the Spirit of God that Paul wants us to understand.

Death did not break that union. Through the power of that Spirit, Jesus Christ was raised from the dead bearing with him all that belongs to Jesus as divine Son of God and bringing to us all that belongs to Christ as the presence and power of the divine Spirit of God. Pentecost is not a replacement for Jesus Christ, but always the manifestation of Jesus Christ through the presence and power of the Holy Spirit.

Our vision of Christ is illuminated by the Spirit of Christ poured out at Pentecost (Acts 2). For those who were intimately acquainted with Jesus, such as the disciples, the Christ of Pentecost was familiar and friendly. If, on occasion, they sometimes longed for the days when they had him to themselves, they now lived for the days in which his power and presence could be experienced by so many others. Jesus Christ is alive and well! And he continues his ministry in the world through the Holy Spirit which came upon the believers at Pentecost and continues to abide with and empower Christians throughout the world.

2

A VISION OF HEALING
AND HOPE

One of my former students, now an ordained Methodist pastor, told me of an encounter with a veteran of the Vietnam War whom she visited in the hospital. He was bitter and cynical, and carried a hatred for the Vietnamese as well as anger against God. When released from the hospital he began to attend the church where she was pastor. One Sunday, during the celebration of the Lord's Supper, there was a time of "passing of the peace," where members of the congregation moved about sharing with one another the peace of Christ. Following the service, this man came up to the pastor and said, "I have had a marvelous healing experience!" As he recounted it, he had approached a woman in the congregation and said, "The peace of the Lord be with you." This woman responded, "And with you also," but in the Vietnamese language! Embracing her, he reported feeling a release and deliverance from his anger and bitterness and a deep inner healing and peace with God.

In telling me this story my friend said, "The incredible thing is that

we do not have anyone attending who is Vietnamese, and there was no
one in our congregation that morning who could speak Vietnamese!"
We understood this to be a personal Pentecost experience for this man.
I see it also as a form of Christopraxis, where a vision of healing and
hope was released through the power of Christ's presence in the
context of human life and love.

A Vision of Life in the Midst of Death

There is no gospel of suffering, no good news in pain. Sorrow has no
healing power, and in death is found no vision of hope. The cross on
which Jesus died was an end, not a beginning. Those who had hoped
the most were those who lost the most. Those who kept their wits about
them in order to perform the "last rites" of burial were moved more by
compassion than by hope. Death and dying is an ancient art, practiced
with patience and rituals transmitted from generation to generation.
For all of the practice humanity has had, nothing new has been learned
through dying. Nor was crucifixion a novelty, despite the occasional
injustice of a good man being put to death. We shrink from the brutality
of the cross, but find no meaning in gazing upon it.

There is no praxis in crucifixion, no vision of victory, no revelation
of truth. It is a darkness in which no light shines. A crucifixion without
a resurrection is a cross without redemption, agony without atonement.
Even the empty tomb, discovered by faithful followers as well as by
fearful guards, produced no joy and brought no deliverance. It was the
vision of Jesus himself, triumphantly and vibrantly alive, that shattered
the spell of death and healed their hurting hearts.

Thus is born the praxis of Christ, not a spiritual vision in the minds
of the believers, not a ghostly apparition that plays games with our
senses, but an undeniable presence with transforming power. This was
not a spiritual resurrection, dangling in the empty space created by a
recent loss.

For forty days the resurrected Jesus Christ moved in and out of the
lives of those who had known him in his living and dying, and who now
came to know him in his resurrection presence and power. While
appearing to them, he confirmed to them the reality of his living
presence as that of the same Jesus who had died, and spoke to them of

the kingdom of God (Acts 1:3). There is no mention made of any mighty works that Jesus performed, such as healing the sick or raising the dead. Instead, we read that he promised that they would be "baptized with the Holy Spirit" and would receive power to be his witnesses, and then he ascended into heaven before their eyes (Acts 1:5-9). Suddenly, as they were gathered for the Pentecost festival, they were filled with the Spirit and gave witness to all who had assembled in Jerusalem concerning this Jesus who was crucified, raised from the dead and made "both Lord and Christ" (Acts 2:36).

This is where Christopraxis begins. For in giving witness to Jesus Christ under the power of the Spirit every person heard in his or her native tongue. This miracle was not so much that of *speaking* in foreign tongues, but in *hearing* the story of Jesus in each person's native language. If we assume that Jesus of Nazareth could only speak in his mother tongue of Hebrew or Aramaic, with perhaps some acquired ability in Roman and Greek language skills, the risen Jesus Christ through the praxis of the Holy Spirit can now be heard in every human tongue! A wounded-in-the-spirit man hears Christ speak to him a word of peace in the Vietnamese language, and has a vision of healing and hope.[1]

A Vision of Christ in the Eyes of the Blind

It is worth noting that the first recorded miracle of healing following the sermon Peter preached on the day of Pentecost took place in the precincts of the temple. As they entered the temple to observe the stated hour of prayer, Peter and John were accosted by a man lame from birth who lay daily at the gate of the temple seeking alms of those who entered (Acts 3:1-10). The contradiction between the temple as the holy place of God's presence and the presence of the man deformed in body since birth is striking and tragic. The temple worship had become a practice of religion without a praxis of healing and hope. Those who served the temple had no vision of the afflicted as the objects of God's special love and concern. The afflicted had no vision of God beyond the maintenance of their pitiable condition through an appeal to the guilty conscience of the healthy for a daily dole of alms. Lack of vision is an affliction that blinds the eye and binds the spirit.

Empowered by the Spirit of Christ, Peter altered his customary practice and made a strategic intervention. Peter "looked intently at him . . . and said, 'Look at us . . . I have no silver or gold, but what I have I give you; in the name of Jesus Christ of Nazareth, stand up and walk.' " Taking the man by the hand, he raised him up and, "jumping up, he stood and began to walk, and he entered the temple with them, walking and leaping and praising God" (Acts 3:4-8).

Peter placed himself directly in the line of the man's vision, limited as it was by the expectation of a few alms, and summoned the man to look directly at him. Peter made no attempt to correct the man's limited vision nor to instruct him in faith. Instead he created a target within himself as a focal point for the man's impaired vision—"look at us"—and thus provided an immediate encounter between the man and Jesus Christ.

Three truths emerge from this incident to reveal something of what I mean by "Christopraxis."[2]

First, there is no Christ for the world other than the Christ who is present in the form of the Holy Spirit indwelling persons and empowering them for witness and ministry. There is no point in gazing into heaven as the disciples did at Jesus' ascension, as though we could have a vision of Christ by looking away from the earth. The angels rebuked the disciples for this mistake, and we can assume that it was meant to be a word of warning for each of us in our own time and place (Acts 1:10-11). Nor should we attempt to direct the attention of others to a Christ who stands above or apart from our own presence, as though an invisible Christ were more easily seen and grasped than an embodied Christ! Christ is not present in those who are not indwelt by the Spirit (Rom 8:9). But as Paul said, "If the Spirit of him who raised Jesus from the dead dwells in you, he who raised Christ from the dead will give life to your mortal bodies also through his Spirit that dwells in you" (Rom 8:11). If the world is to have a vision of Christ in its blindness to God, it must look into the face of those who have the Spirit of Christ.

Second, we can discern from this incident the fact that Christ is revealed to us through his work in the lives of others with whom we live and to whom we minister. Peter and John cannot see Christ by looking into a mirror. The healed man, leaping and praising God, becomes their vision of Christ! In his healing they see the work of Christ—the praxis of Christ—as the continued ministry of God's Spirit in restoring lost humanity to health, wholeness and praise of God. Those who perform service to God in the temple without a vision of humanity in its brokenness and blindness lose their own vision of God. The practice of religion as service to God without the praxis of religion as God's service to humanity becomes vain and useless, to both God and humanity.

The third truth is revealed in the healing of the man. The power of the Spirit is identified as the person and presence of Jesus of Nazareth as the source of the healing. "In the name of Jesus Christ of Nazareth, walk," Peter exclaims. In the praxis of the Holy Spirit not only is there a manifestation of a Spirit of Pentecost but of the Spirit of Jesus, the very incarnation of God. This is why in the previous chapter I took such pains to show that it is the Christ of Pentecost who is the praxis of Pentecost. Here we see a vision of the historical Jesus emerging far beyond that of historical memory.

In the praxis of Christ following Pentecost we now have a vision of Christ in retrospect, uncovering what was hidden from those who accompanied him in his earthly life and ministry. In this vision our own eyes are opened to see more clearly the inner logic of the gospel as Christ's obedient service of God in reaching out to a lost humanity while, at the same time, offering up a true service to God from the side of humanity through his own life of prayer, worship and obedience unto death.

The ministry of Jesus prior to his death and resurrection is viewed from the perspective of the praxis of Pentecost as it took place in the period immediately following the giving of the Holy Spirit at Pentecost (Acts 2). For this reason the accounts of Jesus' earthly life and ministry as recorded in the four Gospels were written after the early Christians had experienced the praxis of the risen Christ. Jesus did not become the Messiah (the Christ) through resurrection. Rather, because he had already become the Messiah as the incarnate Son of God, Jesus Christ is the foundation for the praxis of the Holy Spirit. This is the vision of Paul as well as the writers of the four Gospels.

A Vision of Christ's Messianic Ministry

A careful reading of the New Testament leads to the conclusion that the ministry of Jesus revealed his messianic mission, even as his mission disclosed the fact that in his person he is the Son of God, thus linking messianic office with the one who has come from God himself. Luke directs our attention to the fact that in receiving his apostolic commission through baptism, Jesus was "full of the Holy Spirit," and that he said of his own mission, "The Spirit of the Lord is upon me, because he has anointed me to bring good news to the poor. He has sent me to proclaim release to the captives and recovery of sight to the blind, to let the oppressed go free, to proclaim the year of the Lord's favor" (Lk 4:1, 18-19).

This direct quotation from Isaiah (61:1-2; 58:6) is a self-conscious identification on the part of Jesus with God's own mission to the world as repeatedly promised by the Old Testament prophets.

For Luke, himself a Gentile convert and companion to the apostle Paul, Jesus' nature is clearly demonstrated in his messianic mission, which is universal in scope and empowered and directed by the Spirit. Luke has already heard Paul preach his mission sermon at Antioch of Pisidia, where Paul argues that the resurrection of Jesus Christ established the fact that Jesus is the Son of God as promised in Psalm 2, "Thou art my Son, today I have begotten thee" (Acts 13:33 RSV). This cannot refer to David himself, argues Paul, because he died and was not raised. Jesus, however, has been raised from the dead and so is indeed the divine Son of God through whom forgiveness of sin and fulfillment of the law of Moses is achieved (Acts 13:36-39). The following sabbath Paul was confronted by the Jews who sought to contradict this message. In response Paul states that the mission of God is intended also for the Gentiles. In support of this astounding claim Paul cites the command of the Lord as given by Isaiah (49:6), "I have set you to be a light for the Gentiles, so that you may bring salvation to the ends of the earth" (Acts 13:47).

Luke's experience with Paul was undoubtedly formative for his own mission theology, so that in giving the account of the last words of Jesus on earth before his ascension, Luke provides the explicit promise for which Pentecost is the fulfillment. "But you will receive power when the Holy Spirit has come upon you; and you will be my witnesses in Jerusalem and in all Judea and Samaria, and to the ends of the earth"

(Acts 1:8). We are not surprised then to find that when Luke writes his account of the life and ministry of Jesus as the first part of his two-part work, he presents Jesus as the divine-human Savior whose genealogy is traced back to Adam, who, along with Eve, was the founder of the race (Lk 3:8). Further, Luke shows that the Gentiles (all nations) would have an opportunity to accept the good news of salvation through Jesus (Lk 2:32; 3:6; 24:47). It is clear that Paul understood his own apostolic ministry as transferred from Jesus to him through the Holy Spirit. This is so important that Luke records three accounts of Paul's conversion (Acts 9:1-19; 22:1-21; 26:2-18). Two of these are told by Paul himself, where he testifies to the fact that he received his apostolic commission directly from Jesus, which included the specific reference to the mission to the Gentiles.

Matthew presents Jesus as the teacher of the kingdom of God and Lord of the new community, while Mark focuses on Jesus as the Son of God whose ministry was characterized by mighty works as the presence of God's power and kingdom. John, in his Gospel, takes us behind the scenes of Jesus' earthly ministry to show us the divine origin and nature of this man who was the very incarnation of the living God (Jn 1:1, 14). These several trajectories of theological tradition are interrelated and complement one another.

While the apostle John may have developed his theology of Incarnation more systematically in his Gospel following the writing of the other Gospels, there are antecedents of this theology in Paul, as we have noted above, as well as in Matthew. "All things have been handed over to me by my Father," says Jesus in Matthew's account, "and no one knows the Son except the Father, and no one knows the Father except the Son and anyone to whom the Son chooses to reveal him" (Mt 11:27). As evidence that he was the Son of God with full authority to forgive sins, Jesus healed the paralyzed man, to whom he had already said, "Your sins are forgiven" (Mk 2:5). On another occasion the demons were heard to testify to the fact that Jesus was "Son of the Most High God" (Lk 8:28).

Before John wrote his Gospel with a theology of the Incarnation there was a ministry that pointed to the person of Christ as representing a quality and character attributable only to God himself. It is true that the ministry of Jesus was intended to manifest the work of God in him through the power of the Spirit, rather than as *prima facie* evidence of his deity. No reference is made to any ministry of Jesus prior to his baptism and the descent of the Spirit upon him as a visible sign of his messianic anointing. This should not lead us to conclude that his messianic anointing was the only source of his ministry. The event that took place at his baptism is the public manifestation of a Spirit-conception that Luke is careful to include in his account of Jesus' birth (Lk 1:26-38). All of the Gospel accounts make it clear that it is as the Spirit-anointed one, the Messiah, that he fulfilled the mission for which he was sent. It is as Messiah that he was obedient even unto death. "Was it not necessary that the Christ [Messiah] should suffer these things and then enter into his glory?" said Jesus to the two on the road to Emmaus on the day of the resurrection (Lk 24:26).

It is also true, however, that Jesus linked his authority to forgive sin and to reveal the inner being of God to his own personal relation to God as the Son of the Father (Mk 2:5; Mt 11:27). The resurrection did not merely validate his ministry as the Messiah, it validated the incredible truth that Jesus of Nazareth (born of woman!) is the very Son of God (Rom 1:3). Hidden in his ministry as the Messiah was the personal origin of that ministry grounded in his conception and birth as the Son of God. What the disciples began to see clearly is that his ministry was truly from God. It was the nature of this ministry that convinced them of this reality, not the story of his virgin birth. This story has its credibility in the nature of his ministry, and of the power of God manifested in his ministry, culminating in his resurrection from the dead.

It is noteworthy that only in the Gospel of John, which was written after the Synoptic Gospels and Paul's own letters, do we have a clear theology of the Incarnation.[3] Following Pentecost and the ministry of the Spirit through the early church, a theology of the Incarnation as the source of that ministry gradually became clear. The continuity between the Spirit released at Pentecost and the historical Jesus was an essential link in that theology. The mission of the Spirit in creating the new community of faith could not be separated from the mission of Jesus as the Anointed One—the Christ who came in the power of the

Spirit to inaugurate the kingdom of God. But even more important was the continuity between the Christ as the Anointed One and Jesus as the one who had his own source in the very being of God—the divine Logos who became flesh, as John wrote (1:14). Without this continuity we no longer have the basis for a theology of Incarnation, only for a theology of divine inspiration. Or, as some have suggested, we have a "Spirit Christology" rather than a "Logos Christology."[4]

What took place in the healing of the man lame from birth following Pentecost (Acts 3) is recognized as the praxis of Jesus Christ of Nazareth. There is no gospel other than that of Jesus Christ as the praxis of God's Word of revelation and reconciliation. There is no divine service, neither in the sanctuary nor in the streets, which is not the service of Jesus Christ.

A Vision of Christ's Twofold Service of the Gospel

The true vocation, or calling, of Jesus was grounded in his personal being as the Son of the Father. In assuming the role of the servant he fulfilled this inner life of service and thus revealed the true service (*latreia*) that mediates between God and humankind. He did not become a Son through his obedience and service, but because he was a Son he learned obedience and thus became the source of salvation for others (Heb 5:8-9).

The root of the diaconal ministry of Jesus is found in his ministry of service grounded in his life as the Son to the Father. He is the true *leitourgos,* or minister of God (Heb 8:2). This *latreia,* or service of Christ, is a primary event in the sense that it is the actuality of community between human beings and God from which all possibility of community proceeds. Here again we must say that the true diaconal ministry of Christ is not formed by some general principle of servanthood, or service. Rather he is the minister (*diakonos*) of God and of human persons because he is the servant (*leitourgos*) of God. Jesus serves the Father on behalf of the world. He does not serve the world on behalf of the Father. His calling (vocation) is not to meet the needs of the world, but to serve the Father, who loves the world and who sends Jesus into the world (Jn 3:16).

This distinction is essential for a proper understanding of one's calling into the ministry of Christ. "I have just been extended a call from a church to become their pastor," a student preparing to graduate from our seminary told me with excitement and almost disbelief. Without casting a shadow on this bright and shining moment, I replied, "That's wonderful, Steve! Let's get together and talk about it, because a calling to serve Christ in a pastoral charge is one of the most important events in your life."

And so we did. When I probed further as to what this student's understanding of a theology of a call to serve a church might be, I drew a blank. "All I know about a call is that you have to have one before you can be ordained in my denomination," Steve told me. He confessed that this had never been discussed in any of the three courses in systematic theology and that his one course in pastoral theology talked about the polity of the church, administration of the sacraments and how to conduct oneself as a member of the clergy. The protocol for responding to a call from a church warranted one lecture, but there had been no discussion of a theology of a call.

I shared my own experience of "receiving a call" immediately upon graduation from seminary and how I had understood that as a mandate to serve that church and to become its minister. Not more than three or four years went by, I told Steve, before I felt an increasing sense of despair and even failure. The needs and demands upon my time, emotional resources and spiritual life were incessant and unrelenting. I had allowed my ministry to become identical with my calling.

As it turned out, my ministry was threatening to devour me with its insatiable appetite for my limited resources. There was even the vague sense of a death wish pervading the desperation that drew me deeper into the void. "But this ministry is God's calling," I said to myself. "To step back or to step out for the sake of my own emotional and physical health would be to abandon my calling." Perhaps my ministry would kill me, but if so, then at least I would die as a martyr and not as a failure.

The dreadful thing about such a spiral of despair is that it drives one deeper into isolation. This simply could not be talked about openly (so I thought), especially with other ministers, who were probably each fighting their own demons but telling success stories in order to bolster their egos. When we did talk about problems, as I recall, it was more often to complain than to confess. It was easier to blame those who made our ministry more difficult than to share our own sense of failure.

The turning point came, I told Steve, when I began to reflect upon the life and ministry of Jesus. I wondered how Jesus could give himself permission to stop healing and to remove himself from the incessant demands upon him with good conscience. I pondered the story of Lazarus (Jn 11). If Jesus had any obligations to persons beyond his own small band of disciples, it was certainly to Mary and Martha, and to their brother Lazarus. Yet at the very moment when Lazarus became sick unto death, and the sisters sent for Jesus, he "stayed two days longer in the place where he was" (11:6).

The message sent to Jesus, however, was loaded with the language of obligation: "Lord, he whom you love is ill" (11:3). "Jesus," they seemed to be saying, "Lazarus is dying and you have the pills in your pocket to heal him. If you love him, come immediately." I read this into the text because, as a pastor, I have received many communications that demand priority.

As I reflected on this incident I began to understand that Jesus' ministry was not connected to ministry-related incidents but to his obedience and service to the Father. "My food is to do the will of him who sent me and to complete his work" (Jn 4:34). "I can do nothing on my own. As I hear, I judge; and my judgment is just, because I seek to do not my own will but the will of him who sent me" (Jn 5:30). It then became clear. Jesus' calling was not to serve the world but to serve the Father. It was the Father who loved the world and who sent Jesus into the world. Jesus did not have to love Lazarus more than he loved the Father. In his service to the Father, he would be sent to Lazarus because of the Father's love.

From this I determined that our calling is not to serve the world but to serve God through our participation in Christ's ongoing ministry. I have only one calling, and that is through my baptism into Christ, to serve God in Christ.[5] Where and how I fulfill that calling is determined by where God is sending me.

This church, I told Steve, is following the concept of a call that it has acquired through its own history of institutionalizing the ministry of Christ. It is extending to you a call. What you can say to them is: "You were calling out to God to send to this church a minister. God heard your call and is sending me. I am not coming to be your pastor simply because of your call, but because my calling to serve God in Christ placed me at God's disposal to send me where he wills."

Now I urged Steve not to dump all of this on the calling committee, but to prepare them for his own coming as one called to serve God. It is God who gives his ministers sabbaticals even as he gave his Son, Jesus, a sabbatical every so often.

The christological basis for a theology of calling into ministry rests upon the ministry of Christ as the one who provides the service (*latreia*) of love and obedience to God on behalf of the world. The humanity of Christ stands as representative of all humanity in this service to God.

Christ performs this latreia through his true humanity in a twofold way. First, he is faithful in his service of the Father by extending the gospel to the world. In pledging his own humanity to and for others, as we have seen, he is the bearer of divine love, compassion and mercy toward persons who have no righteousness of their own. Christopraxis is thus more than advocacy, it is a ministry of the grace of God to those who are without grace. It is a ministry of the love of God to those who are unloved, and even unlovable. It is a ministry of the forgiveness and healing of God to those who are condemned and broken. It is a ministry of help to the helpless, of caring to the uncared for, and of food for the hungry, clothing for the naked and shelter for the homeless. This ministry constitutes the *vita apostolica*, the apostolic life of the church in its being sent into the world as the bearer of the life and mission of Christ.

This is the ministry of God himself to those in the world who are "without God" and thus whose own humanity is distorted and deformed. It is the ministry of one who has already pledged his own humanity, and so it is a ministry with no strings attached. This divine latreia has as its goal the humanizing of humanity. Its criterion is not merely human need, but divine love. Its justification is not in the response it produces, but that it is a fulfillment of divine intentionality.[6]

The second movement of this latreia of Christ is the offering of the true service of praise, worship and thanksgiving from human beings to God. The healing of the ten lepers was an act of Christopraxis by which

Christ mediated the healing power of God to each of them in their concrete situation. Only one returned to give thanks—a fact Jesus noted with some amazement (Lk 17:10-19). Yet there is no indication that the divine latreia of healing was revoked for the nine who did not return to give thanks. Jesus himself offered up this service of thanksgiving to God as a vicarious intercession and mediation on their behalf. Here he pledged his own humanity not only as an advocate but as their priest, offering up on their behalf what they failed to do in their own humanity. Thus the church pledges itself to the humanity of those who are oppressed as well as to the oppressors for the sake of the true humanity of both as an act of reconciliation. A service of repentance as well as a service of compassion is bound up in the humanity and ministry of Christ through his church.

Christopraxis is the continuing humanity and ministry of Christ expressed through this twofold latreia. This is a diaconal form of service through which the humanity and the humanizing of others is seen as the object of Christ's own ministry in the world. The church has been granted a share in this service of Christ by extending its own life into the world where those "without God" in the sense of being under torment and bondage are touched with healing and helping actions. Christopraxis unites advocacy and *diakonia* so that actions of "being there" are accompanied by actions of "bringing there" tangible assistance and deliverance. Christopraxis as the praxis of the ministry of the church takes seriously both the kerygma and didache of Jesus—that the kingdom of God is given to the poor, the oppressed and the powerless, and that Christ himself is present in the act of ministry to such as these (see Mt 25:31-46).

The man who lost his faith in God and his trust in humanity through the horror of war in Vietnam needed his own Pentecost in order to have a vision of healing and hope. Some woman, who will forever be nameless and unknown to him, uttered the words of Christ, "And peace to you also." The fact that he heard these words in Vietnamese is a miracle of Christ's praxis through the power of the Holy Spirit, and a sacrament of the "real presence" of Christ to the church in its gathered communion with the Lord.

3

A VISION OF FORGIVENESS AND FREEDOM

Halvard Solness, the master builder in Ibsen's play, admits that he is afraid to climb the scaffolding of a tower that he has built.

HILDA: Afraid of falling and killing yourself?

SOLNESS: No, not that.

HILDA: What, then?

SOLNESS: Afraid of retribution, Hilda.

Raised in a pious home, Solness worried that the structure that he built might be a tower of Babel, a symbol of his rivalry with God. "I pretty well got the idea that He wasn't pleased with me."[1]

Sunday after Sunday, many Christians who gather for worship corporately confess their sins and are granted absolution through some liturgical formula: "Almighty God, our heavenly Father, has had mercy upon us, and has given His Only Son to die for us, and for His sake forgives us all our sins." Or, in less liturgical language, upon confession of sin by the congregation, the pastor might say: "If we confess our sins, he is faithful and just to forgive us all our sins. I declare to you on the authority of Jesus Christ that your sins are forgiven. Now turn to hymn number 398."

Sunday after Sunday, many Christians confess their sins and receive absolution, only to live each day with the nagging thought, "I pretty well have the idea that he isn't pleased with me!" While the confession may have been sincere and from the heart, the assurance of forgiveness rings hollow. And into this hollowness comes the echo of a bad conscience, accusing and scolding, if not condemning. And so confession becomes a ritual without reality and forgiveness a pronouncement without peace. Again and again we look to the cross in hopes of finding that elusive peace, only to come away wounded and weaker. As pastors responsible for spiritual care and the "cure of souls," many of us are troubled and baffled by the failure of the preaching and practice of religion that leaves people so lacking in spiritual health and psychological wholeness.

To announce forgiveness of sins and grant absolution without the praxis of forgiveness that results in restoration of spiritual and emotional health may be close to religious malpractice! A physician who diagnoses a malignant tumor but sends the patient home with a declaration of health without curing the disease would be liable for damages and would soon be a defendant in a malpractice suit. Christopraxis means internalizing the truth of forgiveness and freedom as a standard for daily life.

The forgiveness of Christ has its source in God and its effect in the human soul. Its source is the mercy and grace of God incarnate in Jesus Christ, which takes the consequence of sin into the very inner life of God in order that it may be healed and overcome. The effect of forgiveness is the restored relation between humans and God, with both spiritual and psychological well-being restored to the self. Absolution from sin in a praxis mode is more than a proclamation, it is a plausible peace that floods the self with freedom and restores broken relationships.

The Gospel of Forgiveness

The dilemma of all humans since the Fall of Adam is death, the consequence of sin. Sin caused death, and so death must be overcome in order that this fate, which came upon all, be removed. "Therefore, just as sin came into the world through one man, and death came through sin, . . . so death spread to all because all have sinned" (Rom 5:12). The death of Christ Jesus on the cross could have no meaning except that, following the resurrection of Christ, it be seen as the removing of death as the condemnation due to sin. "If Christ has not been raised," argues Paul, "you are still in your sins" (1 Cor 15:17).

The good news of the gospel is not only that death as the human dilemma caused by sin has been overcome through the death of God's Son, but that the human person Jesus of Nazareth has been raised from the dead and affirmed to be the Son of God in power (Acts 2:22-24; Rom 1:3-5). Not only through his death but through his resurrection and life Jesus continues to be the advocate for humanity before the Father. This is why the gospel of forgiveness begins with Pentecost as the praxis of the Spirit of the resurrected Christ. The vision of forgiveness and freedom that belongs to the forgiven person is not from the perspective of the cross but from the experience of the resurrection. The vision of the cross as atonement for sin is always seen from the perspective of the forgiven person who has experienced transformation from death to life. The cross by itself condemns, it does not convert.

"Wait just a minute!" cried a pastor who was sitting in a Doctor of Ministry seminar where I made that statement. "We have a cross on the wall of our sanctuary behind the altar as a symbol of Christ dying for our sin. We have at least a dozen hymns in our hymnal which speak of the cross and the shed blood of Christ as the atonement for our sins. What about this chorus which we love to sing?

At the cross, at the cross where I first saw the light,
And the burden of my heart rolled away,
It was there by faith, I received my sight,
And now I am happy all the day."[2]

"Let me ask you a question," I replied. "If Jesus had remained in the tomb and not been raised from the dead, would we still be able to sing that hymn?"

"Of course not," he shot back, "but the Bible clearly says that Christ died for our sins on the cross, and I happen to have my Bible open to

1 Peter 2:24, which reads: 'He himself bore our sins in his body on the cross, so that, free from sins, we might live for righteousness; by his wounds you have been healed.' What do you say to that?"

Well, the lecture took exactly the turn that I had hoped, and what follows in this chapter is a greatly expanded development of my response.

The question that plagues most of us who are in ministry is, Why, despite our preaching on the theme of God's forgiveness through the death of Christ and the atonement for sins completed on the cross, does the power of sin, guilt and shame seem to have such a stranglehold on those who believe that truth? Why are so many Christians turning to psychotherapists to find relief for their emotional problems? Why are the marriages and family relationships of church members so dysfunctional and so often abusive? Why, if we confess our sins each Sunday and receive the good news of our forgiveness, is there so little reconciliation, so little justice and so little peace in our world, not to mention in our lives?

I believe it is because we offer a concept of forgiveness without the praxis of forgiveness and freedom.

The Spirit of the resurrected Christ is the Spirit of Pentecost, and as such is the basis for the renewal of life for those who receive the gospel. The atonement from sin that occurred through the death of Christ for the sins of the world can be announced only as a gospel of Pentecost. Christ is risen! Because he lives you will also live! Christ comes to you in your place and time, clothed in your own humanity, speaking your own language, sharing your own culture and custom, liberating you from the fear of death, the condemnation of sin and the inhuman burdens and oppressions of life.

Peter's first sermon at Pentecost reached its climax with the astounding claim that Jesus of Nazareth who was crucified at the people's urging had been raised from the dead. The good news for those who acknowledge that Christ has risen is that, through baptism in the name of Jesus Christ, they will receive forgiveness of sins and the gift of the Holy Spirit (Acts 2:38). Later, while preaching in the house of the Roman centurion Cornelius, Peter again proclaimed the resurrection of Christ and the forgiveness of sins. At this point, his sermon was interrupted by the

Holy Spirit coming upon all who heard his words! Recognizing that the coming of the Holy Spirit was already a work of the risen Christ in the lives of those who received the gospel, Peter commanded them to be baptized in the name of Jesus Christ despite the fact that they were uncircumcised Gentiles (Acts 10:34-48).

The praxis of forgiveness of sin through the coming of the Holy Spirit rendered circumcision obsolete as a criterion for participation in God's salvation. A theology of circumcision now must give way to a theology of spiritual baptism into Christ. The older theological manuals are superseded and a new theology must be written that takes account of the praxis of Christ through the Spirit.

The gospel of the forgiveness of sins is itself grounded in the gospel of the resurrection of Christ and the gospel of the Spirit of Christ which came at Pentecost and continues to come wherever and whenever this gospel is proclaimed. The assurance of forgiveness is given by declaration, and also by the presence and power of the Spirit of Christ in the lives of those who belong to Christ.

In the first recorded sermon following his conversion, Saul of Tarsus proclaimed the gospel of the resurrection followed by the invitation: "Let it be known to you therefore, brethren, that through this man forgiveness of sins is proclaimed to you, and by him every one that believes is freed from everything from which you could not be freed by the law of Moses" (Acts 13:38-39 RSV). For Saul this gospel of forgiveness was a personal reality that he received through the gift of the Holy Spirit at a time when he was actively persecuting Christians and opposing Christ. Blinded by the light that struck him to the ground on the road to Damascus, Saul received the Holy Spirit through the prayer of Ananias, and recovery of his sight (Acts 9:1-18).

Saul, later changing his name to Paul, never tired of recounting the dramatic change that came in his life through his encounter with Jesus Christ. The gospel that he preached was first of all experienced in his own conversion. Not only was he wrongly attempting to achieve a righteousness before God through the law, but he was persecuting Christ through his attempt to hunt down Christians and put them to death. Despite this, Paul says, he received mercy and forgiveness, and God was "pleased to reveal his Son to me" (Gal 1:16). Paul understood his own personal Pentecost as a praxis of forgiveness through the gift of the Spirit of Christ. He then saw the objective basis for this forgiveness with respect to the law to be in the death of Christ for sin, so that death as the consequence of sin could be destroyed in his resurrection. Jesus was "handed over to death for our trespasses," Paul wrote, and "raised for our justification" (Rom 4:25).

The scriptural evidence is compelling in leading us to understand that forgiveness of sins is much more than a forensic formula pronounced by a judge who grants a pardon while we remain secretly uneasy and self-condemned in our hearts. Rather, forgiveness is a praxis of the Spirit of Christ wherein we are set free from the self-accusation and shame that result from our alienation from God as the source of life.

In the psychological account of his struggle with sin Paul acknowledges the ambivalence and despair of attempting to free himself from this torment, and then cries out: "Wretched man that I am! Who will rescue me from this body of death? Thanks be to God through Jesus Christ our Lord! . . . There is therefore now no condemnation for those who are in Christ Jesus. For the law of the Spirit of life in Christ Jesus has set me free from the law of sin and of death" (Rom 7:24-25; 8:1-2).

The declaration of absolution from sin apart from the transforming, healing and liberating praxis of the Spirit is indeed spiritual malpractice. To pronounce health where there is still sickness is spiritual fraud. To leave people at the cross without praying through to Pentecost is spiritual bondage, not freedom. Solness, the tormented character created by Ibsen, represents the pernicious fruit of a piety that poisons and a theology that is toxic.

The vision of forgiveness and freedom that Pentecost promises is not without effort; it is strange to us and not easily received. For we judge ourselves most severely and are our own most relentless critics. We need more than a spiritual high; we need a spiritual guide, one who both exhorts and comforts, one who believes in us when we hardly believe in ourselves. "And by this we will know that we are from the truth and will reassure our hearts before him whenever our hearts condemn us; for God is greater than our hearts, and he knows everything" (1 Jn 3:19-20).

The Spirit of Christ at Pentecost shines on Jesus and we see him in a new light, close by our side. Not only was he raised from the dead, says the apostle Paul, but we too now walk in resurrection renewal of life. "God put this power to work in Christ when he raised him from the dead. . . . You were dead through the trespasses and sins in which you once lived. . . . But God, who is rich in mercy, out of the great love with which he loved us even when we were dead through our trespasses, made us alive together with Christ" (Eph 1:20; 2:1, 4-5).

The Gospel of Encouragement

Nevertheless, I am reminded, we do continue to sin. Even the apostle John warns us, "If we say that we have not sinned, we make him a liar, and his word is not in us" (1 Jn 1:10). At the same time John says, "If anyone does sin, we have an advocate with the Father, Jesus Christ the righteous" (1 Jn 2:1). The Greek word translated "advocate" is *paraclete*, which can mean one called to the side of another, one who exhorts, or one who encourages. It is the resurrected Christ through the power of the Holy Spirit who comes to stand with us as our advocate.

The form of Christopraxis by which the Spirit of Christ continues to minister in the world is rooted in Christ's own ministry of *paraclesis*. Despite the variety of forms in which the word *paraclesis* is used in the New Testament, scholars generally agree that the original meaning of exhortation or encouragement is qualified by the mode of Christ's own presence "alongside" of and on behalf of those to whom this exhortation or encouragement is given. The specific promise of Jesus to his disciples is that he would not leave them as orphans but would send "another paraclete," the Holy Spirit, to be with them (Jn 14:16). The intention of Jesus' words is clear. Even as he has been their advocate, standing with them and for them, even in their instability and unfaithfulness, so he will continue to do this through the presence of the Holy Spirit.

The disciples must have been caught in the crossfire of the accusations hurled against Jesus. He was charged with violating the strict intent of the law of Moses; he was reviled as unworthy and unacceptable due to his associations with those rejected as irreligious and immoral. Jesus was even charged with being a despised Samaritan and possessed of a demonic spirit (Jn 8:48; Mk 3:30)! His own family came to him and sought to take him back with them because some thought that he had lost his mind (Mk 3:21).

For the disciples, these accusations and threats were sufficient to cause them to have doubts of their own. Questions arose in their own minds as to whether or not they were doing the right thing. Yet one thing held them secure. The unimpeachable peace and serenity of Jesus served as a healing presence and strong encouragement to their own instability and uncertainty. They heard him warn those who sought to undermine the commitment of his disciples: "If any of you put a stumbling block before one of these little ones who believe in me, it would be better for you if a great millstone were fastened around your neck and you were drowned in the depth of the sea" (Mt 18:5-6). As their paraclete, or advocate, he warned others not to tamper with their faith in him or trouble them with their insinuations. At the same time his own spirit of inner peace and security touched their fearful and wavering spirits with healing and enabling power. As the incarnate Word of God, Jesus not only preached and taught, but he moved alongside to heal and help.

Theologians tend to speak of two forms of the ministry of the Word of God—kerygma, the Word proclaimed, and didache, the Word taught. This formula tends to leave paraclesis, or the paracletic ministry of encouragement or exhortation, to the Holy Spirit. This way of thinking separates the rational form of the Word from the relational. It tends toward a presentation of the gospel through preaching and teaching as though the task is fully completed if one is faithful to the *content* of the Word. The human response to the Word of God is thus primarily a rational one, so that the emphasis is on what one understands as true, not on how one lives truthfully and authentically. If the Holy Spirit is considered at all as part of the gospel, it is to enlighten the mind, or bend the will, rather than to complete the gospel of forgiveness through producing health and wholeness at the level of the emotional and relational self.

We need to see the paracletic ministry of Christ as critical to the praxis of the Word of Christ as proclaimed, taught and experienced. Word and Spirit must not be separated as though Word were primarily mental and objective while Spirit is primarily existential and subjective. A better way of looking at the praxis of kerygma, didache and paraclesis would be as follows. Were God to come to me only in the mode of kerygma, that could mean "God has come: be silent before him—my realities and interests do not really matter." The reality of the kingdom takes precedence. Were God to come only in the mode of didache, that could mean "God has come: the road on which life has brought me no longer is important; he has another way for me." When God comes to me in the mode of paraclesis, it dawns upon me: "God has come and he wants to live in my place and my situation." God enters my situation in its concrete historical reality, and he appears in it for that very purpose. Through the paracletic presence of the Holy Spirit, Jesus himself takes up my cause as his own.[3]

Through this ministry of Christ in the power of the Holy Spirit, I am not simply addressed with the demands of the kingdom of God; I am grasped by the love of God as Father, upheld by the intercession of God as Son, and made to share in the inner life of Godself through the indwelling Holy Spirit. This paracletic ministry of Christ through the Spirit does not leave me as an individual, but incorporates me into the fellowship of the body of Christ, the missionary people of God.[4] As part of this body and mission, I too share in the apostolic life of Christ in being "sent" into the world.

From this we can see that the paracletic ministry of Jesus is grounded in the incarnation. Becoming truly human, he became and is the advocate for all that is human, pledging his humanity on behalf of all others. This advocacy is more than an instrumental one, performed for the purpose of effecting legal atonement. Yes, he did die on the cross in full payment of the penalty of sin and so made atonement. But atonement without advocacy does not empower those for whom Christ died so as to recover their own humanity in full fellowship with God and each other. The advocacy of Christ for humans is the pledge of his humanity as the continuing representation of human persons to God. The continuing humanity of the resurrected Christ is the basis for the ministry of paraclesis carried out by the Holy Spirit. The resurrection of Christ affirms his humanity and also ours as having an objective possibility of reconciliation to God.

Thus the Spirit has no incarnation of its own, nor does the Spirit become incarnate in the humanity of the church as the body of Christ. The church participates in the humanity of the risen Christ as the objective basis for its own fellowship with God. So also the continuing humanity of Christ as the paraclete takes place through the life and humanity of the church in its apostolic mission.

We have seen the problem with a dichotomy between Word and Spirit in the pronouncement of absolution from sin where the truth of forgiveness is upheld without regard for truthful forgiveness as measured in spiritual and psychological health and wholeness. Under this form of teaching and practice, Christians tend to have all sorts of emotional problems that are not dealt with as part of the praxis of the gospel of Christ. One can even go so far as to suggest that the proclamation of the gospel of Christ without regard to the affective, or feeling level, of those who hear and respond contributes to emotional disorder and dysfunction.

To say to a person who is naked and hungry, "Go in peace; keep warm and eat your fill," without supplying their bodily needs, writes James, is without spiritual merit (Jas 2:16). To use more contemporary language, it is a form of spiritual abuse. Likewise to tell a person suffering from emotional distress to "read the Scriptures, pray and obey God," is another form of spiritual abuse. To tell a victim of spouse abuse, whether psychological or physical, to be obedient, submissive and to pray to God, without making intervention and providing security and safety from the abuse, is another form of spiritual malpractice. In these ways, churches and pastors can actually contribute to the disorders among Christians without truly making intercession for them. This is a failure of the paracletic ministry of Christ.

The incarnation of God in Jesus is the pledge of the humanity of Jesus Christ on behalf of all human persons. Thus Christ is the advocate of all persons, not only those who are "in Christ." "Through Christ," all persons have an advocate with the Father. This enables Paul to say: "All this is from God, who reconciled us to himself through Christ, and has given us the ministry of reconciliation; that is, in Christ God was reconciling the world to himself, not counting their trespasses against them, and entrusting the message of reconciliation to us" (2 Cor

5:18-19). The apostle John holds the same view. Immediately after writing that "we have an advocate with the Father, Jesus Christ the righteous," he adds, "and he is the atoning sacrifice for our sins, and not for ours only but also for the sins of the whole world" (1 Jn 2:1-2).

The praxis of Pentecost begins its theological reflection from the perspective of this paracletic ministry of the Spirit of Christ taking place in the world before it takes place in the church. That is to say, Christ is not first of all contained by the nature of the church so that only when Christ is shared by the church does the world encounter him. Rather, as Thomas Torrance has put it, "Christ clothed with His gospel meets with Christ clothed with the desperate needs of men."[5]

This paracletic ministry of Jesus, of course, presupposes the kerygma as the announcement of this act of reconciliation. But even as the incarnation provides the basis for the kerygma in the humanity of Jesus Christ as the ground of reconciliation, so the continued humanity of Christ provides the ground for the paracletic ministry of the Holy Spirit and the kerygmatic message. Christ is present as the advocate of the people who had not yet heard the good news. The praxis of Christ is that of encouragement and support for those who need help and support in hearing and believing the gospel of forgiveness. The gospel of encouragement is the work of Christ through the power of the Holy Spirit enabling and empowering persons to receive the gospel of forgiveness. Forgiveness of sins is grounded in the gospel of reconciliation, which includes the healing of estrangements and the overcoming of disorder.

The Gospel of Reconciliation

The kerygmatic form of the gospel of reconciliation is that "all this is from God, who through Christ reconciled us to himself and gave us the ministry of reconciliation; that is, in Christ God was reconciling the world to himself, not counting their trespasses against them, and entrusting to us the message of reconciliation" (2 Cor 5:18-19). This is the gospel of Christ's reconciliation accomplished through death and resurrection. This is the gospel that is proclaimed as completed and sealed as God's work of grace to be received unconditionally and freely.

Paul also described the paracletic form of this gospel of reconciliation when he wrote to the Thessalonians and said:

> Our message of the gospel came to you not in word only, but also in power and in the Holy Spirit and with full conviction. . . . We were gentle among you, like a nurse tenderly caring for her own children. . . . As you know, we dealt with each one of you like a father with his children, urging and encouraging you and pleading that you lead a life worthy of God, who calls you into his own kingdom and glory. (1 Thess 1:5; 2:7, 11)

Paul is not satisfied with a proclamation of forgiveness alone. He knows that forgiveness has already been accomplished from God's side, and that God "does not count trespasses" against persons who are sinners (2 Cor 5:19). But forgiveness has not yet been accomplished until there is reconciliation from the human side toward God and toward one another. This is why Paul found such encouragement in remembering the transformation of the lives of those in Thessalonica who had received the gospel of Christ. "Our coming to you was not in vain," Paul writes to them, because "when you received the word of God that you heard from us, you accepted it not as a human word but as what it really is, God's word, which *is also at work in you believers*" (1 Thess 2:1, 13, emphasis added).

The pronouncement of absolution from sin is not only a kerygmatic pronouncement, it is a paracletic process! To give assurance of pardon and forgiveness to persons based on God's reconciliation to the world through Christ is not wrong. But it is incomplete without the assurance that arises from within the lives of those who hear this word. The word of absolution from sin based on the work of Christ in salvation history is premature apart from the praxis of forgiveness as the work of Christ in the hearts and lives of people through the presence and power of the Holy Spirit.

Let me say it as clearly as I can. A vision of forgiveness and freedom comes from the burning light of Pentecost before it can be seen in the sunless shadow of the cross. This has enormous theological significance, both for the proclamation of the gospel of Christ and for the spiritual formation of Christ in the lives of people.

It is precisely this point that I attempted to make in my lecture to the pastors when I said that the cross condemns, but never converts.

Our theology of conversion must not depend upon shaming people by thrusting the cross in their faces. Rather, conversion is the gracious gift of sharing in the life of the resurrected Lord Jesus Christ. The cross bears witness to the end of sin's power while the Spirit bears witness to our being called the children of God, "and if children, then heirs, heirs of God and joint heirs with Christ—if, in fact, we suffer with him so that we may also be glorified with him" (Rom 8:17).

The apostle Paul understood the death of Christ on the cross through the enlightened eyes of faith after encountering the risen Christ on the Damascus road. His gospel was not of human origin, but was "received through a revelation of Jesus Christ" (Gal 1:11-12). "Christ died for our sins in accordance with the scriptures," says Paul, and thus places the cross squarely at the center of his gospel. But the cross does not stand alone. He goes on immediately to say, "he was buried, . . . he was raised on the third day in accordance with the scriptures, and . . . he appeared to Cephas, then the twelve" (1 Cor 15:3-5). The resurrection, followed by direct encounter with his disciples as the living Lord, constitutes the entirety of the gospel.

By setting the death of Christ for sin apart from his resurrection, Paul charges that some have cut themselves off from the very forgiveness of sin that the cross obtained. "If there is no resurrection . . . then Christ has not been raised; and if Christ has not been raised, then our proclamation has been in vain and your faith has been in vain. . . . If Christ has not been raised, your faith is futile and you are still in your sins" (1 Cor 15:13-14, 17).

While Paul does not mention Pentecost in his letters, his theology of forgiveness and freedom issues out of the Spirit of Jesus Christ that releases persons from bondage to sin and transforms them into Spirit-filled Christians and witnesses. This burning light of Pentecost shines upon the cross of Christ for Paul. His spiritual transformation preceded and made possible his theological transformation. He can sniff out the poisonous fumes of a theology that brings death rather than life with unerring instinct. His warning to the Galatian Christians who have fallen under the spell of those who seek to bind their freedom in Christ back to the dead letter of the law is theologically perceptive and pastorally corrective: "You foolish Galatians! Who has bewitched you?

. . . Are you so foolish? Having started with the Spirit, are you now ending with the flesh?" (Gal 3:1, 3).

A theology that is not continually enlightened by the praxis of Christ at work in the transformation of human lives can become a toxic theology. A theology that does not begin and end with grace from both God's side as well as from the human side is a theology that "binds heavy burdens" (Mt 23:4) and sets a "yoke of slavery" (Gal 5:1) on those who look for freedom and forgiveness. A spiritual piety that is produced by such a theology poisons rather than purifies.

All too often people become less whole and less human under the influence of a theology that does not understand that "take up your cross" must be preceded by "the Spirit of life in Christ Jesus has set you free from the law of sin and of death" (Rom 8:2).

The crippling and abusive tactics of contemporary cults have long been known for drawing people into legalistic and sometimes cruel and even sadistic rituals that are dehumanizing. Profesor Ronald Enroth, a sociologist at a Christian college, has documented dozens of cases where Christian churches and organizations have spiritually intimidated their own members. These churches are actually practicing spiritual abuse, says Enroth, and induce guilt, fear and behavioral modification to bring members into line with their particular version of Christian discipleship.[6]

Behind these abusive tactics lies a toxic theology that is a contemporary variation upon the teachings that the apostle Paul condemned and warned against in his pastoral letters (see 2 Tim 3; 4:14-15).

The litmus test of theology is not only what it says of God but what it does to persons when it is preached, taught and practiced. The theology of Pentecost humanizes and heals, for it is a theology of resurrection and life, not of death and despair.

Christopraxis in the mode of paraclesis is a summons and invitation for humanity to become truly human; it is an exhortation to move out of the place of sorrow and humiliation into a community of reconciliation, peace and dignity. Christopraxis as a form of the real presence of Christ is a pledge of comfort and consolation to the oppressed and the broken. It may have to take the worldly form of the presence of Christ in many cases, or the nonreligious form of Christ's presence in the world, as Bonhoeffer came to see it.[7] The praxis of forgiveness must first of all be a praxis of reconciliation and restoration of humanity in the world before it can have authenticity in the liturgy of the church.

Christopraxis means that this paracletic ministry of Jesus is a pledge of his humanity to and for all human persons in the concrete historical, social and moral dilemma of their existence. Since he is the advocate for humanity, the criterion for what is authentically human is his own humanity, not a general principle of humanity. In his paracletic ministry Jesus pledges his own humanity, which has already passed through judgment and the penalty of death to and for the humanity of all persons. Jesus' advocacy is not only for the best of humanity, leaving the rest to their own fate; rather, he is the advocate for all of humanity, bringing every human person into the place where no human distinctive, whether racial, sexual or social, can serve as a criterion for relation with God or with one another.

For the church Christopraxis means that actions which involve advocacy for the full humanity of persons have a priority and authority grounded in the humanity and ministry of Christ himself. The strategy of paracletic ministry is nonnegotiable in terms of advocacy for persons who suffer discrimination, oppression and human torment of any kind. This strategy is not derived from ideological concerns nor from general principles of humanity itself. The strategy of advocacy as a form of Christopraxis is God's own strategy, enacted in Jesus Christ and through Jesus Christ for the sake of the world.

The ministry of Jesus demonstrated the praxis of God's ministry of reconciliation. There was no arbitrary distinction in this ministry between what was spiritual and what was physical. There was as much concern for healing the body as healing the soul, with no clear priority established. On some occasions, Jesus first proclaimed the forgiveness of sins before healing someone (for example, the paralytic; see Mk 2). On other occasions, Jesus offered healing and hope with no mention of repentance and faith. Here is the ground for a theology of social justice and human concern. The gospel of Christ cannot be separated from the praxis of Christ.

To separate evangelism and social justice as two issues to be debated and then assigned priorities is to split humanity down the middle.

Theologically, it is a denial of the Incarnation of God. In assuming humanity in its condition of estrangement and brokenness, Jesus produced reconciliation in his own body, so that no longer can we see humanity apart from its unity in Jesus Christ. To approach persons in the context of their social, physical and spiritual existence and offer only healing and reconciliation for the spirit is already a betrayal of the gospel as well as of humanity.

The praxis of Pentecost as the gospel of reconciliation seeks to make peace in the form of efforts at reconciliation wherever humanity is torn apart and tormented. This demands strategies of intervention where there is emotional distress, domestic violence, child abuse, economic impoverishment, hunger, political oppression, spiritual bondage, social injustice and every structure, ideology, force or religion that dehumanizes humanity.

The tactics by which this strategy must be carried out are contingent upon many factors, including resources, short-term versus long-range objectives, not to mention the specific sense of the leading of the Holy Spirit. As Barth once said, the church may have to engage in tactical withdrawal from the world at times, but never strategic withdrawal.[8] Jesus himself made tactical moves both toward and away from confrontation with the world, but never strategic withdrawal. Having pledged his humanity for the sake of the humanity of others, he was the faithful paraclete until the very end. The humanity of Christ and his ministry in and for the sake of the world constitutes the criterion for the humanity and the ministry of the church.

For all of the global issues that cry out for a gospel of reconciliation, we cannot escape the fundamental fact that each person, in his or her own way, is seeking and longing for peace with God.

Why do so many people feel that God continues to bind them to their faults, failures and sins long after the words of forgiveness have been spoken? Why is the vision of God for so many distorted by self-incrimination and shame? Why do we continue to count against ourselves what God discounts? Why, like Ibsen's Solness, do we shrink from climbing the scaffolding of our lives in order to have a broader and more liberating vision? Where do we get the idea that God "isn't pleased with me"?

Each of us, in the end, must come to terms with the "scaffolding" of life that we are building. We may have found the power to build it, but not the empowerment to live in it with confidence toward God and contentment with ourselves. There is in Christopraxis a liberating vision toward which we still move.

4

A VISION OF EMANCIPATION AND CONSECRATION

*T*he woman stood before Jesus, humiliated and condemned already in the eyes of her accusers. "Caught in the very act of adultery," they said, savoring the sweetness of self-righteous rectitude. "By the law of Moses we ought to put her to death by stoning. What do you say about her?"

Drawing a line in the sand, which placed her on his side, Jesus replied, "Let him who is without sin among you be the first to throw a stone at her." And when, one by one, her accusers had disappeared, he said to her, "Neither do I condemn you; go, and do not sin again" (Jn 8:1-11 RSV).

But you know that she did—of course she did! There is no reason to believe that this woman would be able to live a life without sin any more than any of us could, despite Jesus' dramatic intervention, which saved her life. Spirituality engendered by a crisis tends to crumble under the incessant waves of boredom and banality that wash over us when we are back on the same old beach. Sins of sensuality may be the only medication for unrelieved loneliness and unendurable despair. Threats of future punishment do not ordinarily empower the will to abstain from that which satisfies immediate hunger.

I picture the scene when her accusers come back to Jesus, outraged to discover that this same woman has once again fallen into sin. This time they accuse Jesus of subverting the law and undermining justice. "Don't you realize that this woman is a scandal to us and an embarrassment to you? By exempting her from the just demands of the law—she admitted her guilt!—you condone wickedness and show that you are not of God" (Jn 9:16).

In my scenario I hear Jesus say two things: "First, go and bring her to me; I am the one person she will have no fear of meeting, for I am already on her side. Second, she will learn that I did not only free her from the law, but bound her to me. I am the vine, she is the branch. She who abides in me, and I in her, she it is that bears much fruit, for apart from me, she can do nothing" (with reference to Jn 15:5).

The unconditional grace of God that Jesus offered to this woman carries with it the unconditional demand that her life become attached to the life-giving vine of God's redemptive and enabling love. Grace does not subvert the law by offering unwarranted freedom. Rather the law itself is grounded in God's gracious freedom to uphold the life of his own children. Thus Jesus could say that he did not come to break the law, but to fulfill it (Mt 5:17). This is why Paul said that Jesus is the "end of the law" (Rom 10:4) and that the purpose of the law was to lead people directly to Christ (Gal 3:23-24).

Using this story as a paradigm of Christopraxis through the power of the Holy Spirit, we see why we need a new vision of emancipation and consecration. It is not enough for us to be liberated from bondage, we must also be consecrated through belonging.

When we place the story of the healing of Mary Magdalene in sequence with that of the woman caught in adultery, we see more clearly the working out of this praxis of saving and sanctifying grace. Mary is liberated from bondage through exorcism of the "seven demons" (Lk 8:2). Mark tells us that she was among the several women who accompanied Jesus during his ministry, assisting and ministering to him. She is among those who stood by him during his crucifixion and is with the group who went to the tomb on the first day of the week to anoint his body for burial (Mk 16:1).

She may even have been the first person to encounter the risen Christ, whom she at first mistook for the gardener. In this encounter she received the empowerment to be a witness, going to the disciples and saying, "I have seen the Lord" (Jn 20:1-18). Luke describes the gathering of believers following the resurrection and ascension of Jesus as including "the women," among whom Mary Magdalene surely would have been included (Lk 1:14). Waiting with the rest of the 120 for the baptism of the Holy Spirit and the power promised to them through the Holy Spirit (1:8), Mary would have experienced Pentecost as the continued liberation, consecration and empowerment of Christ in company with the others (Acts 2).

"Christians are not perfect, just forgiven," reads the bumper sticker of the car ahead of me with the fish symbol prominently displayed in the rear window. But is forgiveness a license to drive with reckless regard for the lives of others? Are not Christians to be consecrated as well as converted sinners? We must look more closely at what it means for the praxis of the Spirit of Christ to consecrate as well as to emancipate.

The Praxis of Sanctification

When I talk about the praxis of Christ through the power and presence of the Holy Spirit in our lives, I am referring to what has been called the doctrine of sanctification. The Reformers stressed justification by faith through Christ's atoning death, apart from works, based on the free grace of God. While justification gave assurance of forgiveness of sins and freedom from condemnation as an objective basis for salvation, sanctification was seen as the subjective aspect of salvation, having to do with one's life and behavior as a child of God.

In other words, sanctification has to do with a life of holiness in conformity to the character and life of God, who is the Holy One. It has its roots in the command given to Israel: "You shall be holy, for I the LORD your God am holy" (Lev 19:2). Jesus is the incarnation of the holy God, and was recognized, even by the demons, as the "Holy One of God" (Mk 1:14). Following his resurrection, Jesus appeared to his disciples and breathed on them, saying: "receive the Holy Spirit" (Jn 20:22). All who receive the Holy Spirit are sanctified by that Spirit, according to Paul. Even the Gentiles become an acceptable offering to God, "sanctified by the Holy Spirit" (Rom 15:16). In each of Paul's letters to the churches he urges conformity to Christ in every aspect of life. "As God's chosen ones, holy and beloved, clothe yourselves with compassion, kindness, humility, meekness, and patience" (Col 3:12).

As the minister *(leitourgos)* in the heavenly sanctuary (Heb 8:2), the resurrected Christ continually fulfills his divine service *(latreia)* on behalf of both the Father in heaven and the community here on earth. The true order is the existence of the structure of community as his living body. Christ, the head of the body, continues to function through the agency and power of the Holy Spirit as the Spirit of Christ himself. The nature of this ministry is a sanctifying one, so that those who constitute the community can be called sanctified ones *(hagioi)*. The facts of human culture, race, ethnic and gender identity, ideologies, as well as principalities and powers are now radically conditioned by the priority of that which sanctifies by inclusion rather than by exclusion.

The original structure of sanctification as the holiness of God that determines the true order of the community of Christ is now revealed as a polemic against the exclusiveness that is the mark of the old order. Jesus encounters the world as the "Holy One of God." His is a holiness that goes out seeking to include the lost. It is a holiness that sanctifies by an act of inclusion rather than by a principle of exclusion. The inner power of sanctification is relatedness, experienced immediately by Jesus as the koinonia that he shares with the Father and the Spirit. The exclusive holiness that properly belongs to God alone has opened out into the world through the incarnation, resurrection and Pentecost, so that all humanity can share in this koinonia of holiness.

Unfortunately, the doctrine of sanctification has often led to division and conflict between churches and to frustration and confusion for many Christians. In this chapter, I will consider sanctification as a continuing praxis of Christ through the Holy Spirit, with specific emphasis on the power of holiness to liberate, consecrate and empower Christians.

The Praxis of Liberation

Our contemporary culture is rapidly discovering what many pastors have known for a long time. The power of addiction produces emotional, spiritual and physical cripples who seem to be driven only deeper into their problem by words of condemnation and challenges to reform. Whether or not we call it sin, addiction dehumanizes and paralyzes Christians and non-Christians alike.

The holiness of God became incarnate in the humanity of Jesus of Nazareth. Henceforth, holiness humanizes and liberates humans from the powers that seek to oppress and possess them. Liberation from these powers and from the dehumanizing effect of addiction is the praxis of Christ experienced as sanctification. Let us look at some texts of Scripture that speak of this liberation.

From the first pages of Genesis to the last book of Revelation, the theme of liberation is foremost in the story of God's relation to humanity. Even before sin enters to mar the good of God's creation, there is a story of liberation. Adam, the earth creature, is bereft of human relation and benumbed by futile attempts to find a counterpart among the senseless creatures God produces from the earth. "It is not good that the man should be alone," said the Lord God. "I will make him a helper as his partner." Failing to find that counterpart for the man among the animals, the storyteller laments, "but for the man there was not found a helper as his partner." The man is cast into a deep sleep and the counterpart is fashioned from his side. Awakening out of his lonely existence, he cries out: "This at last is bone of my bones and flesh of my flesh" (Gen 2).

This story of liberation is a story of divine grace that is not viewed as a remedy for sin, but as the very gift of life and the sole condition on which human life rests. The sin that follows is a sin against this grace, and a fall back into bondage from which only the original word and power of grace can liberate. This is the gospel of liberation that precedes the doctrine of sin!

The theme of liberation occurs over and over again throughout the whole of the continuing story of God's struggle to redeem humanity and form a people to share God's own glory and eternal life. The great redemptive event of the Old Testament is an act of liberation through the exodus of those who had been slaves and who were destined for a "land of promise" in fulfillment of the covenant with Abraham, Isaac and Jacob.

At the conception of Jesus, Mary sings a song of liberation. "He has brought down the powerful from their thrones, and lifted up the lowly; he has filled the hungry with good things" (Lk 1:51-53).

In his first sermon in the synagogue at Nazareth, Jesus read from the prophet Isaiah:

> The Spirit of the Lord is upon me, because he has anointed me to bring good news to the poor. He has sent me to proclaim release to the captives and recovery of sight to the blind, to let the oppressed go free, to proclaim the year of the Lord's favor. (Lk 4:18-19)

After reading the passage, Jesus claimed to be the fulfillment of this messianic promise of liberation by saying, "Today this scripture has been fulfilled in your hearing" (4:21).

To the Jews who believed in him, Jesus said: "If you continue in my word, you are truly my disciples; and you will know the truth, and the truth will make you free" (Jn 8:31-32). Becoming angry at the insinuation that they were not already free, they revealed their bondage by rejecting his word and sought, in the end, to put him to death by stoning (8:59).

The vision of Christ through Pentecost is of one who broke out of the prison of death; the God who raised him "freed him from death, because it was impossible for him to be held in its power" (Acts 2:24). The gift of the Holy Spirit came as the power and praxis of forgiveness, healing and new birth into God's kingdom. The first miracle following Pentecost was one of liberation from the paralysis of physical affliction with the result that the healed man enters the temple, "walking and leaping and praising God" (Acts 3:1-10). The second miracle following Pentecost was one of liberation from the paralysis of self-possession and self-existence, with the result that "the company of those who believed were of one heart and soul, and no one said that any of the things which he possessed was his own, but they had everything in common" (Acts 4:32 RSV).

The vision of Christ for Saul of Tarsus, who experienced his own personal Pentecost on the road to Damascus, is of one who liberated him from his blindness to the spirit of the law and gave him the gift of liberty through the Spirit. "Who will rescue me?" cries Paul in the midst of his struggle with a self that teases and torments him with deceptive impulses and desires. "Thanks be to God through Jesus Christ our Lord! . . . For the law of the Spirit of life in Christ Jesus has set me free from the law of sin and of death" (Rom 7:24-25; 8:2). To the Galatians, who appear to have succumbed to the spirit of slavery engendered by the law, Paul writes: "For freedom Christ has set us free. Stand firm, therefore, and do not submit again to a yoke of slavery" (Gal 5:1).

John's final vision in his "Revelation of Jesus Christ" is that of the slain Lamb who is worthy to open the door of heaven and break the seals that bind the vision of liberation from the powers of suffering, destruction and death.

In all of the various events and experiences that produce the theme of liberation from beginning to end of the gospel of God, one aspect remains constant. Liberation is a revelation of the praxis of God rather than an achievement of humanity. As a praxis of God, liberation takes place in the history of humanity, not above it or beyond it. Through the incarnation of God, liberation of humanity from the "pains of death," as Peter put it, and from the "works of the flesh," as Paul viewed it, takes place from below because it comes from above. That is, liberation is a revealed praxis through the working of God in the event of the life, death and resurrection of Jesus Christ. It is revealed through the actuality of the new humanity of Christ and through the coming of the Spirit of Jesus Christ through and following Pentecost.

Liberation is a praxis of Christ and a gospel of Christ that seeks to liberate humanity in its total experience of living under the domination of evil, whether it be from supernatural or natural powers. This theology of liberation has its sources in the praxis of Christ, not in a praxis of ideological or political encounter. There is another kind of liberation theology whose primary agenda is salvation in history through conflict and confrontation, as though one could be liberated from evil structures and systems by opposing them ideologically and politically. The salvation of God does indeed call into judgment the evil structures of society and promises ultimate liberation. The praxis of Christ, however, releases the power of the Holy Spirit first of all within human persons to effect liberation and produce the fruit of liberation, the sanctification of humanity. The seeds of struggle for liberation at the historical level alone have no potential to bear the fruit of lasting and eternal freedom. At the same time, it must be said that the gospel of Jesus Christ is also a gospel of liberation.[1]

It is beyond the scope of this chapter to provide an analysis of the nature of addiction and the steps to recovery. An abundance of resources are now available on this subject.[2] The praxis of Christ as the power of sanctification, however, requires that the church not only demand holiness of its members but also offer the resources of liberation from addictions that dehumanize its members.

Two things may be said at this point. First, the church must become a community of redemption and healing where those who are in bondage are permitted and encouraged to express their needs without fear of rebuke or condemnation. "I do not condemn you," Jesus said to the woman caught in adultery. Before persons can find liberation from their sinful addictions the church needs to be liberated from its self-righteous and condemning spirit. Programs that offer the most effective help to those suffering from the many forms of addiction that afflict people are seldom found within the church. At most, some churches have sponsored such programs as adjuncts to their congregational life and programs of ministry.

Many churches are unwilling to become a community of healing and a resource of empowerment for those who are caught up in addictive bondage because of the fear that their own holiness will be compromised. This is a failure to understand the true character of holiness as revealed through the praxis of Christ. For the sake of preserving its own image of holiness, the church often forces its members to conceal or deny their struggle against the very addictions which the gospel of Christ seeks to overcome. Liberation as a praxis of sanctification begins with repentance on the part of the church in order that it might truly become a "communion of sanctified ones." Where there is no liberation there is no praxis of the Holy Spirit, and no sanctifying power.

The second thing that must be said is this. Addiction, as one form of sin, isolates and alienates persons—it dehumanizes them. The breaking of the bondage of any addiction takes place when one is empowered to move out of that isolation and enters into relation with others who practice unconditional acceptance while providing a structure of accountability and reinforcement. The liberating power of the praxis of Jesus always begins with personal encounters, not with public proclamation.

There is no record of what actually happened to the woman to whom Jesus said, "Go and sin no more." I have suggested that liberation from the demand of the law that she be put to death would, in and of itself, have no redemptive effect in her life *apart* from continued relation to Jesus. One might hope that some of the disciples provided a context of love and belonging for her to find healing and enabling grace. If so, she too may have been part of the company who experienced the praxis of Pentecost!

Where there is authentic liberation there will also be sanctification, a holiness that humanizes and consecrates our human relationships.

The Praxis of Consecration

A pastor, whom I will call Larry, asked my counsel with regard to a situation in his church that had caused a great deal of anguish for him personally as well as for the members of the church. When a new choir was formed, a man from the congregation volunteered and was accepted as a regular member. While this man faithfully attended the church, it was well known that he had been divorced and that he and the woman with whom he was living had never been legally married, though they presented themselves as a typical family, including the three children from her former marriage.

"The crisis came," Larry told me, "when I confronted the man with this situation and asked him to drop out of the choir. I told him that as long as he was living with a woman without legally being married to her, his presence in the choir compromised the ministry of the entire choir. He accepted this fact and withdrew, remaining in attendance at the church. When other members of the church found out about it, the thing blew up in my face. Even the choir director, who was a strong supporter of my ministry, accosted me the following week and said, 'Pastor, how could you do such a thing? Don't you have any compassion?' "

As Larry went on to describe the events of the following weeks and months, it became clear that he was also in a crisis, both theologically and personally. He had barely survived in his role as pastor with the help of a denominational official who intervened and stabilized the conflict.

Larry defended his action by saying that it was a matter of principle and that the character and integrity of his own ministry were at stake in allowing a man to participate in the morning worship service in the choir while living with a woman to whom he was not legally married. "I think that I do have compassion," he told me, "but how could I give approval to a relationship that was clearly wrong in the sight of God? I may have handled it wrong, and I have admitted that, but I am not able to approve of a relationship not consecrated by marriage."

I probed gently. Would he have permitted the man to remain in the choir if he had walked in a week later with a marriage certificate signed by a local justice of the peace and duly recorded with the proper legal authorities? "Yes," he replied, "that would have resolved the whole problem."

I pressed further. Does the civil authority have the power to consecrate what he called an unconsecrated relationship in God's eyes? He hesitated. "I don't like to think of it that way," he replied. "I think that it is a matter of obedience to God, and that living together without being married is disobedience and thus a sin before God. I felt that allowing him to sing in the choir would compromise my own pastoral leadership and lower the spiritual quality of the church's ministry."

I have discovered that most pastors eventually feel caught in similar situations where they are expected to show compassion while, at the same time, they uphold standards of holiness and biblical principle. It might be the matter of remarriage for persons who have been divorced, or the marriage of a Christian believer to an unbeliever. It may be the issue of allowing a member of the church board who suddenly is revealed to be an alcoholic to continue in a leadership position. Whatever the circumstances, the issue of what constitutes a standard of holiness and what can be viewed as consecrated by God becomes a test of pastoral integrity and congregational maturity.

What are the criteria for determining what God consecrates as holy in such difficult situations? Let us look at the praxis of holiness as reveled through the ministry of Jesus and then through the pastoral wisdom of the apostle Paul.

Through Jesus Christ the holiness of God is perceived in the context of the love of God. In Jesus we see a fusion of love and holiness that severely judges the evil that dehumanizes humanity while tenderly seeking the good of humanity in its most pitiable condition. For Paul, this priestly ministry of Jesus is the radical content of a theology of Pentecost. The Spirit of Jesus is the Holy Spirit, who sanctifies by bringing persons into relation with Jesus, the "holy one" of God. The Spirit of Pentecost is the Holy Spirit because the holiness of God has become human in Christ, and his humanity continues to be the bearer of holiness. The Spirit of Pentecost is the Spirit of this same Jesus Christ, the Holy One of God.

On one occasion a woman came in from the street and stood behind Jesus, weeping. She bathed his feet with her tears and dried them with her hair. The Pharisee, who was Jesus' host, was scandalized and said: "If this man were a prophet, he would have known who and what kind of woman this is who is touching him—that she is a sinner" (Lk 7:38-39). In response, Jesus reminded him of her ministry to him, a ministry not shown even by the host, and pointed to her great love and consequently to the forgiveness of her sins. The holiness of Jesus consecrated the life and actions of the woman while she was still a sinner. Consecration is not a certificate of holiness granted to the righteous, but a relation to Jesus, regardless of the direction from which one comes!

This truth enabled Paul to eliminate the distinction between the profane and the holy, which tended to separate people from each other and from things in this world. Paul's theological reflection upon the "humanizing holiness" of Jesus Christ led him to set aside many of the Old Testament holiness codes as no longer applicable or necessary. Paul himself, who was formerly a "blasphemer, a persecutor, and a man of violence," received mercy and grace as an example "to those who would come to believe in [Christ] for eternal life" (1 Tim 1:13, 16). In response to those who continued to use the Old Testament regulations to condemn others, Paul wrote that "everything created by God is good, and nothing is to be rejected, provided it is received with thanksgiving; for it is sanctified by God's word and by prayer" (1 Tim 4:4).

The practical outworking of this theology of consecration through union with Christ led Paul to make a pastoral decision in the case of a married person who becomes a Christian but whose spouse does not. Apparently this situation occurred in the church at Corinth and raised a question in the minds of some regarding the status of the Christian married to an unbeliever. Did the unbelieving partner cause the believing spouse to be "unequally yoked," and should a believing spouse therefore separate from an unbeliever in order to retain status with God? In other words, was this marriage consecrated in God's eyes even though one partner was not a believer? One should not feel compelled to separate from an unbelieving spouse in order to be holy, wrote Paul, "for the unbelieving husband is made holy through his wife, and the unbelieving wife is made holy through her husband" (1 Cor 7:14).

It is clear from this passage that Paul assumes agreement in principle with the assertion that children who belong to parents who are part of God's covenant people are consecrated through that relation, even though they have not yet come to the age of their own understanding and commitment. His argument concerning the status of an unbelieving spouse is based on this assumption.

On the ground that children are "consecrated" in belonging to a family that belongs to Christ, Paul argues that an unbelieving spouse can be likewise consecrated. Not only does the believing marriage partner remain holy when married to an unbeliever, but, according to Paul, the unbelieving spouse is actually consecrated by the relation in "consenting" to stay in the relationship on the same basis that one's children are consecrated. One need not separate from the unbeliever as long as that person "consents" to live in harmony and peace, allowing the Christian partner to serve the Lord. "And if any woman has a husband who is an unbeliever, and he consents to live with her, she should not divorce him" (1 Cor 7:13).

Paul also makes clear that consecration is intended to lead to personal salvation. "Wife, for all you know, you might save your husband. Husband, for all you know, you might save your wife" (7:16).

Consecration is relational holiness; salvation is personal holiness through the indwelling Holy Spirit. The unbelieving spouse is consecrated by consent, not yet by belief.

Quite clearly the consent on the part of an unbelieving spouse implies a willingness to uphold the integrity of the marriage and family life as oriented to God through the life of the believer. We know that the Holy Spirit not only dwells in individuals but also in community, which was the promise to the people of Israel. Consequently, those who consent to live in relationship to persons who belong to Christ, both children and unbelieving spouses, share in the consecration of the Spirit of Christ.

This understanding of sanctification through the Holy Spirit does not contradict Paul's warning to the Corinthians that unholy partnerships might exist where the consecrating power and life of the Holy Spirit are not allowed to rule (2 Cor 6:14-18). Here we see the importance of discernment in the presence of the Spirit as a praxis of sanctification rather than a legalistic separation from unbelievers in order to achieve one's own holiness. The sanctifying presence of the Holy Spirit in relationships becomes the criterion for making decisions in cases where the spiritual life of individuals is not all that clear.

Paul also addresses a situation where a Christian might desire to marry one who does not profess Christian faith and who does not consent to the faith of the prospective partner. In this case Paul says that one is in danger of being "mismated." However, as we have seen, where there is consent, the union may not be "mismating" (1 Cor 7:14). That is, where the praxis of the Spirit creates consent on the part of the unbelieving person, and where both persons participate in Christian community, one could assume that it is the Spirit of Christ which is prompting this consent. To judge all such relationships as unholy may be to judge that which God is consecrating through Christ and would seem to be just as serious as the Pharisees' judgment of Jesus regarding his friendship and relationship with sinners.

The significance of Paul's theology of consecration through the Spirit is grounded in the social and filial bond through which Christ is embodied in the community. Paul's pastoral decision issues from theological reflection on the nature of sanctification as relationship to

God. This relation to God, for Paul, is trinitarian by virtue of the ministry of the Spirit to bind persons to Christ who is the ground of sanctification for humanity through his own relation with the Father.

I used Paul's pastoral teaching concerning the unbelieving spouse (1 Cor 7) in my discussion with Larry. While the situation he faced was different, the issue of consecration where there is not a legal marriage can be considered somewhat similar. The couple who were living together as husband and wife without being legally married were actually considered by the other members of the church as a stable Christian family. They demonstrated the qualities and character of a Christian family, even though they were not married. Larry began to see why the members of the church were so offended at his decision not to allow this man to sing in the choir. The church had already "consecrated" this family by fully accepting them. To treat the man as unconsecrated and not suitable to participate in the worship of the community in the name and Spirit of Jesus was to strike a blow at the very heart of the community itself.

Larry thought that the issue was between the human quality of compassion and his theology of sanctification. He discovered that the real issue was his own theology of holiness in tension with the praxis of the Spirit of Jesus at work in the lives of the people in his congregation. He had attempted to be a prophet, in the sense that the self-righteous Pharisee used the term. In so doing, he failed to be a pastor in the sense of the ministry as Jesus defined it.

A more helpful approach would have been to have quietly counseled the couple to have their union blessed by the affirmation of the congregation, and for their "common-law marriage" to be legally certified. Paul's counsel is apropos at this point: "Let us therefore no longer pass judgment on one another, but resolve instead never to put a stumbling block or hindrance in the way of another" (Rom 14:13).

Without the praxis of sanctification, liberation can leave people untouched and unhealed. The "humanizing holiness" of sanctification prepares the way for empowerment for the sake of restoration into fruitful fellowship and anointing for witness and service to Christ.

5

A VISION OF
ENTITLEMENT AND
EMPOWERMENT

*I*f there is one situation in which the praxis of entitlement and empowerment is most needed within the church's contemporary ministry, it is the role of women. Women who feel called to pastoral ministry and are members of denominations that do not ordain women often express deep personal conflict over their situation. Their questions often are put this way: If the Holy Spirit empowered both men and women at Pentecost to be witnesses in fulfillment of Joel's prophecy (Acts 2:16-17), why does the church disempower women by denying to them the office of pastoral ministry?

Mary approached me immediately following a lecture in which I had presented a theology of the ministry of all of the people of God as the continuing ministry of Jesus Christ in the power of the Holy Spirit. She was visibly disturbed and asked for an appointment to discuss the lecture further. Two days later we met in my office, and it was clear that her disturbance was more than disagreement over something I had said.

"I found Jesus Christ as my personal Savior through a Christian group of students on the campus of the university I was attending," she began. "As I grew in my Christian faith, I felt a strong sense of calling to serve Christ and began to work in my local church as a volunteer staff member with the youth ministries board. Feeling the need for more formal theological training, I applied to the seminary and came here to get a master's degree in Bible and theology."

"Sounds like you have a clear sense of God's leading in your life," I responded. "What's the problem?"

"During my first year of seminary course work, I caught a vision of what God wanted me to become, a pastor of a church where I could minister the Word of God through preaching and teaching. The problem is this," she responded. "I went home this summer and shared this with my local church and was told by the pastor that I should not expect to be ordained, as this was contrary to the Bible's teaching. He told me that women were not allowed to have pastoral authority over men and that I should seek some other ministry in fulfillment of my calling.

"I thought at the time that I had accepted his counsel," she told me, "though I felt something die within me. Then when I heard you talk about the empowering of the Holy Spirit that came upon both men and women at Pentecost, I felt like jumping up and shouting, 'But my church doesn't believe that.' "

Then, looking directly at me for a long time, she asked, "Am I disqualified from the same empowerment of the Holy Spirit as you have in your life just because I am a woman? Are men entitled to be pastors just because they are male?"

Mary felt strongly that she had been called and empowered by the Holy Spirit for pastoral ministry. Now she was told that she was not entitled to the pastoral office of Christ's ministry based solely on her gender. Does the principle of entitlement qualify and restrict the praxis of empowerment?

The Praxis of Entitlement

Among Jesus' contemporaries the concept of entitlement had to do with status and position rather than with personal and spiritual standing. The priests were entitled to serve in the temple on behalf of the people, though both were assumed to be heirs of the covenant promise to Abraham. In the home, parents had entitlement to privileges and authority that the children did not share, even though children were given full standing with the household of faith. At the same time, children were expected to grow to maturity and receive their own full entitlement as adults in the community.

The teaching and practice of Jesus were remarkable for their creative reversal of the principle of priestly entitlement. He forgave the sins of the paralyzed man and claimed entitlement to this authority by virtue of his power to heal (Mk 2). He liberated the sabbath from its confining and restrictive practice, and opened it up to include the ministry of healing. He announced his entitlement for this authority by claiming to be Lord of the sabbath (Mt 12:8). He took the children in his arms and said, "It is to such as these that the kingdom of God belongs" (Mk 10:14).

The apostle Paul's claim that he was entitled to an apostolic ministry and authority was based solely on the fact that he had been called and appointed to this office directly by the Spirit of Jesus. From this we conclude that both entitlement and empowerment for ministry are based on the gift of the Spirit of Jesus Christ. Here we will examine the relevance of this for the issue of the role of women in pastoral ministry as a form of Christopraxis.

Some who approach the issue of the role of women in the pastoral office of the church base their position on a theology rooted in historical precedent. Due to the lack of a tradition of women holding leadership in the church, the argument of precedence militates against a change in the order and polity of the contemporary church, in their judgment. Some who emphasize the continuity of office, such as in the Roman Catholic Church and the Anglican or Episcopal Church, find little support for including women in the pastoral office. Indeed, many have even argued against allowing women to serve as pastors on the ground that the incarnation took place in a male, so only males could have become apostles and only males fulfill the pastoral office.[1]

Those who emphasize the continuity of apostolic teaching based on certain texts of Scripture are similarly bound to an interpretation of

Scripture that, in their view, forever forbids women from holding the highest teaching office in the church. For many Roman Catholic and Protestant theologians, historical theology, tradition and biblical teaching tend to determine the norm for contemporary practice and ministry. What is lacking in these traditions of authority and office is the christological basis for entitlement and empowerment through the praxis of the Holy Spirit in the community of believers as the body of Christ.

The question of pastoral leadership in the church as it relates to the ecclesiastical form of ordination is an issue that must be considered through the praxis of Pentecost, which is the praxis of the Spirit of Christ. The role of leadership in the church can be understood as a praxis of entitlement and empowerment issuing from the life and direction of the Holy Spirit in the community. "Leadership is a function of the Christian community," says Werner Jeanrond, "and not a status over against it."[2]

Entitlement for leadership of the church comes from within the church as constituted by the distribution of Christ's pastoral leadership by the Spirit. Paul makes it clear that *Christ* gives the gifts of ministry to the members of the church by means of the Holy Spirit (Eph 4:7-13). In that same context Paul urges his readers not to consider themselves any longer to be children (lacking entitlement), but as growing up to maturity through Christ (4:14-15). The gifts of ministry, including pastoral leadership, are "activated by one and the same Spirit, who allots to each one individually just as the Spirit chooses" (1 Cor 12:11).

Many denominations and churches, however, increasingly have accepted women as fully qualified for the pastoral office and as having met the same criteria in being called by the Spirit of Christ as have men. This has caused dissension and debate within and between churches. Some theologians have attempted to find in Paul's own teaching and practice some ambivalence so that one text can be played off against another and a decision made in favor of ordaining women, supposedly on the same biblical authority as those who forbid it. For the evangelical church, whose foundation is the authority and infallibility of Scripture, this presents an especially difficult problem. In many cases this has become an issue of biblical authority, with debate over exegesis the decisive factor rather than the qualifications of women to fulfill the pastoral office.

Did Paul actually teach that women are not entitled to receive the gift of pastoral leadership due to their gender, and that this was meant to become the norm in every place and for all time?

Paul apparently felt that he had the "mind of Christ" when he instructed the women in the church at Corinth to "be silent in the churches" (1 Cor 14:34). This apostolic teaching regulated the participation and practice of women in the church at Corinth on the principle of subordination to their husbands. Many scholars assume that Timothy was assigned as an overseer of the church in Ephesus. Paul wrote to him, instructing him not to permit women to teach or have authority over men. Here too they were to "learn in silence with all submissiveness" (1 Tim 2:11-12).

This is a difficult text in light of Paul's practice in other churches of recognizing women who exercised gifts of pastoral ministry, such as in the church at Rome and at Philippi. Recent scholarship has shed important light on these verses from the perspective of the presence of certain Gnostic sects at Ephesus in which women were elevated above men. This could well be the basis for Paul's warning to Timothy to forbid "this kind of teaching" that gave women authority over men.[3]

Some theologians argue that Paul was relying on a rabbinical interpretation of Genesis 2 in his instruction to Timothy (1 Tim 2:11-15), which held that females were inferior and subordinate to males due to a sequence of creation. From this, they conclude that Paul violated his own christological hermeneutic as expressed in Galatians, that "there is no longer Jew or Greek, there is no longer slave or free, there is no longer male and female; for all of you are one in Christ Jesus" (3:28).[4] Regardless of how we interpret the difficult text in 1 Timothy 2:11-15, we should remember that Paul has argued strongly for the priority of the Spirit of the resurrected Christ over rules and regulations based on Old Testament texts. For Paul the praxis of the Spirit of Christ is normative, not formal principles, even those which can be cited as having some origin in a doctrine of creation.

In biblical theology, in both the Old and New Testaments, creation is contingent upon the Word of God. The created world and order came into being "out of nothing" and serve the eschatological purpose of God. God enacted his covenant with human persons in order to prepare a people for his own glory, sharing eternal life with the Father, Son and Holy Spirit.[5] This is why Paul could see clearly that circumcision, as a "sign cut into the flesh," has given way to the circumcision of the heart through Christ's resurrection of the flesh and the indwelling of the Holy Spirit. In the same way the biological (male-female), economic (master-slave) and racial (Jew-Gentile) distinctions grounded in the created order are to lose their power to discriminate under the redemptive power of Christ (Gal 3:28).

All persons, of whatever gender or race, are entitled to receive the gift of the Spirit for the ministry of Christ. As the church moves away from the first century toward the "last century," when Christ will come, we can expect the promise of Pentecost to become more and more evident as the racial, sexual and cultural distinctives are superseded by the new order of ministry inaugurated by Jesus Christ in the power of the Spirit. Historical precedence must give way to eschatological preference.

Like entitlement, empowerment for ministry flows out of the eschatological event of Pentecost, as Peter announced. Pentecost was the inauguration of the "last days" of Joel's prophecy. The church lives in the growing brightness of its approaching glory as the bride of Christ. From the Christ who is coming and who is present in the gift and ministry of the Holy Spirit, the members of the body of Christ receive their authority and power.

The Praxis of Empowerment

The eschatological reality of Christ's praxis in the Spirit and his coming at the end of the age constituted the basis for the apostolic norm in Paul's mission theology. He presented this clearly in his letter to the church at Corinth, where some had challenged his apostolic teaching and authority.

Think of us this way, as servants of Christ and stewards of God's mysteries. Moreover, it is required of stewards that they be found trustworthy. But with me it is a very small thing that I should be judged by you or by any human court. I do not even judge myself. I am not aware of anything against myself, but I am not thereby acquitted. It is the Lord who judges me. Therefore do not pronounce judgment before the time, before the Lord comes, who will bring to light the things now hidden in darkness and will disclose the purposes of the heart. Then each one will receive commendation from God. (1 Cor 4:1-5)

Paul is clearly referring to his apostolic authority rather than to any specific teaching or practice. However, it was his teaching and practice that caused others (who held that the law had priority over the Spirit) to question his authority. Paul was quite willing to submit his practice of not requiring circumcision for Gentile Christians, for example, to the final verdict of the coming Lord Jesus. His assurance came from the reality of the praxis of the Spirit of Christ as experienced in his ministry. In this way we can say that what was normative for Paul was that which could be accounted for by the praxis of the Spirit of Christ and that which could be submitted to the coming Christ.

The principle of expediency allows for exceptions to be made to what is normative practice for the sake of honoring the law of love. Paul argued that "in the Lord Jesus," nothing is unclean in itself (Rom 14:14). At the same time he counseled, "It is good not to eat meat or drink wine or do anything that makes your brother or sister stumble" (14:21). "For though I am free with respect to all, I have made myself a slave to all, so that I might win more of them. . . . I have become all things to all people, that I might by all means save some" (1 Cor 9:19, 22). Where it was expedient to abide by the Jewish laws and customs, Paul did so for the sake of winning to Christ those who were subject to those laws and practices. But these exceptions never became normative criteria for the freedom of the gospel.

Through the principle of expediency, he could insist on temporary and provisional applications of other principles for the sake of the effectiveness and order of the church. So he could approve of the circumcision of Timothy but refuse to have Titus circumcised. Timothy's circumcision was expedient, but not normative. The coming of the Spirit of Christ upon the uncircumcised is normative and will in the end prevail.

If Paul made exceptions in certain cases, on the basis of expediency, do these exceptions then become normative for all times in every century? I think that Paul himself would be astonished at the idea that his practice of expediency where he made exceptions should take precedence over the will of Christ at some other time and place! This would be to operate exactly contrary to the praxis of the Spirit of Christ as he himself understood it.

It is not simply that these teachings are culturally conditioned, so that a less culturally formed principle should be extracted and applied in other situations. This destroys the apostolic character of the words in that context and removes apostolic authority from the church in its present situation. If the resurrected Jesus Christ was the hermeneutical criterion for Paul in his own apostolic teaching, then the resurrected Christ continues to be the criterion for apostolic life and practice beyond the life of Paul.

John Stott, an evangelical theologian with a high commitment to biblical inerrancy and infallibility, seeks to escape the binding implications of Paul's teaching with regard to the role of women in the church by appealing to the culturally conditioned circumstance of the teaching. The requirement of silence, like that of head covering, was a "first-century cultural application" of the requirement of submission, which alone has "permanent and universal validity."[6] The practical implication he draws from this is that women can be ordained to pastoral ministry, but cannot be appointed to positions having authority over men. This would violate the universal principle of submission of women to men, which Stott grounds in a doctrine of creation and not subject to cultural relativism. In this discussion there is virtually no acknowledgment of the fact that the risen Christ is present in the church through the Holy Spirit as a hermeneutical criterion made evident through the actual praxis of the Spirit in setting women apart for this very ministry.

Some churches do not allow women to occupy positions of teaching and pastoral ministry in the local church yet do permit them to hold such positions on the mission field. I expect that Mother Teresa, by her selfless commitment to the poor, has earned "entitlement" to represent Jesus on the streets but would be denied the pastoral office in many denominations on the basis of her gender alone! What takes place in missions is allowed to follow the principle of expediency without becoming normative for the church. This is precisely the opposite of what the apostle Paul practiced in developing his mission theology as the normative theology for the church. If anything, Paul's teaching restricting the role of women in the established churches at Corinth and Ephesus was due to expediency, while his normative practice was to view women and men alike as having the gift of apostolic ministry.

In other places, such as Rome and Macedonia, where the status of women in society was not morally or religiously questionable (as it was in Corinth and Ephesus), Paul seems to view women as sharing equally with men in the ministry of Christ. In his letter to the church in Rome, for example, he commends to them Phoebe, a *diakonos* (not deaconess!). The male ending to the Greek noun indicates that this function of serving had already become an office of ministry.[7] He also mentions Junia as one "of note among the apostles" (16:1, 7). Commentators of the first few centuries found it remarkable that Paul should count this woman as a fellow apostle!

The issue then, contrary to Stott's suggestion, is not between culturally bound practices and universal principles. The issue is between the normative criterion of the Spirit of Jesus Christ disclosed through the praxis of the Spirit of Christ and what is expedient for the sake of maintaining order and effectiveness in the life of the church. According to Paul, the baptism of the Spirit by which persons become part of the body of Christ removes historical discrimination between Jew and Gentile, male and female (1 Cor 12:13; Gal 3:27-28). Through baptism into Christ both men and women share in Christ's praxis of ministry through the Spirit.

Edward Schillebeeckx makes this point emphatic when he says:

The baptism of the Spirit removes historical discriminations. In principle, Christian baptism completely removes all these social and historical oppositions within the community of believers. Of course this is a performative and not a descriptive statement; however, it is a statement which expresses the hope which needs to be realized now, already, as a model in the community. . . . According to Paul and the whole of the New Testament, at least within Christian communities of believers, relationships involving subjection are no longer to prevail. We find this principle throughout the New Testament, and it was also to determine strongly the New Testament view of ministry. This early-Christian egalitarian ecclesiology in no way excludes leadership and authority; but in that case authority must be one filled with the Spirit, from which no Christian, man or woman, is excluded in principle on the basis of the baptism of the Spirit.[8]

Some in the church today may feel compelled to deny the office of pastoral ministry to women on either traditional or scriptural grounds in order to be apostolic. In fact they may be placing a hindrance on the apostolic ministry of Christ in the church today. If the Spirit of the resurrected Jesus is present in the contemporary church, anointing and calling women as well as men to the office of pastoral ministry, then this is surely an apostolic ministry as commissioned by Jesus as the living apostle.[9]

Mission theology has the task of continuing the historical development of theology based on the resurrection of Christ and the present (eschatological) reality of the Spirit of Christ alive in mission. This is the critical task of a reformed theology and continues the tradition of the Reformation. But this also is precisely where academic theology can institutionalize reformed theology as theological canon and end up being quite un-reformed!

I must introduce a caveat at this point. Against those who would use a spiritual hermeneutic and read Scripture through a private interpretation with the claim of being led by the Spirit, we must insist on a more rigorous discerning of the Spirit. The hermeneutical criterion in reading Scripture in light of the contemporary praxis of the Holy Spirit is the resurrected Christ revealed through the Spirit. Near the end of the first century, John clearly saw the need for a closer association of the Spirit with the person of Christ himself. This, as we have seen, is present in Paul earlier, but in the Gospel of John it becomes quite explicit (see chaps. 14–16).

When the Spirit comes, Jesus reminds his disciples, he will bring to remembrance what has been earlier said, and will "guide you into all truth; . . . and he will declare to you the things that are to come" (Jn 14:26; 16:13). He will not speak on his own authority, but he will "glorify me," said Jesus (16:13-14). Though Jesus reminds them that he is going away, he promises that he will come to them, and that when the Spirit comes to them, not only would his presence be with them but also the Father would be present (14:18, 23). This corporate "we" of the triune God is reflected in the corporate nature of the church as the body of Christ. As the church discerns the presence and power of the Holy Spirit, it will also discern Christ Jesus and the Father, for the work of the Spirit and the mission of Christ Jesus is that of God the Father.

The apostolic nature of the church's hermeneutical task is thus fully trinitarian, and also eschatological. Present interpretation of Scripture must be as faithful to the eschatological reality and authority of Christ as to scriptural reality and authority. This is why the hermeneutics of mission theology is a theological hermeneutic and not merely a spiritual hermeneutic.

Jürgen Moltmann suggests that a "hermeneutics of origin" that grounds theology in Scripture alone *(sola scriptura)* must understand that Scripture is grounded in Christ, not only historically but eschatologically. "The hermeneutics of christology's origin must therefore be complemented by the hermeneutics of its effects."[10] Theological hermeneutics seeks what is normative in Jesus Christ as the inspired source of the written Word and the objective reality of Christ as the praxis of the Holy Spirit in the context of mission.

The criterion for the praxis of the Spirit as discerned in the ministry context is not determined by cultural relevance or pragmatic expediency. It is the work of the risen Jesus Christ that becomes the criterion in the praxis of the Holy Spirit. It is this contemporary work (praxis) of Christ through the Holy Spirit which becomes normative and calls the church into repentance where it has imposed its own normative and binding rules.

The sanctification of the church is a liberating, consecrating and empowering praxis of the Holy Spirit. The holiness of God is a holiness that humanizes through consecration and spiritual empowerment.

A church in which racial and ethnic categories define its constituency is operating out of expediency, and this cannot be normative. A church in which homogeneity of economic, cultural or ethnic groupings occurs naturally is operating out of expediency, and this cannot be normative. A church in which males are granted pastoral leadership and authority to the exclusion of females is operating out of expediency, and this cannot be normative. Expediency, supported by biblical texts, remains expediency, and should give way to full apostolic freedom in creating a church without such hindrances to the ministry of Christ.

The church that denies entitlement to Mary to serve Christ as a minister in the full power of the Holy Spirit may believe that it is applying an absolute principle based on a text of Scripture. If we take the full authority of Scripture as binding, however, we would be compelled to allow the Spirit of the risen Lord Jesus to be the Lord of the church as its head. The Spirit "allots to each one individually just as the Spirit chooses," taught Paul. Mary has solid biblical support for her belief that the Spirit may have chosen her to serve Christ through the pastoral office.

The final examination, Paul warns, will not be exegetical alone, but a revelation in our life and ministry of the actual working of Christ, so that when he comes he will find his own Spirit working in and through us. This "working" is a praxis of Christ through the power of the Spirit. By this praxis we will be examined. "Examine yourselves to see whether you are living in the faith. Test yourselves. Do you not realize that Jesus Christ is in you?—unless, indeed, you fail to meet the test! I hope that you will find out that we have not failed" (2 Cor 13:5-6).

PART 2

MISSION THEOLOGY

6

A PAULINE
PERSPECTIVE

With this chapter we have reached a turning point in the book. The methodology by which the sequence of chapters has been laid out attempts to follow faithfully the inner logic of the praxis of Pentecost. First we have explored the vision from Pentecost as the praxis of Christ, giving healing and hope, forgiveness and freedom, entitlement and empowerment.

The early Christians first experienced the presence and power of Christ in their lives and then produced theological reflection based on that experience. The concern in this book has been not only to expound the several facets of the gospel of Christ but to trace out the theological trajectory on which the life and mission of the church can be renewed in its vision of Pentecost as the praxis of Christ. In this chapter I will develop more fully the basic thesis of the book, which can be stated as follows.

Pentecost is the source of the mission theology of the church, even as mission theology leads directly to a theology of the church. That is, a theology of the church emerges out of mission as the church understands its nature as grounded in God's own mission inaugurated through Israel and consummated in Christ. This means that mission has a theological priority in determining the nature of the church and its relation to the mission of God for the world.

If the mission of Christ through the presence and power of the Spirit determines the nature and ministry of the church, then we should expect a mission theology to be the source of that renewed vision and life. This is exactly what we will find when we examine more closely one of the more dominant theologies of the New Testament, the mission theology of the apostle Paul. While there are other theological themes and trajectories in the New Testament, we will concentrate on Paul's mission theology because it represents the main focus of the book of Acts in depicting the emergence of first-century Christianity through missionary expansion beyond the early church in Jerusalem.

The Praxis School of Theology

Paul's first encounter with Jesus Christ occurred on the Damascus road (Acts 9) after the Pentecost event. Immediately following his experience, Paul underwent a radical reorientation of his theology under the tutoring of the praxis of the Spirit of Christ. This is what I call the "Praxis School of Theology." Following this encounter, where he received his own revelation of the gospel of Christ (Gal 1:11-12), Paul was thrust into the mission of Christ by the Holy Spirit (Acts 13), where he developed further his theology of redemption and the mission theology of the church.

Paul's conversion experience on the Damascus road may have been his own personal Pentecost; he spoke of it often in growing wonder at the grace of God that called him and saved him. While not present at the actual Pentecost event (Acts 2), Paul had what we may call a "blue-collar" Pentecost. He experienced the dramatic power of the Spirit in the marketplace, the public square, the industrial part of town. It was a working Pentecost, where the Spirit of Christ continued working for the salvation of persons in the most unlikely places, such as the jail in Philippi (Acts 16) and the Areopagus in Athens (Acts 17). Paul was not so much interested in speaking by the Spirit in an unknown tongue, though he had that gift (1 Cor 14:18), as he was in preaching the gospel of Christ in a language that could be understood and would result in a manifestation of the Spirit in human lives. Paul taught that it was Christ who was to be glorified through the Spirit, not those who had the gifts of the Spirit.

The corpus of New Testament literature that is attributed to Pauline origin and influence represents, by many standards, the normative theology of the church and its ministry. While Paul attributed the same divine status to Jesus of Nazareth as did John in his later incarnational theology, it is also noteworthy that Paul's mission theology followed the praxis of the Spirit of Christ rather than the official theology of the Jerusalem community. Indeed, he takes special pains to point out that he did not receive his theology from any human person but directly from the Lord through revelation (Gal 1:12). Only after waiting three years following his conversion, by his own account, did he finally go up to Jerusalem to visit Peter, and then only for fifteen days. During this time he consulted with no other apostles, though he did acknowledge a brief conversation with James (Gal 1:18-19).

Following his visit to Jerusalem, Paul apparently spent some time back in Tarsus. Barnabas found him there and brought him to Antioch, where he spent a year teaching and ministering (Acts 11:25-26). By this time Paul had developed the inner theological relation between the outpouring of the Spirit at Pentecost, his own encounter with the risen Christ on the Damascus road and the mission of God in Jesus Christ accomplished through his life, death and resurrection. Only then was Paul ready to be sent out on the first extended missionary journey (Acts 13). The praxis of the mission of the Spirit of Christ became Paul's theological tutor.

Based out of Antioch, rather than Jerusalem, Paul spent the remainder of his life either on his missionary journeys or in prison. Formerly schooled in the theology of the prestigious Gamaliel (Acts 22:3), and armed with the impressive credentials of a Pharisee, Paul underwent a theological as well as a spiritual conversion (Phil 3:5-11). Paul reinterpreted his understanding of the Old Testament law in accordance with his revelation of Christ through the Spirit. When he observed the Spirit at work among the Gentiles who had not been circumcised, he concluded that circumcision no longer had any necessary merit. When confronted with confusion and disorder in the churches due to an overeager and competitive exercise of the gifts of the Spirit, he argued not for less of the Spirit but for more of the Spirit and less of human pride and self-seeking.

Paul wrote to the Corinthian Christians, the most notorious offenders in this regard, reminding them that though there are a variety of gifts, there is but one and the same Spirit. There are varieties of service, but the same Lord (Jesus), and there are a variety of workings, but the same God who inspires them all in everyone (1 Cor 12:4-7). This trinitarian theology is formulated as a means of grounding the manifestation of the Spirit in Christ and the ministry of Christ in God the Father.

When we remember that Paul's ministry and the writing of this letter preceded the writing of the four Gospels, we see the emergence of a trinitarian theology from within mission theology. To be sure, what came to the early disciples following Easter as a commission directly from the risen Lord was part of the oral tradition that Paul would have learned immediately following his conversion. Yet, more than any other witness to the resurrection, Paul carried out this commission of Christ and so was led to develop a theology of the continuing mission of Christ through the Spirit.

The praxis of the Spirit of the risen Christ constituted the "new school of theology" for Paul. As he proclaimed the gospel of a crucified and resurrected Messiah, he witnessed the convicting and transforming power of the Holy Spirit. He reminded the church at Thessalonica of this compelling testimony to the power of the gospel when he wrote, "Our message of the gospel came to you not in word only, but also in power and in the Holy Spirit and with full conviction; . . . you turned to God from idols, to serve a living and true God, and to wait for his Son from heaven, whom he raised from the dead—Jesus, who rescues us from the wrath that is coming" (1 Thess 1:5, 9-10). This is the Praxis School of Theology!

Having his own apostolic authority grounded in the Spirit of Christ that encountered and taught him, and having followed the Spirit in his mission itinerary and strategy, he had to argue the essential unity of the Spirit, of Christ and of God. The nature of God, if we are to use that language, was not for Paul a matter of specifying three natures contained within one deity. Rather, the nature of God is manifested in his working, or his ministry through the Spirit and through the Son, Jesus Christ.

Paul would have been keenly aware of the confession of Israel, "Hear, O Israel: The LORD our God is one LORD" (Deut 6:4 RSV). Monotheism was deeply embedded in the theology and experience of Israel. Jesus himself came under severe attack because he appeared in the eyes of the Pharisees to compromise this oneness of God in claiming identity with God. At the same time Paul wished to preserve the differentiation between God as Father and Jesus as his Son, "declared to be Son of God with power according to the spirit of holiness by resurrection from the dead" (Rom 1:4). This differentiation between Jesus Christ and God the Father was essential to Paul's understanding of God's working "from below," so to speak, in providing a basis through adoption for all to experience this "Spirit of sonship" and so become children of God.

> For all who are led by the Spirit of God are children of God. For you did not receive a spirit of slavery to fall back into fear, but you have received a spirit of adoption. When we cry, "Abba! Father!" it is that very Spirit bearing witness with our spirit that we are children of God, and if children, then heirs, heirs of God and joint heirs with Christ—if, in fact, we suffer with him so that we may also be glorified with him. (Rom 8:14-17)

The concept of the universal fatherhood of God as Creator of all humans who bear the divine image is not the basis for Paul's "theology of sonship." Through sin this filial relation has been lost and must be recovered through a "new creation" (2 Cor 5:17) and adoption into relation with God through Christ as our brother. Even the law could not effect this transformation, argued Paul, "For God has done what the law, weakened by the flesh, could not do: by sending his own Son in the likeness of sinful flesh, and to deal with sin, he condemned sin in the flesh, so the just requirement of the law might be fulfilled in us, who walk not according to the flesh but according to the Spirit" (Rom 8:3-4).

Paul's argument in his epistle to the Roman church is that both Jew and Gentile must experience fellowship with God through Christ in the power of the Spirit, and so inherit the Abrahamic promise. For the Spirit of God does not work independently of Christ in producing children of God. Rather, the Spirit of God works through Christ, so that Christ's own Sonship is reconstituted by the "Spirit of holiness" in his resurrection (Rom 1:4).

Even as Luke records the account of the conception of Jesus as a creation of the Spirit ("The Holy Spirit will come upon you," 1:35), so Paul attributes the reconsecration of Jesus to divine Sonship in the resurrection to the "Spirit of holiness" (Rom 1:4). This same Spirit of God, so prominent in the Old Testament as the formative power of the children of Israel, and so instrumental in the conception and resurrection of Jesus, is viewed by Paul as the creative power through which both Jew and Gentile (literally, all nations) are enabled to enter the kingdom of God. It is the "law of the Spirit of life in Christ Jesus," writes Paul, which "has set me free from the law of sin and of death" (Rom 8:2). If the Spirit of God dwells in us, continues Paul, then Christ is in us. It is "the Spirit of him who raised Jesus from the dead" who gives us life in our mortal bodies (Rom 8:9-11).

Paul's Revelation Theology

Paul will not yield his authority as an apostle to those who heard the spoken words of Jesus prior to his death and resurrection. He fully accepts the teachings and acknowledges them in the context of his own teaching. But he claims that the same Jesus is now revealing his will through the mission of the Spirit, so that Paul can claim the same source for his teaching as an apostle as do those who have their source in the remembered words of Jesus.

This must have been an astounding claim at the time that Paul first made it the face of those who were eyewitnesses to what Jesus said and did before his resurrection and ascension! It would be one thing to say that the Spirit is the agent of redemption, whereby the hearts of men and women are opened to hearing the gospel of Christ. It is quite another thing to claim, as Paul did, that the Spirit is the very revelation of the work of Christ opening new dimensions of truth as a basis for theological reflection upon what has already been revealed.

Paul's theology of the Holy Spirit goes far beyond a theology of renewal through an experience of the Spirit. Some understand Pentecost as simply a theology of a Spirit-filled life, or a theology of the baptism of the Spirit. For Paul, the Spirit is the Spirit of Jesus Christ working so as to reveal truth, not merely to excite feelings and to stimulate worship.

At the same time, however, Paul's theology of revelation through the Spirit does not seem to be a kind of "word revelation" or "Rhema revelation" that is popular today among some pentecostal Christians. The Spirit may also have given revelation through the gift of discernment and prophecy within the context of the Christian assembly. Paul does not deny that the Corinthians also experienced this (1 Cor 12). But these "words" of revelation seem to be largely words that enhance and enable other aspects of his ministry rather than become a basis for theological reflection. Paul does say that he received "his gospel" in a private "revelation of Jesus Christ" (Gal 1:12). And he says that he "went up by revelation" to Jerusalem after fourteen years to defend his gospel before those who were apostles before him. We are not told the manner in which Paul received these revelations. We do know that on other occasions the Lord seemed to speak to him in dreams and visions (Acts 16:9; 22:17; 27:23).

What is clear, however, is that Paul did not base his argument for his apostolic authority on these private revelations alone, but upon the work of the Spirit among those to whom he ministered Christ. What became undeniable, so that even those in Jerusalem had to acknowledge it, was that the Spirit of Jesus was doing "signs and wonders" among the Gentiles, and that many had come to believe that he was the Messiah through Paul's ministry. This was a critical issue at the Jerusalem conference, where Paul was sent by the church at Antioch, along with Barnabas and others, to address the question of circumcision for the Gentile converts (Acts 15). Paul did not argue his case based on his personal revelation experience, but on the grounds of the manifestation of the Spirit of God through his missionary activity among the Gentiles.

For Paul, the fruit of the Spirit's work was evidence of the work of the Spirit. To the Christians at Thessalonica, Paul wrote, "our message of the gospel came to you not in word only, but also in power and in the Holy Spirit and with full conviction" (1 Thess 1:5). These early Christians "turned to God from idols, to serve a living and true God, and to wait for his Son from heaven, whom he raised from the dead—Jesus, who rescues us from the wrath that is coming" (1 Thess 1:9-10).

Paul's Redemption Theology

Behind Paul's Christology is his theology of God's mission through the Spirit by which the Spirit of God in creation is united with the Spirit of God through Christ seeking the restoration of the whole of God's creation. In the formula "Christ Jesus" Paul encompasses the whole of the messianic mission of God as the Father who sends the Spirit and begets the Son. He incorporates in this formula the cosmic significance of Christ's death and resurrection as an atonement for the sins of the whole world and "life for all" (Rom 5:18). In saying "Christ Jesus" Paul captures the liberating and reconciling power of the Spirit of God as a vital and compelling agent of transformation, overcoming the power of sin, canceling the power of evil, and creating a new humanity within every nation, tribe and culture (Eph 2:11-22).

Paul's redemption theology originates in the mystery of God's own eternal and gracious election of all humanity through his own incarnate humanity, Christ Jesus. It culminates in the eschatological vision whereby God's gracious election of humanity through his Son is fulfilled through the Spirit's work of effective calling so that "every knee should bend, in heaven and on earth and under the earth, and every tongue should confess that Jesus Christ is Lord, to the glory of God the Father" (Phil 2:10-11). For Paul, to say "Christ Jesus" is to experience the depth of the mystery of God's own love for the Son, the Son's own love for the Father, and the Spirit's work of love in enabling us also to become children of God.

This is why Paul uses the language of adoption to indicate that even as Christ was raised from the dead to "become a Son of God" in power, so we too will become "joint heirs" with Christ through our resurrection and adoption. "The whole creation," says Paul—and here we see again the cosmic dimensions of his theology—"has been groaning in labor pains until now; and not only the creation, but we ourselves, who have the first fruits of the Spirit, groan inwardly while we wait for adoption, the redemption of our bodies" (Rom 8:22-23).

Paul's redemption theology enabled him to escape what later became known as "modalism," where the identity of God as Father and Son are collapsed into the Spirit. The Holy Spirit is the present and continuing work of God's redemption through adoption into the divine Sonship of Christ. Christ continues his apostolic ministry as Lord, seated at the right hand of the Father (Col 3:1). Paul has no problem with this differentiation within the work of God, for God is known as the one God in all his working.

For the Israelite the unity or oneness of God's being was not mathematical but organic and synthetic. God's work is one with his being, and so to praise his work is to praise him. To acknowledge the Spirit of Christ is to acknowledge Christ, and to acknowledge Christ is to acknowledge the Father, one God in all his works! Paul writes to the Roman Christians, "I appeal to you, brothers and sisters, by our Lord Jesus Christ and by the love of the Spirit, to join with me in earnest prayer to God on my behalf" (Rom 15:30). This is a trinitarian understanding of the inner relations between God as Father, Son and Holy Spirit.

Here we see how a mission theology laid the foundations for what later became the trinitarian confession and theology of the church. Jesus claimed an identity between himself and the Father due to the works of the Father manifest in him. Later, John remembered Jesus saying, "Do you not believe that I am in the Father and the Father is in me? . . . Believe me that I am in the Father and the Father is in me; but if you do not, then believe me because of the works themselves" (Jn 14:10-11). The works and the words bind the identity of Jesus and the identity of the Father into a unity of divine revelation. In like manner the Spirit claims identity with Jesus. Jesus promises that the Spirit, "whom the Father will send in my name," will "remind you of all that I have said to you" (14:26). When the Spirit does come, Jesus told them, "He will glorify me, because he will take what is mine and declare it to you. All that the Father has is mine. For this reason I said that he will take what is mine and declare it to you" (16:14-15).

These words of Jesus recorded by John were written long after Paul had developed his mission theology with its intrinsic trinitarian structure. What the disciples had first remembered concerning Jesus' promise of the Spirit, and no doubt shared as oral history, became for Paul an actual experience of hearing the words of Jesus as from the contemporary Lord.

This apparently accounts for Paul's self-conscious distinction between words directly reported to him by the disciples and his own teaching, which he claims has the same authority. For example, to the Corinthians he wrote, "To the married I give this command—not I but the Lord, . . ." followed by a teaching Jesus gave before his crucifixion. But then he added, "To the rest I say—I and not the Lord . . . "; here he does not have a direct citation from Jesus. Yet Paul does not make this distinction for the purpose of giving greater authority to the words spoken by Jesus before his crucifixion than to the words he speaks on behalf of Jesus. For he concluded by saying, "I think that I too have the Spirit of God" (1 Cor 7:10, 12, 40). "Now the Lord is the Spirit," wrote Paul, "and where the Spirit of the Lord is, there is freedom" (2 Cor 3:17).

Paul's Christological Hermeneutic of the Spirit

Invariably when I teach this praxis theology to pastors the question comes up: "Isn't it dangerous to rely so much on the Holy Spirit as a criterion for our interpretation of the Word of God? I have people in my church who feel led of the Spirit to say and do all kinds of crazy things! This all sounds very subjective to me."

"That depends on how we understand the relation between the Spirit and Jesus Christ," I reply. "The objective reality of the Holy Spirit is the person of the risen Christ." This is what Paul meant when he wrote: "There is one body and one Spirit, just as you were called to the one hope of your calling, one Lord, one faith, one baptism, one God and Father of all, who is above all and through all and in all" (Eph 4:4-6).

In the face of the confusion and disorder resulting from the manifestation of the Spirit in the New Testament church, one might think that Paul would have retreated from his emphasis on the Spirit and fallen back upon some guidelines and regulations derived out of the historical memory of Christ when he was on earth. Quite the contrary. Paul might have been embarrassed over the misuse of the freedom to walk in the Spirit on the part of some Christians, but he would not retreat from the criterion of the risen and coming Christ as having authority in the church through the praxis of the Holy Spirit. What this did require of Paul was the development of a christological hermeneutic of the Spirit.

A christological hermeneutic is the criterion by which the church is to recognize and affirm the testimony of the Spirit to the unity of Christ in his historical incarnation and his eschatological manifestation. Let me expand on this further.

While Paul appears to have had no direct knowledge of Jesus Christ prior to his death and resurrection, his Christology takes seriously the historical aspect of the person, life and ministry of Jesus as the Son of God. At the same time, it is also true that Paul does not appear to have had a concept of the incarnation of a preexistent Logos such as came later through the gospel of John.[1]

Incarnation as a theological doctrine appears to have emerged after Paul's theology of mission and the church. However, we must not minimize Paul's view of Christ as having both "descended and ascended" in assuming human form. Paul includes an early christological hymn in his letter to the Philippian church, which expresses clearly the idea of incarnation, as Christ, "though he was in the form of God, did not regard equality with God as something to be exploited, but emptied himself, taking the form of a slave, being born in human likeness" (Phil 2:6-8). This descent, however, is included with the description of the exaltation of Christ through resurrection and ascension as the glorious power of God over all things on heaven and earth (Phil 2:9-11).

By the time that John had developed fully the theology of the Incarnation, Paul had already grounded the mission of the church in the continued ministry of the incarnate, crucified, resurrected and coming Christ. During this present age, Christ continues to be the source of the ministry of the church as his body (Eph 1:22-23). The church exists with Christ as its head as the "dwelling place of God in the Spirit," said Paul (Eph 2:22 RSV). But not only is Christ Jesus the cornerstone of the church (Eph 2:20), as the source of its ministry in the power of the Spirit, he is the one who continues to be commissioned with the task of the church's ministry. This ongoing ministry of Christ as the ministry of the Son to the Father will continue, said Paul, up to the end of this age, when he will deliver the kingdom to God the Father, after "destroying every rule and every authority and power" (1 Cor 15:24-25 RSV).

The resurrection of Jesus was the cornerstone of Paul's Christology, while for John it was incarnation. Both, however, attributed to Jesus of Nazareth the personal status of divine Sonship and thus grounded the ministry of the Spirit through the church in the relationship of the Son to the Father.

The theology of the Incarnation of God in Jesus of Nazareth was not then developed in order to establish the nature of the church, but rather to undergird the mission of the church through the Spirit as the continuing mission and ministry of God through the Son—Jesus Christ.

The claim that the praxis of the Spirit revealed the truth of Jesus Christ was, for Paul, the basis for his mission theology. He could no longer require circumcision when he saw that the Spirit of Jesus worked equally among the circumcised and the uncircumcised. He could no longer require the observance of sabbath and cultic laws of the Old Testament when he saw that Christ himself is the substance of the righteousness to which these laws pointed (Col 2).

Having the Spirit of Christ is to have the substance of Christ, Paul argued. In this way, theological reflection upon the law and prophets became a christological hermeneutic. The law was now interpreted through Christ, so that those who have the Spirit of Christ cannot be judged by anyone—for "we have the mind of Christ" (1 Cor 2:15-16). "Do not let anyone condemn you in matters of food and drink or of observing festivals, new moons, or sabbaths. These are only a shadow of what is come, but the substance belongs to Christ" (Col 2:16-17).

Paul's profound grasp of the trinitarian relations between Holy Spirit, Christ and God the Father is the ground for his teaching. His theological reflection is more substantive than merely ethical instruction. What was at stake was the very heart of the revelation of God through the law and the prophets, as well as through the incarnation of God in Christ.

The Spirit does not reveal truth beyond or outside of that revealed through Jesus Christ. In the manifestation of Christ Jesus through the Spirit's power, the complete revelation of God through Christ comes into clear focus as to its mission and purpose. The mission of Christ as the continuing mission of God through the power of the Spirit thus has hermeneutical significance in interpreting the Word of God. The effect of the Word of God is bound to its source; thus the truth of Scripture, for example, is not established solely by its inspiration (God breathed), but in its execution, in its effect. Isaiah has already clearly stated this: "So shall my word be that goes out from my mouth; it shall not return to me empty, but it shall accomplish that which I purpose, and succeed in the thing for which I sent it" (55:11).

Paul is very conscious of this eschatological aspect of the Word of God. Writing to the Corinthian church he speaks of the apostolic "stewardship" of the mysteries of God.

> Moreover, it is required of stewards that they be found trustworthy. But with me it is a very small thing that I should be judged by you or by any human court. I do not even judge myself. I am not aware of anything against myself, but I am not thereby acquitted. It is the Lord who judges me. Therefore do not pronounce judgment before the time, before the Lord comes, who will bring to light the things now hidden in darkness and will disclose the purposes of the heart. Then each one will receive commendation from God. (1 Cor 4:2-5)

Two points emerge out of this text. First, Paul does not claim that his own personal revelation stands as an absolute truth apart from its verification by the Lord Jesus himself. This is what it means to say that all revelation from God is ultimately grounded in Jesus Christ, both historically and eschatologically. The praxis of the Holy Spirit as a contemporary witness to that revelation constitutes the inner logic of both the historical and the eschatological Christ.

Second, Paul does theological reflection not only in retrospect to what has already been revealed through Israel and the historical Jesus, but prospectively in light of the coming of Christ Jesus, the Lord, with the Spirit of Christ now present as the "first fruits" of that appearance (Rom 8:23). These first fruits are revealed through the mission of God by the Spirit's working. Mission theology is both contemporary and contextual in its time and place.

As a church planter and pastor Paul found it necessary to provide a theological justification for his ministry as an apostle, and therefore for the nature of the church as a ministry of the Spirit of Jesus. While not present at Pentecost as a believer in Christ, he nonetheless became the preeminent theologian of Pentecost. He stood his ground against those whom he called pillars in the church in Jerusalem, arguing that Jerusalem had become the "Hagar" of Abraham, producing the child of the bondslave, not the child of promise and freedom (Gal 2:9; 4:22-32). Through the Spirit, wrote Paul, we have been set free, and so we should walk by the Spirit because we "live by the Spirit" and bear the "fruit of the Spirit" (Gal 5:5, 16, 22, 25).

Mission Theology and the Nature of the Church

The church exists as the missionary people of God—that is its nature. The mission of the church is to embody in its corporate life and ministry the continuing messianic and incarnational nature of the Son of God through the indwelling of the Holy Spirit. The nature of the church is determined in its existence as the mission of God to the world. The church's nature, as well as its mission and ministry, have their source in the life of the triune God—Father, Son and Holy Spirit.

The mission and nature of the church have their source in the mission of God through the incarnate Messiah continuing in the world through Pentecost. This requires a theology that views the nature and mission of the church as a unity of thought and experience. Paul was careful to do this in his formulation "one body . . . one Spirit . . . one Lord . . . one baptism" (Eph 4:4-5). Paul makes it clear that the ministry of the Holy Spirit is essential to a knowledge of Jesus as the incarnate Lord. "No one speaking by the Spirit of God ever says 'Let Jesus be cursed!' and no one can say 'Jesus is Lord' except by the Holy Spirit" (1 Cor 12:3). But he also warns, "Anyone who does not have the Spirit of Christ does not belong to him" (Rom 8:9).

The nature of the church, argued Paul, could not rest merely upon a historical link with Jesus and the twelve disciples, but upon the Spirit of the resurrected Christ who has "broken down the dividing wall of hostility" and created in himself "one new humanity in place of the two" (Eph 2:14-15). The critical phrase for Paul with regard to the nature of the church is "new creation." This is "from God, who reconciled us to himself through Christ, and has given us the ministry of reconciliation" (2 Cor 5:17-18). The connection between the old covenant and the new covenant is a real one, but also one that is eschatological in nature. The relation is not predicated upon historical necessity but upon covenant faithfulness on the part of God.

When Paul was challenged as to the authority by which the Gentile churches were operating, he argued that with the death and resurrection of Jesus Christ a new age has broken into the old, so that these eras now overlap. As David Ford puts it:

> The new is being realised now through the Holy Spirit, so the most urgent thing is to live according to the Spirit. It certainly involves present eschatological freedom, hope beyond death and the significance of the Church in history. . . . But as regards contemporary ecclesiology there are two implications that seem most important. The first is that the determinisms of history are broken by the gift of the Spirit as the down payment of what is to come. If God is free to open history from the future then the future need not mirror the past. In the Church this combines with the message of the cross to allow for discontinuities and innovations. The criterion for something is no longer whether that is how the Church has done it in the past or even whether Jesus said it (cf. Paul on his means of subsistence) but whether it embodies the new creation and its vision of love. . . . For Paul the content of eschatology is christological and the final reality is face to face.[2]

This led Paul to suggest a quite radical discontinuity between the old order and the new marked by the death and resurrection of Jesus Christ. The discontinuity is only claimed from the side of historical, religious or ethnic priority. On the side of God's election and gracious covenant as fulfilled through Jesus Christ and the coming of the Holy Spirit, there is real continuity. Paul's own apostolic authority and commission rested on this fact as well as did his theological hermeneutic.

No longer could circumcision be a criterion for belonging to the kingdom of God when the circumcised Messiah died and his circumcision did not save him. No longer can the regulations and rituals of the law bind persons with cultic power now that the Spirit of the resurrected Christ has become the new law (Rom 8). These things were only "shadows," but the "substance" belongs to the Christ who died and is now alive (Col 2:17).[3] Through this christological hermeneutic Paul is able to find trajectories of theological tradition in the Old Testament that strongly support his own mission theology.

There is a strong sense of continuity in Paul's theology, but this continuity rests solely in the relation between the Spirit given at Pentecost, the Spirit of Christ who confronted him on the Damascus road, and the Spirit of the historical Jesus who died and was raised again. Thus Paul makes no clear distinction between Spirit of God, Holy Spirit, Spirit of Jesus and Spirit of Christ. Each of these ways of speaking refer to the unity of Word and Spirit as revealed through Jesus, descended from David according to the flesh, and Jesus Christ, raised from the dead and declared to be "Son of God in power according to the Spirit of holiness" (Rom 1:2, 4 RSV).

For Paul, the nature of the church could be established only through continuity and discontinuity. He developed his theology of the church as a theology of the mission of the Spirit as the continuing mission of Jesus as Son of God. In his letter to the Roman church, in particular, Paul cites the faith of Abraham before he was circumcised as the basis for justification. So then it is through faith in the promise of God by which righteousness comes (continuity), not through the Mosaic law (discontinuity), as many of Paul's contemporaries claimed (Rom 4). Not only that, through faith both Jews and Gentiles become heirs of the promise given to Abraham by which "all the families of the earth" should be blessed. Through this Jesus Christ, who is descended from David according to the flesh but declared to be Son of God in power through the resurrection (Rom 1:4), a new relation of continuity is established between the Jew and Gentile as well as between the old covenant and the new covenant (Gal 3:23-29).

The organic connection between the church (new covenant) and Israel (old covenant) is now established through Christ, even though the forms of the old cannot be required as a condition for participation in the new. Nor does one's standing in the former community of Israel automatically grant a place in the new community of the Spirit. "Even we [Jews]," says Paul, "have come to believe in Christ Jesus, so that we might be justified by faith in Christ, and not by doing the works of the law" (Gal 2:16 RSV). Between Isaac and Ishmael is the barren womb of Sarah, so that Isaac is the child of promise and grace. The continuity is solely due to the promise, fulfilled through grace, not due to natural process or religious standing.

In the same way, between the church and Israel is the tomb of the Messiah. The resurrected Christ is the "child of promise," so that both Jew and Gentile have access to the Father through him. Paul stresses the point that the offspring promised to Abraham was singular, not plural. Christ is actually this promised offspring. The continuity between the church and Israel is thus through Christ alone, so that all who belong to Christ through the Spirit, both Jews and Gentiles, are "Abraham's offspring, heirs according to the promise" (Gal 3:16, 29). This continuity is not established through historical succession but through the resurrection of the Messiah (Christ) and the sending of the Holy Spirit.

The Roman Catholic theologian Edward Schillebeeckx echoes this theme when he says:

> The continuity between Jesus Christ and the church is fundamentally based on the Spirit. The ministry is a specific sign of this, and not the substance itself. Whereas in the early church ministry was seen rather in the sign of the Spirit which fills the church, later, people began to see the ministry in terms of the ecclesiology which regards the church as the extension of the incarnation. People moved from a pneuma-christological view of ministry to a theology of ministry based directly on christology.[4]

The determination of the nature and mission of the church does not emerge from a Christology that is merely historical in nature. As the Greek Orthodox theologian John Zizioulas has suggested, even Jesus has to be free from his past history in order to bring to the present history of the church his eschatological presence and power.[5]

Colin Gunton warns against seeking to establish direct links between historical events, even those which belong to the historical Jesus, and the being of the church in the contemporary age. The result of attempting this, he argues, leads to the question of the authority by which the church is constituted. If the church is historically determined in its authority, it will either seek some kind of institutional connection with the past or create a strongly clerical ecclesiology based on a link with the twelve disciples, neglecting the role of the Holy Spirit as the present authority of Christ.[6]

When we grasp the heart of Paul's mission theology, we are struck by several things. First, Paul became the theologian of Pentecost, transforming it from a festival into a foundation for the life and growth of the church. Second, Paul became the primary theologian of the apostolic church, defining the gospel of Christ as an imperative of mission before it became a subject of proclamation in the church. Third, Paul produced an authentic praxis theology, discovering anew the truth of the gospel in the context of Christ's ministry in the world.

This enabled Paul to become a truly cosmic theologian, discarding the myopic lens through which one looks at God from a window on earth. Paul saw the whole cosmos, including this planet earth, as embraced by the incomprehensible love and grace of God, and all under the promise of redemption in Christ (Rom 8). Cosmic in vision, alive in praxis, apostolic in spirit and pentecostal by nature, the church thrives where its mission theology flourishes freely.

7

AN APOSTOLIC MANDATE

Did Paul have moments of regret that he did not know Jesus of Nazareth to be the Messiah before he was crucified? I can well imagine Paul scolding himself for missing the opportunity to have direct historical knowledge of Jesus. Surely he must have experienced rejection from the other apostles who had these credentials while he did not!

Peter stood among the believers following the ascension of Jesus and stipulated that only one of those who had been followers of Jesus from his baptism until his resurrection and ascension could be eligible to become an apostle (Acts 1:15-22). Paul's lack of experience in this area plagued him throughout his entire missionary career. Writing to the Galatians, he defended his apostolic authority and commission by arguing that it had come directly from the risen Christ, if not from the historical Jesus (Gal 1:11-24). He was careful to point out that he had not had any contact with the former disciples in Jerusalem for three years following his conversion, and then only for fifteen days spent with

Peter (1:18). If others could claim that the risen Christ appeared to them, so could Paul. As one "untimely born," Paul wrote, "he appeared also to me" (1 Cor 15:8).

Later Paul wrote to the Corinthians and, by his own admission, embarrassed himself by finding it necessary to argue for his apostolic credentials by referring to the many things that he had accomplished though the power of Jesus Christ and how much he had suffered for his sake (2 Cor 10—12). Finally, Paul argued, the "signs of a true apostle" were performed among them by the power of the Holy Spirit in his life (2 Cor 12:12).

In the end Paul seems to have proved his point. Even Peter wrote of Paul's apostolic witness, called him "our beloved brother Paul," and commended his letters as having wisdom and authority as do the "other scriptures" (2 Pet 3:15-16). Paul wrote that he had laid a foundation in Jesus Christ beside which there can be no other. Be careful, he warned, how each person builds upon it (1 Cor 3:10-11).

One of my students returned from an interseminary retreat and reported this statement in a discussion with a Roman Catholic seminarian: "The Catholic Church has apostolic authority through the official teaching of the Papal Father who sits in the chair of Peter. You Protestants have broken from that authority and substituted the Bible, which has become a kind of 'paper Pope,' with each denomination deciding for itself what has authority. How can you call your church apostolic?"

"I was quite unprepared for that," John told me. "I certainly had read about apostolic succession and the rejection of that position by the Reformers in my church history class. I knew why I didn't believe in apostolic succession, but I had never really thought about what it meant to be apostolic in a contemporary sense."

John is not alone. There is a growing concern among the pastors I have taught in our Doctor of Ministry seminar that the apostolic gift seems to have been neglected, if not rejected outright, in the contemporary church. Did Paul intend that apostles, along with prophets, evangelists, pastors and teachers, be considered gifts of Christ to the church as stated in his letter to the Ephesian church (Eph 4:11)? If so, in what way can we understand the gift of apostolic ministry to be relevant for our churches today? These and similar questions arise in our discussions.

In this chapter I will answer these questions and present a new vision for the apostolic mandate for the church based on the mission theology and nature of the church following Pentecost.

The Apostolic Foundation of the Church

The church, as Paul was later to write, is "built upon the foundation of the apostles and prophets, with Christ Jesus himself as the cornerstone" (Eph 2:20). Peter described Christ as a "living stone" and Christians as "living stones" built into a spiritual house (1 Pet 2:4-5). Institutional theology tends to ground its nature in historical continuity with the apostles, with the incarnation as the cornerstone. Because the first-century apostles were no longer living, apostolic succession was instituted as the only link between the ruling bishop and the original apostles.

The Protestant church rejected this "mechanical" succession of apostolic authority through the *office* of apostle, and grounded the apostolic nature of the church in the *message* of the apostles, that is, in the gospel to which the apostles gave witness. Paul himself seemed to move in this direction when he wrote to the Galatian church, "But even if we [apostles] or an angel from heaven should proclaim to you a gospel contrary to what we proclaimed to you, let that one be accursed" (Gal 1:8).

The Reformers saw the apostolic foundation as permanently grounded in the gospel of Jesus Christ, his death and resurrection as fulfillment of the law and the only basis for salvation from sin and the granting of eternal life. The church is apostolic when it has this gospel, on biblical authority, as the content of its proclamation and assurance for its faith. To this extent both the Roman Catholic and Protestant traditions represent a theology of the church that grounds the apostolic nature of the church on some connection with the first-century apostolic life and witness.

For the Roman Catholic Church, its apostolic authority lies in direct succession back to Peter as the first apostle. In somewhat the same way the Protestant church bases its apostolic nature upon the witness and teaching of the first-century apostles, secured by the placing of these writings within the canon of Scripture.[1]

A theology of the church that is based on some kind of historical continuity with the incarnation through the first-century apostles tends to marginalize the Pentecost experience and to view the manifestation of the Holy Spirit with some suspicion. This suspicion extends to the role of the Holy Spirit in the interpretation of Scripture as well as to the manifestation of the Spirit in the life and mission of the church. For example, in the first chapter of his *Systematic Theology* the Princeton theologian Charles Hodge states that the Holy Spirit has no part in determining the rule of faith, but only in its application. Many consider an exegesis of the Scripture under the contemporary guidance of the Holy Spirit too subjective and unreliable.

For mission theology, however, the apostolic nature of the church cannot be so easily determined by appeal to apostolic succession or to apostolic teaching of the first century secured by Scripture alone. We have already described Paul as the theologian of Pentecost. His own apostolic authority was argued on the basis of an encounter with the risen and ascended Christ. His apostolic teaching was grounded in the claim that he had the "mind of Christ," and that this mind was given to him in the form of the Spirit of Christ (1 Cor 2:10-16).

Since Christ is the cornerstone, as Paul suggested, and since this cornerstone is a living stone, as Peter reminds us, the apostolic nature of the church is grounded in a living apostle, who is Jesus Christ. The book of Hebrews identifies Jesus as the "apostle of our confession" (Heb 3:1). The chief apostle of the church is Jesus Christ, and his apostleship continues through the age of the church until the end of the age.

Jesus Christ as the True Apostle
In describing the sequence of events that will occur in connection with the day of resurrection, Paul argues that Christ, having been raised from the dead, constitutes the first fruits of all who have died and who will be raised at his coming.

> But each in his own order: Christ the first fruits, then at his coming those who belong to Christ. Then comes the end, when he hands

over the kingdom to God the Father, after he has destroyed every ruler and every authority and power. . . . When all things are subjected to him, then the Son himself will also be subjected to the one who put all things in subjection under him, so that God may be all in all. (1 Cor 15:23-24, 28)

This describes clearly the apostolic nature of Jesus' own apostolic ministry. As the Son of God he was given the messianic task of inaugurating the kingdom of God to rule over all things. When this is completed, he will then be relieved of his apostolic mission and continue in the eternal relation he has with the Father as the Son. Until then, Jesus continues to be the apostolic source of the church's life and mission in the world through his power and presence as Holy Spirit. Pentecost, therefore, is the eschatological manifestation of the apostolic nature of the church as the continuing praxis of Jesus' apostolic authority to the end of the age.

Paul is clearly aware of this with respect to his own apostolic authority and ministry. To the Corinthians he wrote that he and other apostles were entrusted with a stewardship of the mysteries of God as servants of Christ. In this stewardship Paul did not consider himself accountable to any other human person in an absolute sense, nor did he consider himself to be the absolute authority.

I am not aware of anything against myself, but I am not thereby acquitted. It is the Lord who judges me. Therefore do not pronounce judgment before the time, before the Lord comes, who will bring to light the things now hidden in darkness and will disclose the purposes of the heart. Then each one will receive commendation from God. (1 Cor 4:4-5)

"I think that I have the mind of Christ," Paul said as a basis for his apostolic teaching. He was so sure of that fact that he could stand over and against the other apostles who challenged him on the grounds that he was subverting the Jewish law. These other apostles had received their calling directly from Jesus before his death and had been recommissioned by him immediately following his resurrection. This is not enough, argued Paul. Because Christ is a living Christ and because he continues to exercise his will and authority through his Spirit, the mind of the apostle must be open to the will of Christ as revealed through the Spirit in every contemporary situation.

Luke also introduces this apostolic and pentecostal authority when he juxtaposes the "eyewitness" category of apostolic credentialing in selecting a successor to Judas (Acts 1) to the event of Pentecost where the Spirit descends upon the 120 in the upper room (Acts 2). In fulfillment of the promise of the risen Christ Jesus at his ascension, the Spirit now comes upon them to send them out empowered to be witnesses. Eyewitnesses to the historical event of Jesus prior to his crucifixion can also become pentecostal witnesses. But it is no longer necessary to have been present as a witness prior to the resurrection, because in the resurrection and giving of the Spirit of the resurrected Christ Jesus, this continuity is established personally through Christ. This is Paul's argument for his own apostolic authority.

Mission theology is apostolic theology when it seeks to define and make clear the apostolic work of Christ in the present century rather than in the first century. Institutional theology tends to look back to the first century of Christian experience as normative and apostolic. Mission theology looks toward the "last century," or the century in which Christ can be expected to return, as normative and apostolic. The last century is not the one just passed, but the one that will mark the end of the age. Moving ever closer to this last century, the church expects the kingdom of God to be present in ever new and renewing ways.

The vision given to John can be understood as a judgment against the church in its failure to allow the Spirit of Christ to prepare it to be the church that Christ will find when he comes. The message to the "seven churches" is couched in language that suggests that the church should be preparing to receive the Christ who "stands at the door and knocks," being renewed in the power and presence of the Spirit (Rev 1—3). This Christ who stands at the door of the church and knocks is the true apostle of the church, and calls the church into apostolic life and ministry.

The church itself should seek to become the church that Christ desires to find when he comes, a church where distinctions of race, religion, ethnicity, economic and political status and gender identity will no longer be found, neither in it nor in its apostolic life. This is what Paul clearly had in mind in writing to the Galatians, "There is no longer Jew or Greek, there is no longer slave or free, there is no longer male and female; for all of you are one in Christ Jesus " (Gal 3:28). This surely was not a description of the first-century church, but Paul believed that it should be a description of the "last-century" church if it continues to grow into its own true nature under the apostolic ministry of Christ through the Spirit.

Following the reading of the messianic promise of the anointing of the Spirit from Isaiah (61:1-2; 58:6), Luke records Jesus as saying, "Today this scripture has been fulfilled in your hearing" (Lk 4:18-21). Mission theology operates in the eternal present so that with the coming of the Spirit to each contemporary day, the "today this is fulfilled" comes to pass. Because the Spirit is the Spirit of the resurrected Christ Jesus and also the Spirit which forms the life and ministry of the church, there is continuity with both past and future.

This is the breakthrough that Jürgen Moltmann has contributed with his book *The Church in the Power of the Spirit,* where he suggests that the messianic mission of Jesus is not entirely completed in his death and resurrection. Through the coming of the Spirit, his history becomes the church's gospel for the world. The church participates in his mission, becoming the messianic church of the coming kingdom. There is, says Moltmann, a "conversion to the future" through which the church enters into the messianic proclamation of the coming of the kingdom. Moltmann suggests that we can view the "sending of the Spirit" as a "sacrament of the Kingdom."

> In so far as Jesus as the Messiah is the mystery of the rule of God, the signs of the messianic era are also part of his mystery. In so far as the crucified and risen Jesus manifests the salvation of the world determined on by God, proclamation and faith and the outpouring of the Holy Spirit on the Gentiles are also part of this salvation. . . . It also follows that a christological-ecclesiological rendering of the term—Christ and the church as the primal and fundamental sacrament of salvation—certainly touches on a further sphere covered by the New Testament but does not go far enough, especially if the church of Christ is only understood in its sacraments and not at the same time in the context of the eschatology of world history.[2]

Apostleship as an Eschatological Orientation

The eschatological nature of apostleship rests upon the eschatological nature of the Holy Spirit as the Spirit of the resurrected Christ Jesus. Pentecost is thus an apostolic event, since it constitutes the sending of the witnesses into the world to testify to the power and presence of the kingdom of God. But the resurrected Christ Jesus was himself sent into the world by and from God the Father, so that incarnation is connected to Pentecost through the inner logic of the apostolic sending that constitutes the mission of Jesus as the Son of God. The church's continuity with the incarnation is through Pentecost, not through historical precedent or memory.

Paul was very clear about this continuity between Pentecost and incarnation, not as a historical or institutional projection from the past into the future but as the continuing mission of God. This mission of God is apostolic as represented by the sending of Israel into the world as a special people of God through whom the Messiah would come. The messianic anointing of Jesus by the Spirit continued this apostolic continuity. In this sense Jesus is the "true apostle." The messianic mission is given to the one sent by the Father, the divine Son of God incarnate. Following Pentecost, the sending Father, the sending Son and the sending Spirit constitute the apostolic mission of God through which the church is drawn into its mission and discovers its nature.

The church does not *drive* the kingdom into the world through its own institutional and pragmatic strategies. Rather, it is *drawn* into the world as it follows the mission of the Spirit. The church is constantly being re-created through the mission of the Spirit. At the same time it has historical and ecclesial continuity and universality through its participation in the person and mission of Christ Jesus through the Spirit.

All apostolic authority and witness are grounded in the living and coming Christ, not only in the first-century Christ. A mission theology is apostolic when it recognizes the eschatological praxis of the Spirit in the present age and interprets this in accordance with the Jesus Christ who is the same yesterday, today and forever (Heb 13:8). The author of Hebrews reveals the priestly nature of Jesus as mission theology when he argues that Jesus is a priest after the order of Melchizedek, and not of Aaron (Heb 6—7). Melchizedek was "without genealogy, having neither beginning of days nor end of life" (Heb 7:3).

The priestly ministry of Jesus is not grounded in continuity with the office or lineage of Aaron but in the praxis of the Spirit as the priestly work of God through him. In the same way Paul views his own apostolic authority as grounded in the apostolic nature of Christ, who continues his apostolic ministry through the Spirit. Apostolic authority is eschatological, not merely genealogical.

Wolfhart Pannenberg makes a significant contribution to the apostolic form of mission theology when he writes:

> In this age of historical consciousness, therefore, the church needs a new concept of apostolicity that will allow it to recognize without reservation the difference between the age of the apostles and its own day, without thereby losing its connection with the mission of the apostles. Attention to the eschatological motif in the early Christian apostolate can help us do this. The only criterion of apostolic teaching in this sense is whether and to what degree it is able to set forth the final truth and comprehensive universality of the person and work of Christ in the transforming and saving significance of his resurrection and the power that gives light to the world.[3]

While continuing to hold to the apostolic foundation in the first century, Pannenberg suggests that there was an eschatological motif among these apostles lighting the way forward to the transforming power of the resurrection.

This is what I have called the apostolic nature of Christ's continuing ministry through the Spirit as a power that will transform the church itself more and more into what it should be at the end. Pannenberg goes on to suggest what this might mean in terms of the apostolic life of the church in this present age.

> It follows that the true *vita apostolica* is to be sought in the life of the church's leaders and in the life of individual Christians who let themselves be permeated by the final, all-encompassing, liberating, and transforming truth of Jesus. The *vita apostolica* does not mean copying the way of life of the apostolic age or what we think that way of life was, and it certainly cannot be lived by borrowing this or that form of life from the regulations of the apostles. That which was

apostolic then may be irrelevant today or may even be a hindrance
to our apostolic tasks. This insight enables the church to be free to
live in its own historicity as opposed to that of the apostolic age and
still remain in continuity with the mission of the apostles.[4]

This is a helpful insight. The apostolic continuity of the church must
be found in its life under the transforming power and presence of
Christ rather than in its conformity to the form of the church in the
first century. The transferred apostolic life of the church, as I have
suggested above, is to be found in the continuity of the living apostleship of Christ Jesus in the sending of the witnesses issuing out of
Pentecost. This is a continuing *vita apostolica,* or apostolic life, because
of the eschatological nature of the Holy Spirit who continues the
mission of the incarnate Son of God, Christ Jesus, to the "ends of the
age." This is why mission theology is apostolic theology and this is why
the church is the missionary people of God.

Those who seek to repristinate first-century Christianity as a basis for
the polity, worship and style of the church in the present century
actually become nonapostolic and finally irrelevant to the apostolic
mission of the church today. As Pannenberg suggests, that which may
have been apostolic in the first century may actually be a hindrance to
the apostolic mission of the church today.

For example, some churches refuse to use instruments of music in
the worship of the church because this does not follow the practice of
first-century Christianity. Other churches attempt to pattern their
financial, organizational and administrative structures after the first-
century church with the claim of being a New Testament church. More
seriously, and even tragically, some churches refuse to allow women to
exercise the gift of pastoral leadership and ministry because the twelve
disciples were all male. These attempts to remain in continuity with
first-century patterns of Christianity actually may be hindering Christ's
apostolic ministry for today. Christ, who comes out of the future, stands
knocking at the door of the church while its occupants gaze passively
into the past through stained-glass windows.

A theology of the church that attempts to order its life and ministry
on the basis of historical precedence alone loses its apostolic character
to the extent that it attempts to project and protect its origins out of

first-century ecclesiology. The Spirit of Christ Jesus provides this continuity so that the task of mission theology is always a hermeneutical one.

In the present mission of God in the world through the church as the people of God, theology must recognize the eschatological signs of the coming Lord Jesus and read the Scripture in light of its testimony to the same Lord Jesus. This is Christ Jesus, descended from David according to the flesh, conceived by the Spirit of God, crucified, dead and buried, risen and ascended to the right hand of God the Father, and present as the coming One through the power of the Spirit. Mission theology is a living theology *(vita theologia)*, continually reading the authoritative Scriptures in light of the authority of Christ's ministry in and through the church as the mission of God.

The apostolic authority of Christ as emerging in the present out of the future demands that the church repair and reclaim the lives of people broken by sin and crushed by failure. The question of remarriage for persons who have been divorced, for example, is a question of the apostolic authority of the church to acknowledge those things which have died, and to restore to life persons who have brought judgment down upon themselves as well those who are innocent victims. As the apostle of God's promise of healing and hope, Jesus acted with full authority in renouncing disorder, disease and demonic dehumanization of people. With the same authority he brought people out from under the crushing judgment of the letter of the law and opened up the pathway to life in its fullest for all who came to him.

The Apostolic Mandate for Mission Theology
The most remarkable statement of a mission theology in the New Testament is found in Paul's epistle to the Romans. In this letter, Paul presents the most systematic and profound explication of the gospel to be found throughout all his writings. What makes this letter a statement of mission theology is the occasion that prompts its writing, probably from Corinth, while Paul is awaiting the further collection of money that he had pledged to take personally to Jerusalem for relief of the Christians (Acts 20:2-3; 1 Cor 15:25-27; 16:1-5; 2 Cor 8). Paul specifically alludes to this projected trip to Jerusalem near the end of his letter to the Romans (15:25-27).

What has prompted the letter, however, is not this project, for he makes no appeal for money. Rather, he has determined that his next mission should be to Spain, and he intends to do this by way of the church in Rome, where he evidently expects both spiritual and material assistance in order to be "sent on by you" (Rom 15:24, 28-29).

Paul's mission theology was anchored on the one end by the gospel that he had received directly from Christ by revelation through personal encounter (Gal 1:12). It was anchored on the other end by the Spirit's mission of making Christ known in regions not already evangelized by this gospel:

> For I will not venture to speak of anything except what Christ has accomplished through me to win obedience from the Gentiles, by word and deed, by the power of signs and wonders, by the power of the Spirit of God, so that from Jerusalem and as far around as Illyricum I have fully proclaimed the good news of Christ. Thus I make it my ambition to proclaim the good news, not where Christ has already been named, so that I do not build on someone else's foundation. (Rom 15:18-20)

Paul has already preached his gospel as a fulfillment of Isaiah's messianic prophecy: "I have set you to be a light for the Gentiles, so that you may bring salvation to the ends of the earth" (Is 49:6; Acts 13:47). This is Christ's apostolic and messianic mission, which continues the trajectory of God's mission as revealed in the Old Testament. This is God's mission through the Spirit of the Messiah (Christ) by which the church as a missionary people of God continue the purpose set forth in the calling and consecration of Israel in the Abrahamic blessing (Gen 12). The gospel through which mission receives its mandate is truly Christ's gospel, and as such it is also God's gospel from the beginning.

The church exists in the center of this continuum between gospel and mission, as the body and presence of Christ. The apostolic mandate is to move from the gospel through church to mission. From the perspective of mission, the theological mandate then reflects back to the gospel, through the church. In this way the church cannot be the church simply by encasing the gospel in its liturgical practice, nor can the church be the church by defining itself solely by mission, without accountability to the gospel. The apostolic mandate, as we have seen from Paul, is rooted in God's original purpose for all people as revealed through the Abrahamic covenant, of which the children of Israel became the "suffering servant."

Schematically, it would look like figure 1.

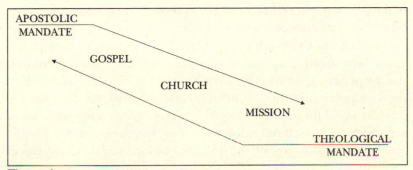

Figure 1.

The theological mandate falls upon the church from the side of mission and is Spirit-led through the church to gospel truth. The apostolic mandate falls upon the church from the side of the gospel as God's mission, not from mission imperatives diagnosed out of contemporary needs and manufactured out of sociological and technological pragmatics and possibilities.

In faithfulness to his apostolic mandate Paul envisions Spain as the next mission horizon for the gospel. He could have made his plans to go directly to Spain and bypass the church in Rome. His mission theology, however, includes the church as strategic and instrumental for this mission. He writes to the church in Rome for the sake of seeking their investment in this mission. He does this so that the church can itself demonstrate its apostolic and missional character. In making this attempt, however, Paul now must fulfill the theological mandate, reflecting back on the gospel from the perspective of the projected mission to Spain.

Paul does not define the church as a theological treatise but in the context of the gospel and mission as constitutive of its life and purpose. Jesus as the beloved Son, anointed by the Spirit, completes the messianic mission given to Israel in his own self-offering for the sins of the world. The Holy Spirit, as the contemporary presence and power of this messianic kingdom promise of redemption, creates the missionary people of God out of every nation, tribe and culture. This is to fulfill Christ's mission of reconciliation of the world to God.

The church will always be tempted to make itself and its confession of faith the agenda and content of its theological reflection. If it does this, it loses its apostolic witness and authority. For the church to be apostolic it must also follow the Holy Spirit's leading through the apostolic mandate of mission. An apostolic church clearly understands the gospel as the mission of God originating in God's redemptive purpose for all humanity, fulfilled through Christ Jesus and released into the world through the Holy Spirit. The church is apostolic when it does its theological reflection from the standpoint of already being invested in mission beyond the doctrinal and parochial boundaries of the church.

Apostolic theology emerges out of the apostolic task. This theology can be found by those who discover anew the mission of Christ in the praxis of the Spirit. This theology can be written only by those who discover the gospel anew in the praxis of mission.

Does Christ continue to stand at the door of the church and knock, seeking to give the gift of apostolic ministry to the church? I believe that he does. Even as pastors, teachers and evangelists are given to the church to equip the members for Christ's ministry, so apostles are given. But even as the church must be pastoral in each aspect of its life and ministry, so it can and must be apostolic.

The theologians of the church must be apostolic in experiencing the praxis of Christ through the power of the Holy Spirit, becoming theological pathfinders through the modern jungles of myth and magic that seek to confuse and captivate people's minds and spirits. Apostolic theology brings clarity and conviction to the ministry of Jesus Christ that is taking place beyond the institutional safety net of polity and program. That takes theological nerve!

The pastors of the church must be apostolic in preaching a theology of the incarnate and present God, interpreting the Word of Christ through the praxis of the work of Christ. Apostolic proclamation seals the tomb of sins forgiven and unbinds forgiven sinners to live freely and unfettered in the bright light of resurrection truth. That takes theological insight!

The members of the church must be apostolic in their calling to be disciples of Jesus Christ as the true apostle and head of the church. Apostolic discipleship is the life of costly grace, saying with Paul, "I want to know Christ and the power of his resurrection and the sharing of his sufferings by becoming like him in his death, if somehow I may attain the resurrection from the dead" (Phil 3:10-11). That takes theological faith!

The apostolic church must be *truthful* in its praxis as well as in belief. At times, when the church seeks to protect and identify itself as the *true* church, it forgets to be a truthful witness. The church can be apostolic and truthful, said the Roman Catholic theologian Hans Küng, only when it helps people "to be truthfully christian, to be truthfully human." That is, "to remain free from all claims except the radical will of God as revealed in Jesus Christ." He notes further:

> Wherever, among individuals or groups, there is a truthful church, there occurs a necessary demythologising and de-demonising, a deepening and humanising of the world and of man; there dawns something of that complete justice, that eternal life, that cosmic peace, that true freedom and that final reconciliation of mankind with God, which one day God's consummated kingdom will bring.[5]

This then is the answer to the question of the apostolic foundation of the church. It comes in the form of another question. Is the church that baptized you into Christ and that affirms your calling as Christian disciple *truthful* in its praxis of Christ? If so, then it is the true church and faithful to its chief apostle, Jesus Christ.

8

AN EMERGING
CHURCH

For more than seventeen years I have had discussions with over two thousand pastors who have enrolled in a Doctor of Ministry program in order to advance their own competence in ministry and to bring back new concepts and strategies to make the ministry of their churches more effective. While strategies of church growth are high on their shopping list, the felt need is expressed more in terms of spiritual renewal for their own lives as well as for the church.

For some the spiritual vitality that marked their earlier ministry has already succumbed to the fatigue of the long-distance runner. Anxious to get out of seminary and into the ministry, "where the rubber hits the road," many pastors look back and see a lot of skid marks. Where once the tank was full and the level road stretched out before them, they now discover that they are "running on empty," and the climb is mostly uphill.

"My church is like a dead battery," one pastor confessed to me. "And it's like they are all plugged into me, hoping for a recharge."

How do you revitalize a church whose most recent accomplishment was a glorious celebration of its founding a hundred years ago? What can you do when the church you helped plant ten years ago spends more energy and time bickering over a remodeling plan for the sanctuary than spreading the good news to its unchurched neighbors?

When these questions are asked, what appears to be a search for a theology and strategy for renewal comes down to a theology of the emergence of the church from within its own institutional and historical existence. The situation of the contemporary church is not so different from the emerging of the first-century church following the Pentecost event. The church has its roots in the redemptive history of God's covenant reaching back to the origins of Israel as the chosen people through whom God's blessing would extend to "all the families of the earth" (Gen 12:3). At the same time the church does not emerge from these roots but from the creative power of God's Spirit, which comes into the present from the future.

The church does not emerge out of its past. When it attempts to do this it resorts to strategies of resuscitation rather than experiencing the power of resurrection. In its attempts to be contemporary the church usually arrives a decade, if not a generation, too late. The renewed church emerges in the present out of its future. As in the case of everything related to the creative life and power of God, the future of the church exists first and then its present.[1]

In this chapter I will examine this process of emerging, first from the "old wineskins" that threatened to restrict the "new wine" of Pentecost, and then from the tenacious tentacles of the church's own institutional survival. Finally, we will see the emerging church as the empowered church, with the resurrection life of Christ flowing into it from above.

Emerging: From the Old Wineskins

The anxiety of the disciples of John the Baptizer was one of the first signs that the mission and ministry of Jesus was threatening to the old order. Approaching Jesus, they asked: "Why do we and the Pharisees fast, but your disciples do not fast?" Jesus' reply was pithy and pointed: "No one sews a piece of unshrunk cloth on an old cloak, for the patch pulls away from the cloak, and a worse tear is made. Neither is new wine put into old wineskins; otherwise, the skins burst, and the wine is spilled, and the skins are destroyed; but new wine is put into fresh wineskins, and so both are preserved" (Mt 9:14-17).

The preservation of the old wineskins is not only sensible but significant. The older skins have many uses, but fermenting new wine is not one of them! The emerging church is not carried into the future in the old containers. The shape of the church is determined by the praxis of the Spirit. Blessed is the church that bursts with this new wine!

When we trace out the emerging church during the period immediately following Pentecost, the struggle between the old wineskins of historical continuity and the fermenting, and sometimes explosive, power of the Spirit becomes evident. Paul's mission theology was clearly on the side of the new wine, while the church at Jerusalem sought to contain and give shape to this spreading movement.

James, Peter and John, the three "pillars" in the church at Jerusalem, had strong ties with the Jesus of Nazareth whom they knew before his death and resurrection. Peter and John, of course, were among the twelve disciples and represented the continuity of that tradition. Though James, the brother of Jesus, was not known as a believer prior to Jesus' crucifixion, quite obviously he had his own natural ties to him. The early Christian community at Jerusalem would likely have granted these three a leadership role based on their prior relationship to Jesus. It soon became apparent, however, that their theological reflection at this early stage was committed to maintaining continuity with the "tradition of the twelve," even though they gave strong testimony to the fact of the resurrection and experienced the coming of the Spirit at Pentecost.

Peter, who preached the first sermon following Pentecost, did not become the theologian of Pentecost, for he does not appear to have grasped the praxis of Pentecost as formative for the nature of the church, as did Paul. In his sermon at Pentecost Peter recounted the historical facts of Jesus' life, together with some Old Testament Scriptures that could now be interpreted as predicting this event. He quotes the promise of the Spirit found in Joel, telling them that they are witnessing its fulfillment. Even Stephen's sermon, which led to his martyrdom, is basically a recitation of the Old Testament events that have now culminated in the resurrection of Jesus as the crucified Messiah (Acts 7).

While Peter later became open to the inclusion of Gentile believers through the ministry of the Spirit in the house of Cornelius (Acts 10), he may have subordinated this ministry of the Spirit to the nature of the church as he saw it, grounded in historical continuity with the Jewish Messiah and the law of Moses. At Antioch, Paul eventually felt compelled to rebuke Peter for acting contrary to this gospel of freedom when he withdrew table fellowship from the Gentile Christians over the issue of circumcision (Gal 2:11-21). Peter had some difficulty accepting the fact that the resurrection power of Christ actually broke into the present through the Holy Spirit in order to liberate believers from bondage to the law that had come to an end in Christ.

Luke, who was in the praxis school of theology with Paul, sees in Pentecost the fulfillment of the Old Testament promise that the Spirit of God would usher in the Day of the Lord with a special anointing falling upon a Davidic son. Luke cites the promise of Isaiah (61:1-2; 58:6) in connection with Jesus' announcement of his own mission (Lk 4:16-21). Following the resurrection Luke records the transferal of this apostolic mission from Jesus to the disciples in the promise of the Holy Spirit with a consequent mission of witness to the end of the earth. Pentecost then occurs as the formative event of the missionary people of God through which the church comes into being (Acts 1–2).

In Matthew's Gospel we have a similar progression from chapter 10, which records the selection and commission of the twelve with their empowerment to perform signs and wonders, through chapters 25 and 28, culminating in the Great Commission. The eschatological vision of Matthew 25 sees all nations gathered at the glorious throne of the Messiah, from which will be selected those who have responded to the apostolic witness. While Matthew does not identify the Holy Spirit as the formative power of this transfer of apostolic mission to the disciples, as Luke does, it is the mission of God through Jesus into the whole world that lays the foundation for what later became the church following Pentecost.

From the life of the early Christians in Jerusalem, it is clear that they expected a rather sudden return of Christ to set up the eschatological kingdom of God. They thus devoted themselves to the formation of a communal life in anticipation of this event. So, despite the tendency to maintain continuity with the earthly history of Jesus, the Jerusalem community also had a vision of the eschatological nature of the church, awaiting the triumphant and glorious return of Christ.

Near the end of that century John received the extraordinary vision on Patmos that looked forward to the consummation of Christ's victory over the forces of evil, leading him to write the book of Revelation. Peter also, though at first unsure of Paul's eschatological vision of the freedom of the Spirit, could finally write of the "inheritance that is imperishable, undefiled, and unfading, kept in heaven for you, who are being protected by the power of God through faith for a salvation ready to be revealed in the last time" (1 Pet 1:4-5). The Petrine tradition eventually makes it clear that the church is an eschatological reality in the present time, born anew to a living hope through the resurrection of Christ, for a "salvation ready to be revealed in the last time" (1 Pet 1:3, 5).

This emerging church, therefore, struggled to assimilate the vision of a resurrected Messiah into the form of the Jewish tradition where the Messiah would fulfill the expectations of the old covenant. The new wine was fermenting, and the old wineskin was threatening to come apart at the seams.

Following the conversion of Saul of Tarsus, and his subsequent activity in planting churches in Gentile territory through the manifestation of the power of the Holy Spirit, these trajectories of mission theology through the early witnesses became a vibrant force among the early Christian community. Though it did not take place without a struggle.

While Paul does not specifically refer to the coming of the Holy Spirit at Pentecost, it is clear that he has experienced a personal encounter with the Spirit of the risen Christ in his own personal Pentecost. Paul's clear testimony to the power of the Spirit of Christ in his life and thought provides the basis for saying that Paul begins his theological reflection out of the Pentecost event as a continuing reality and praxis of the Spirit of Christ.

Becoming a companion of Paul on some of his missionary journeys, Luke provided a vital connection for Paul's theology by relating the Spirit of Pentecost to the Spirit of God active in the conception of Jesus as well as in his earthly ministry (Lk 1). Luke later makes explicit what we find implicit in Paul's mission theology, beginning his account with the Pentecost event (Acts 2). In this way Pentecost became a theological praxis for the formation of the church and its ministry.

A theology of the renewal of the church must begin with a theology of the emerging church, with the "new wine" of the Spirit's praxis allowed to give new shape and vitality to the church's life and ministry. The church must be prepared to "lose its identity" and find it again in the Christ of Pentecost. Its renewal begins with its new birth from above. At the same time, the church must preserve the old wineskins by allowing them to carry and serve the old wine at the banquet where those gathered from "the streets and the lanes . . . the poor, the crippled, the blind, and the lame" are brought in by the Spirit of Christ (Lk 14:21).

Emerging: With Theological Clarity

I have found that pastors, for the most part, are inoculated with enough theology at seminary to provide lifelong immunity. As a generalization this is not fair, I realize. At the same time, despite theological controversies that rock the foundations of many denominations and some churches, the manuals to which most pastors refer in seeking wisdom for their daily ministries are not theological but practical. It would indeed be strange to find the words *theology* and *renewal* in the same book title, not to mention in the same thought!

This is too bad. For it takes theological nerve, not spiritual verve, to follow the praxis of the Spirit! The church in renewal is an emerging church, not only from old wineskins that form its identity but with theological clarity as to its mission and nature. Failure of theological nerve is not so much the mark of a novice as the mentality of a technician. A good technician can push the launch button for an exploratory mission in space. But it is the daring visionary who designs the mission, who swings with the stars and traces orbits in the skies that have never before existed in the human mind.

Renewal is at first a theological venture of tracing the orbit of the Spirit that connects the future to the present, and then consecrates as it corrects the past.

"What no eye has seen, nor ear heard, nor the human heart conceived," wrote the apostle Paul, "these things God has revealed to us through the Spirit; for the Spirit searches everything, even the depths of God" (1 Cor 2:9-10). If our theological manuals are written only by technicians and not by those who are "struck by the Spirit," then it is no wonder that they are good only for conformity or controversy. These books are not what is referred to by the television commercial: "Don't leave home without it!"

The small boy pacing up and down on the sidewalk with a duffel bag slung over his shoulder attracted the attention of a passerby. "Are you waiting for someone?" he asked the boy.

"No," he replied, "I'm running away from home."

"But why then are you still in the neighborhood?"

"Because I'm not allowed to cross the street," the boy replied.

The apostle Paul "crossed the street," so to speak. In so doing he not only broke with his own Jewish tradition but refused to come under the tutelage of those who preceded him in the "school of the apostles" at Jerusalem. Refusing to bring Gentile Christians under the old wineskin of the Jewish law, Paul emerged from the confrontation with a theological clarity that can be found today wherever there is an emerging church.

The emerging church experienced its first theological crisis in the conflict between Paul's mission theology and the more institutional theology of the Jerusalem church. The tendency in the Jerusalem theology to live by historical and institutional continuity with the past is also a strong element in the contemporary theology of the church. An institutional theology of the church is one in which organizational, institutional and historical factors tend to set the theological and mission agenda of the church. I will argue that Paul's mission theology began with a quite different theological basis in the praxis of the Spirit and produced a more vital and creative understanding of the church as a missionary people rather than an organizational entity.

In referring to the Jerusalem theology, I remind the reader of the

position taken by the elders of the church in Jerusalem with regard to
the requirement that Gentile Christians be circumcised in accordance
with the Jewish law in order to be fully accepted into the church. Paul's
letter to the Galatians provides our most direct knowledge of this
position. After assuring the Galatian church that his own apostolic
authority and the gospel that he proclaimed did not originate with the
apostles at Jerusalem (chap. 1), Paul rather sarcastically refers to the
three "pillars" in the Jerusalem church—James, Peter and John. Fourteen years passed before he had a private meeting with them (chap. 2).
He asserts that they fully consented to his ministry to the Gentiles, and
even accepted Titus, who was not circumcised (this probably refers to
Paul's trip to Jerusalem, described in Acts 15).

Despite this apparent concession to his ministry, Paul refers to an
incident that later took place in the church at Antioch when "certain
people came from James" and urged the Jewish Christians to separate
from the uncircumcised Gentile Christians at table fellowship. Not only
was Peter involved in this defection, according to Paul, but Barnabas
was persuaded as well and withdrew fellowship from the Gentile Christians. Paul testifies to his outrage at this violation of the gospel of Christ
and states that he rebuked Peter publicly over this matter (Gal 2:11-14).

The conciliatory tone of the Acts 15 meeting soon dissolved into
polemics and opposition to Paul. It became apparent that the leaders
of the church in Jerusalem never fully accepted the freedom that Paul
claimed to have in Jesus Christ, where the distinction between Jew and
Gentile had been set aside once and for all through the death and
resurrection of Christ (Eph 2:11-22). This contrast between Paul's
concept of the church and that of the Jerusalem community has been
portrayed clearly by Emil Brunner, among others. The church in
Jerusalem operated more as a theocratic community, imposing the
strictures of the Jewish law upon Christians, in contrast to Paul's
charismatic concept of the church under the leading and direction of
the Spirit of Christ.[2]

Luke presents both sides of the issue in his account in Acts 15,
allowing the Jerusalem church to have its place as well as the churches
formed under Paul's ministry among the Gentiles by the work of the
Spirit. The theological clarity, however, remained with Paul, and so did

the continued Spirit of renewal and mission that spread across the known world of that day.

While Brunner may have overstated the contrast, there is much truth in what he has said.[3] Paul developed his theology of the emerging church out of the praxis of the Spirit of Christ revealed through the mission of proclaiming the gospel. This is set in contrast to the theological mindset of the Jerusalem community, which, though having experienced the historical event of the giving of the Holy Spirit at Pentecost, nonetheless retreated to a more institutional and legalistic theology of the church. This contrast is not meant to suggest introducing a dichotomy between church and mission. Rather, for the sake of overcoming such a dichotomy I suggest that Paul's mission theology is first of all a theology of the church as the mission of Jesus Christ in the world.

Emerging: With Resurrection Power and Life!

The raising of Lazarus (Jn 11) can easily be seen as a parable of the emerging church. The lament of the sisters upon greeting Jesus expresses so well the mentality of the church whose programs and methods become rituals for baptizing the dead rather than for celebrating life. "Lord, if you had been here, my brother would not have died" (11:32). This is as if to say, "Lord, we were faithful and did our best. We left it in your hands and now it is too late."

Even when Jesus attempted to break through this cordon of negativity by saying, "Take away the stone," they attempted to stop his ministry! "Lord, already there is a stench because he has been dead four days" (11:39).

In the end, however, Lazarus emerged when his name was called, though he was still bound with strips of cloth. "Unbind him," said Jesus, "and let him go" (11:44).

There is a sense in which Pentecost represents the "unbinding" of the church from its "graveclothes." With stunning theological clarity Paul wrote to the church he had planted in Galatia. "Are you so foolish? Having started with the Spirit, are you now ending with the flesh? . . . For freedom Christ has set us free. Stand firm, therefore, and do not submit again to a yoke of slavery" (Gal 3:3; 5:1).

Paul's theology of spiritual freedom says to the Christians in every age: "Unbind the church, and let it go!" This is not to say that the church is free to follow every spirit or every "wind of doctrine" (Eph 4:14). Being freed from the law of sin and death, we are under the "law of the Spirit of life in Christ Jesus," wrote Paul (Rom 8:2).

Paul did not seek to demolish the old wineskins, even though he did not find the new wine of the Spirit of Jesus there. Instead, he saw the law as a tutor leading to Christ (Gal 3:24). The emergence of the church through the resurrection power and Spirit of Jesus Christ corrected and consecrated the old covenant.

How do we unbind the church so that it can emerge with resurrection power and life? Several steps logically follow from a mission theology of the church.

Redefine the mission. The praxis of Christ is discerned in the mission of Christ as defined by God's love for the world. Every church exists as a result of the mission of Christ empowered by the Spirit of Christ. Every church should define its specific mission on a regular basis. A mission statement answers the question: "What ministry of Christ in the world would not take place if we did not exist?" Every church has the purpose to glorify God by extending the gospel of Christ into the world in obedience to Christ's commission. "Go therefore and make disciples of all nations, baptizing them in the name of the Father and of the Son and of the Holy Spirit, and teaching them to obey everything that I have commanded you" (Mt 28:19-20).

The mission of each church, however, is specific to that church's understanding of its role in fulfilling this commission. When the church lives by the purpose of the commission of Christ without defining its mission, it has not yet been unbound. Pentecost unbinds the church by empowering it for specific goals and objectives that flow out of its mission statement. This statement should be formulated through a consensus of the church through its leadership and ordinarily will be no longer than one or two paragraphs.

Using the model displayed in the previous chapter, each church should position itself between the gospel of Christ and its particular mission. This is exactly what Paul did when he redefined his mission as extending to Spain. When the church has grasped its mission clearly it has made contact with the source of its empowerment and is stretching its limbs, preparing for action!

Recalibrate the aim. It is no use having a target if the sight is not properly calibrated. The launching of a satellite into space not only is a "mission" but has specific goals and objectives. Without sufficient launching power, the rocket will never get beyond the pull of gravity and will fall back to earth. But it is not enough to blast off into space; the on-board computers must be carefully calibrated so as to place the satellite in orbit at exactly the right speed and distance.

This metaphor is an apt one, for the mission of a church does not ride on rails, like a train, but moves on a trajectory that requires faith in calculations that take into account the invisible, the unexpected and the untried. Many churches make the mistake of loading a mission on a flatcar and sending it down rails that lead to nowhere. The role of the Holy Spirit is not to provide raw power for launching a mission, but to provide a guidance system by which the church can recalibrate its aim. Paul had to recalibrate his aim several times when he sought to accomplish his mission in Asia. Twice the Holy Spirit told him to go back and to set his sights higher! Finally, in a vision during the night, he heard a man calling out, "Come over to Macedonia and help us" (Acts 16:6-10).

Once the mission statement is clear, the church must pause to "hear the Macedonian call." This requires all the more a consensus of the Spirit on the part of the members of the church. Renewal comes about through listening for this call, not by building new models to send down the same old rails!

Reenergize the cells. Earlier in this chapter I used the metaphor of a dead battery, with the members of the church plugging into the pastor seeking a recharge. One thing I have learned in attempting to jump-start a dead battery is that it is impossible if one of the cells is dead. A dead cell short-circuits the electrical current flowing through a battery.

When the apostle Paul wrote to Timothy, he gave instructions on maintaining the "godliness" of the church. He warned against permitting members of the church to have a "morbid craving for controversy and for disputes about words . . . envy, dissension, slander, base suspicions, and wrangling among those who are depraved in mind and bereft of the truth, imagining that godliness is a means of gain" (1 Tim 6:3-5). The godliness of a church is not its self-righteousness, but its spirit of humility and love.

The Holy Spirit abides not only in each individual member of the church but in the body as a whole. It is not enough for individual members to be filled with the Spirit; the church must be filled with the Spirit as well. What short-circuits the Spirit of renewal is a contrary spirit in the body, manifested by the sparks that fly when contact is made. Paul's counsel to the church at Philippi would make an excellent text for a service of repentance and renewal, reenergizing the cells of the church. "If then there is any encouragement in Christ, any consolation from love, any sharing in the Spirit, any compassion and sympathy, make my joy complete: be of the same mind, having the same love, being in full accord and of one mind" (Phil 2:1-2).

Unleash the people for mission. Jesus walked out of his tomb on Easter morning, having already left his graveclothes behind. He was unbound. Mary Magdalene may have been the first one to greet him, though she had to be jolted out of her own stupor of disbelief in order to recognize him. She must have fallen at his feet and put her arms around him, for Jesus said to her: "Do not hold on to me, because I have not yet ascended to the Father. But go . . ." (Jn 20:17).

When the people of God are empowered, they need to be released for the ministry of Christ and not huddled around the feet of Christ at the altar. We sup with Christ in order to run with him. The church needs to unleash its members and become a sending church rather than a gathering one. When the only theme song of the church is "Blest Be the Tie That Binds," it will get all tangled up in its own apron strings. The Spirit of Christ cannot be tethered to institutional programs nor contained in the straitjacket of ecclesial politics.

Jim Rayburn, the founder of Young Life, in a personal conversation years ago recounted to me his experience as a youth pastor in a church in Texas. "I found out that the kids would only accept me when I met them on their turf and won the right to talk about Christ to them on their terms. I spent most of my time on the playground and in their backyards. Their response to Christ was thrilling and powerful."

The church, however, did not see much of the kids, nor of Rayburn, and became impatient with his ministry. "I was given an ultimatum," Rayburn told me: "Bring the kids back into the youth program of the church or find another job." It did not take long for him to make his decision, and as a result Young Life emerged, while the church remained behind its walls.

The early church, 120 people in all, emerged from behind its walls on the day of Pentecost, and before nightfall "that day about three thousand persons were added" (Acts 2:41). The next day the *Jerusalem Journal* reported something about "a Holy Spirit coming upon these people." Little did they know!

9

A CHARISMATIC DYNAMIC

The higher Christian churches—where, if anywhere, I belong—
come at God with an unwarranted air of professionalism,
with authority and pomp, as though they knew what they were doing, as
though people in themselves were an appropriate set of
creatures to have dealings with God. I often think of the set pieces of liturgy
as certain words which people have successfully addressed
to God without their getting killed. In the high churches they saunter through
the liturgy like Mohawks along a strand of scaffolding who have long since
forgotten their danger. If God were to blast such a service to bits,
the congregation would be, I believe, genuinely shocked. But in the low
churches you expect it any minute. This is the beginning of wisdom.[1]

When the church becomes enthralled with its own expertise, it loses its
capacity to be transformed by the freedom of the Spirit. On another
occasion, Annie Dillard suggested that if we really believe that we have
come to worship God when we attend a divine service, we had better

put seat belts on when we sit down in the pews! I am not sure that this is what Paul meant by "stirring up the gift" when he exhorted Timothy (2 Tim 1:6 KJV). For Paul, the praxis of the Spirit was his theological teacher as much as his innovator in worship.

An Evangelical and Pentecostal Theology?

I teach at a theological seminary whose theological stance is defined first of all in its catalog as "Evangelical Commitment." This is further defined as a fervor that flows out of God's character, the practice of evangelism, engagement with Scripture in the context of the responsible Christian community, godly living and confidence in the unity of God's truth.

This theological stance is also held amid an ecumenical posture, with a multidenominational faculty, student body and constituency. As a result there is a broad continuum of Christian experience and ecclesiological pluralism represented at every level, within the framework of an evangelical theological commitment.

Recently I was asked by a pastor in our Doctor of Ministry program, "Why does a school with an evangelical emphasis not also have a pentecostal theology? I understand that you have a lot of students and some faculty who have a charismatic Christian experience and many who are members of Pentecostal churches. Is Pentecost only an experience and evangelical only a theology?"

"If you have a couple of hours," I responded, "I would like to talk about that. Better yet, I am writing a book and I'll talk about it there!"

He was not the only one asking this question. Several years ago the seminary offered a course titled "Signs and Wonders." It was team-taught by one of our regular faculty and a pastor whose ministry was well known for an emphasis on healing, exorcism and the use of the supernatural spiritual gifts in evangelism. When over two hundred students enrolled and when each class period was followed by clinical demonstrations of healings and exorcisms, a controversy erupted. The theologians were uneasy and questioned the biblical and theological basis for this ministry. Did such a thing belong in an academic curriculum? It appeared to be appropriate to *discuss* such issues in an academic setting, but actually to experience them was a confusion of boundaries, many thought.

At the core, however, the controversy revealed an unresolved question, neatly put by my pastor friend. "Is Pentecost only an experience and evangelical only a theology?"[2]

In this chapter I will show the inner connection between an evangelical and pentecostal theology. Or rather, I will show why a mission theology such as emerged from the apostle Paul's ministry and teaching is both evangelical and pentecostal. I use the phrase "pentecostal theology" in a generic sense, including charismatic and Third Wave theology.

Paul, through his own conversion by the Spirit of Jesus and his missionary activity, became the first theologian of Pentecost and, as we have seen, formulated a dynamic charismatic theology. The Spirit poured out at the first Pentecost provides the theological praxis for a doctrine of the Trinity. Paul argued passionately and profoundly for the unity of God in his work as Spirit within us, Christ with us, and the Father around us. A mission theology cannot be truly evangelical and trinitarian without also being a pentecostal theology. Nor can a pentecostal theology be effective in mission without also being trinitarian in nature.[3]

This is all the more relevant in our day when we see the church divided over doctrinal orthodoxy, which seeks to hold the church accountable to its historical theology and confessions on the one hand, and, on the other hand, a quest for renewal through the manifestations of spiritual enthusiasm and promotion of evangelism through "signs and wonders." I fear that an institutional theology of the church will, at best, be able only to achieve an uneasy alliance with the manifestations of the Spirit that it cannot ignore. At the same time, it will allow disapproval of these phenomena, if not disdain, to permeate its official theology.

Without an authentic mission theology, such as developed by the apostle Paul, the Spirit of Pentecost may flourish but ultimately fail when it does not lead to renewed theological reflection on the grace and mystery of God's inner relation as Father and Son and Holy Spirit. Without such a mission theology authentically produced by those who experience God's mission in relation to the world, an academic theology of the church may reign as the "queen of the sciences," yet finally fall victim to its own paralysis of analysis. It will not be enough to call such a theology evangelical if its only distinctive is that it upholds true doctrine over false, or defines its own theology as orthodox as against other theologies.

Truth in theology is not relinquished when it is open to the Spirit which leads to truth. God's self-revelation through Christ's mission is the criterion for truthfulness. "When the Spirit of truth comes, he will guide you into all the truth; for he will not speak on his own, but will speak whatever he hears, and he will declare to you the things that are to come. He will glorify me, because he will take what is mine and declare it to you" (Jn 16:13-14). The Spirit of truth did not disappear into the ink that binds the Word of God to the printed page. Scripture is true because it is inspired by the Spirit, but the truth of Scripture as Word of God resides in the continued praxis of the Holy Spirit. To break this inner relation of truth is to separate "evangelical" from "pentecostal."

Mission theology is what keeps those involved in the apostolic mandate of mission accountable to the truth of revelation and reconciliation in Jesus Christ as the "once and for all" history of salvation. But mission theology also is "salvation in history," as some liberation theologians remind us. Mission theology has as its truthful content the historical facts of salvation through the incarnation, death and resurrection of Christ, leading to the presence of Christ in the historical present. This salvation of God through Christ intended for the whole world demands an interpretation and application in the living and contemporary history and culture of each person and generation.

Mission theology follows the truth of Pentecost as the manifestation of the Spirit of Christ in the praxis of mission. This is a living truth and a contemporary truth that is being revealed through the encounter between Christ and persons in their own time and place. Systematic and historical theology can only prepare the way for mission theology and allow Pentecost once more to lead the way to the resurrected Christ as the source of all truth.

While loading their guns for the "Battle over the Bible," some theologians may have actually turned their backs on the mission of God with its power encounter with the forces of evil and oppression for the sake of a better aim at other theologians. They are like the Pharisees, who were so intent on discrediting Jesus for the sake of their own orthodoxy that they were blinded to the messianic power of Jesus in healing the eyes of the man blind since birth (Jn 9). Paul's own evangelical theology came "not in word only, but also in power and in the Holy Spirit and with full conviction" (1 Thess 1:5). The truth of the gospel, Paul reminded Peter, was not a human determination of God's law but the divine determination of human reconciliation and liberation, such as was represented by the Jews and Gentiles united in Christ at a common table (Gal 2:11-21).

The word *evangelical* may best be understood as a mission term before it is used as theological jargon. It is time once again to recover its authentic theological content by assigning the task to the mission theologians in the vanguard of the missionary people of God, the church under the power of the Holy Spirit.

But this cannot take place if those who have experienced the mission of God through the Spirit are not encouraged and enabled to occupy primary theological chairs in the church's institutional and educational life. Would Paul, the missionary theologian, be permitted to teach theology in our foremost divinity schools and theological seminaries? Would his DPT (Doctor of Pentecostal Theology) earned through the Extended Education Department of the church in Antioch qualify him alongside the academic doctorates earned in residence under the divinity faculty at the University of Jerusalem? Or would he be assigned to teach in the missiology department, with Bible and theology taught by others who have earned their degrees through academic study and research?

It is a standing joke among theological faculties that the apostle Paul would not stand much chance of a tenured faculty appointment, or even, for that matter, a call to be pastor of a local church. But then, all joking aside, the faculty and the church go right ahead with business as usual, following the accepted and established criteria!

The Pentecostal Movement—A Theological Anomaly

The modern Pentecostal phenomenon, with its emphasis on a personal and corporate experience of the Holy Spirit, is producing astounding claims of growth in churches in North America as well as in countries around the world. Largely a grassroots movement based on the manifestation of signs of the Spirit with a highly experiential form of Christian faith, Pentecostalism tends to move from experience toward theology. Theologians within the Pentecostal movement have in some cases formed their own Bible schools and seminaries. Others have found their way into the more traditional seminary faculties, usually having first of all qualified by a Ph.D. degree from a prestigious divinity school.

The modern Pentecostal movement represents a theological anomaly, when viewed from the perspective of a mission theology as I have defined it. Having direct experience of the mission of God through the Holy Spirit, Pentecostal churches should have become a strong force in developing a mission theology along the lines of the Pauline theology developed in chapter six. This does not seem to have happened for the most part. I believe that there are two reasons for this.

First, the tradition of an academic theology of the church, with its strong tendencies toward developing a theology of institutions (with an emphasis on historical antecedents), produces a dichotomy between objective truth and subjective experience. This is true even in the study of the Scriptures. The Holy Spirit is studied under the theological category of the "order of salvation" rather than given an epistemological and hermeneutical role in theological reflection. Charles Hodge, of the "Old Princeton School" of theology, in the very first chapter of his *Systematic Theology* went so far as to say that the Holy Spirit has no part in determining the rule of faith, but only in its application. As a result the magisterial theology of Reformed orthodoxy and consequently of later "new evangelical" theology captured the main centers of theological training with a strong emphasis on the critical mind of the scholar and objective revelation.

The revival movements of the nineteenth and early twentieth centuries, in both England and the United States, produced a resurgence of Christian faith among the people. The Pentecostal movement swelled this tide of personal religion with its emphasis on the signs of the Holy Spirit as a mark of personal holiness as well as a powerful force in evangelism. Meanwhile, academic theology had already become deeply entrenched in the search for objective truth and the maintenance of its own institutional life and orthodox confessions of faith. The Pentecostal movement simply had no place in the theological academy under these terms.

Second, those who were most influenced by the Pentecostal movement of the Holy Spirit were attracted more to the immediate effects of their experience than to theological reflection upon it. I find it interesting that the Pauline formula "Christ Jesus," with its strong sense of continuity with God's mission through the Spirit in the Old Testament and deep trinitarian instincts, gave way in pentecostal piety to the simple formula "Jesus." The messianic mission represented in the title "Christ" has largely dropped out of the pentecostal vocabulary. Prayers to Jesus come easily to the lips both in devotional worship and in prayers for healing.

Through the Holy Spirit, Jesus has become contemporary as a formula for exorcism and as an object of devotion. But with this is a loss of continuity between the present experience of the Spirit (Jesus) and the messianic Spirit of Jahweh manifested through Israel and united with Christ Jesus in a full trinitarian experience. There was little need for theological reflection, given this radical contemporization of Jesus through the experience of the Holy Spirit. As a result the Pentecostal movement lost its connection with mission theology. This is the anomaly. It has pentecostal experience without pentecostal theology. Where we expect mission theology, we are shown signs and wonders.

The Third Wave Movement—A Charismatic Power Encounter
Professor Peter Wagner at Fuller Theological Seminary acknowledges his own conversion to a pentecostal experience while a missionary in Bolivia, where he saw multitudes coming to Christ through the Pentecostal churches while the more traditional missionary efforts were insignificant, by contrast. Adapting the church growth principles of Donald McGavran to his own pentecostal leanings, Wagner has become one of the most prominent leaders in what he has termed "the Third Wave." Following the emergence of the Pentecostal movement

in the United States in the early part of the twentieth century (the first wave), and following the rise of the charismatic movement in the 1960s (the second wave), Wagner suggests that a third wave of the Holy Spirit's work is now developing. Citing David Barrett, the charismatic Anglican who is the editor of the *World Christian Encyclopedia,* Wagner states that in 1970 there may have been as many as fifty thousand who could be identified as belonging to the Third Wave, while in 1987 there may be as many as twenty-seven million.[4]

The Third Wave is distinguished from the earlier Pentecostal movement, says Wagner, by its emphasis on the filling of the Holy Spirit rather than on a baptism of the Holy Spirit evidenced by the Spirit gift of tongues. The core of the Third Wave, maintains Wagner, is composed of evangelicals who are satisfied with their present ecclesiastical affiliation and desire that it remain intact. This leads to a further distinctive of this movement in that it seeks to avoid divisiveness and disunity. By not stressing the Spirit-filled life as against those who do not have the Spirit, this movement seeks to avoid the tendency of the charismatic movement (second wave), which in Wagner's judgment contributed to a "two class" Christian experience.[5]

One primary distinctive of the Third Wave movement is its emphasis on the supernatural power of the kingdom of God as manifested through "signs and wonders," particularly in the area of physical healing and the exorcising of demons. John Wimber, founder of the Vineyard Christian Fellowship in Anaheim, California, strongly influenced Wagner in this emphasis. Wimber argues that "power evangelism," characterized by the manifestation of "signs and wonders" in the area of supernatural healings and exorcisms, has replaced "program evangelism" as God's strategy for this generation.[6]

To Wagner's credit, he realizes the need to provide theological foundations for this movement, and in his book he attempts this task. Beginning with the assumption that the "signs and wonders" performed by Jesus were done so totally through his humanity as filled with the power of the Holy Spirit, Wagner argues that this provides an incarnational theology by which the same power that Jesus possessed can be transferred to any believer today. This "Passing the Power" (a chapter title in his book) can take place because it is not the deity of Christ that constitutes the basis for his "power ministry" but his humanity.

Even though our human nature is not perfect, unlike that of Jesus, Wagner argues that we can still do the "greater works" (Jn 14:12) because the same Spirit that anointed him has now come upon us through Pentecost.[7] The "power encounters" that result from the manifestation of the Holy Spirit through this approach demonstrate to a skeptical and unbelieving world the reality of the unseen God, Wagner maintains. Thus, church growth and evangelism can best be accomplished through the development of the gifts of the Spirit, particularly the supernatural gifts of healing and exorcism.

The church reaps the harvest of these power encounters and so grows numerically as thousands are added through personal conversion to Christ, who is presented as the Lord and Savior of each individual. With power evangelism tied to discipling and nurture through cell groups and congregational life in the context of celebration in worship, Wagner argues that church growth becomes kingdom growth in fulfillment of the Great Commission in Matthew 28:18-20.

I have dealt with this movement at length because it represents one of the most significant attempts in our modern era to renew and expand the traditional church through an emphasis on the power of the Spirit. If the statistics cited by Wagner are cut in half, we are still talking about twelve million Christians who can be identified as part of the Third Wave movement. The Full Gospel Church in Seoul, Korea, accounts for one million of these if it succeeded in expanding beyond six hundred thousand to one million by 1992, a goal that had been announced by Pastor Paul Yonggi Cho.

My own assessment is critical of the movement's theological basis and basically affirmative of its spiritual impetus. I am encouraged by the attempt, though belated, at developing a theological basis for its ministry focus. I see it as truly grasping the apostolic mandate of carrying out the gospel in a mission to the world, through the church. My criticism would be that it has failed to fully define the nature of a mission theology such as I have attempted to describe above. There is a sense in which the modern church growth movement is also a theology of the church first of all as an institution that seeks to extend its own life through mission.

Wagner begins with the traditional church doctrine of the Incarnation as consisting of the two natures of Christ. He then attempts to ground the power of God in the human nature of Christ to the exclusion of the divine nature. Wagner argues that the Spirit of God performs signs and wonders through the human nature of Christ. Instead of seeing the incarnation as a continuation of God's mission through the divine Sonship of Jesus, by the power of the Spirit, he uses the incarnation as a means of linking the Spirit with our humanity. In seeking to develop a theology of "signs and wonders" he locates the power of the Spirit in our common humanity with Christ. He does not trace out the relation of Pentecost to resurrection and crucifixion, as Paul does in his theology of the Spirit.

Wagner's use of power evangelism as a method to add to the church is exactly what I earlier described as the method of an institutional theology of the church. The gospel is narrowed to fit the task of adding to the church rather than its ministry to the world in its all-embracing reconciliation of human life—social, political and spiritual.

The Third Wave Movement—Its Theological Inadequacy
The inadequacy of Professor Wagner's theology of Incarnation lies in his view that the humanity of Christ is only instrumental. The "signs and wonders" wrought by Jesus are said, according to Wagner, to be primarily manifestations of power, which is an occasion of the Spirit of God. Thus we too, Wagner argues, can expect to be instruments of the Spirit in God's manifestation of power through signs and wonders today. This attempt to ground pentecostal power in the Spirit alone, viewing humanity as only instrumental, does not provide for the sanctification of humanity. Humanity is in need of more than its physical or even emotional healing. The power of sanctification is found in the actual humanity of Jesus Christ as the bearer of the very life of the Son as divine Logos, not merely as a human instrument through which God displayed his divine power.

This theological inadequacy leads to a misunderstanding of the church. It fails to see the church as the corporate form of God's mission to the world in its need for full reconciliation to God and with one another. The emphasis on signs and wonders as a methodology for evangelism and church growth does not grasp the wholistic thrust of the church's life and mission. The miraculous does not violate the natural means by which God's mission finds its way through Christ into the world for the salvation of all. Feeding the hungry, liberating the oppressed, bringing peace and reconciliation to people and between people is never accomplished by the miraculous alone—not in Jesus' ministry, not in Paul's ministry, and not in the church's ministry to the world.

This means that evangelism must not be construed as merely adding members to the church in such a way that the humanity of those evangelized is left unconsecrated. The sanctification of humanity is grounded in the humanity of Christ as a vicarious humanity, by which his priestly ministry includes all who are suffering in their own humanity. Formation of Christ in the world through the Spirit does not take place apart from the world. This can be seen as the thrust of the teaching of Jesus in Matthew 25, where the presence of Christ in the world occurs through ministry to those who are outcasts, through visiting the imprisoned, through ministry to the poor and through clothing the naked.

The Christian mission does not bring Christ to the world. That is not its power. That is the power of Pentecost, where Christ returns in the power of the Holy Spirit. Rather, Christians who are the temple of the Holy Spirit witness by their own presence in the world that Christ has come to the world, and has taken up the cause of the afflicted, the oppressed and the estranged as his own cause. The mandate for theological reflection is pressed upon those who minister to give account of that which is done in the name of Christ, and for the sake of "humanizing humanity" in its estrangement from Christ. Pastoral decisions with regard to people who suffer loss and estrangement demand this kind of mission theology.

As I see it, the charismatic renewal movement did not attempt to develop a clear mission theology as it found its home in churches where a theology of the church was already fully developed, based upon some form of continuity between the church and the incarnation. Because this tradition had its theological foundations sunk deep into the christological controversies and councils of the first five centuries, "ecclesial theology" preempted "mission theology," based on the assumption that the nature of the church is defined more by the incarnation than by Pentecost. Theology was assumed to deal with the "nature of things," and the nature of the church could be defined by reflecting upon the nature of Christ as both human and divine, ontologically one with the preexisting divine Logos.[8] The question of the church's nature rested upon a theology of the Incarnation in terms of the two natures of Christ, the form of his real presence on the altar and his relation to the office of ministry in the church.

The mission and ministry of the church are forced to serve the nature of the church in a theology of the church grounded upon its own institutional existence. When theology tends to define *church* in terms of historical institution, as an object, it fails to see it as a Pentecost event and its relation to the mission of God in the world. No longer existing primarily as a missionary people of God empowered and directed by the Holy Spirit, the church struggles to formulate a theology of missions when it is reminded of the Great Commission (Mt 28). Concerns for orthodoxy in its doctrinal confession have produced a rich but sometimes puzzling tradition of theological reflection. Evangelism then becomes a means to add members to the church. Expressed concern for social and political justice, concern for the poor and the oppressed, and concern for peace and reconciliation between persons not in the church are weak in theological substance.

To this day there rages a debate over the so-called priority of the evangelistic mandate over the cultural mandate, or the relation of evangelism to social action.[9] The root of this problem, as I see it, is the traditional formation of a theology of the church along institutional lines in contrast to the New Testament process of theological development. As a result, the church tends to become inward directed rather than outward focused.

A second criticism can be made of the Third Wave movement with respect to its understanding of power. When the power of the Holy Spirit is seen primarily as a supernatural event and as a power encounter with alien spiritual powers, the "power of God for salvation" as Paul used the phrase (Rom 1:16) becomes trivialized and superficial.

When Luke places the Magnificat of Mary, the mother of Jesus, at the very outset of the announcement concerning the birth of the Messiah, he is envisaging a different kind of power. "He has shown strength with his arm; . . . brought down the powerful from their thrones, and lifted up the lowly; he has filled the hungry with good things, and sent the rich away empty" (Lk 1:51-53).

Luke's gospel account is carefully constructed so that the power of the cross as the baptism of Jesus is foremost. As early as chapter nine Luke tells us, "When the days drew near for him to be taken up, he set his face to go to Jerusalem" (9:51). A few chapters later Luke reminds us, "Jesus went through one town and village after another, teaching as he made his way to Jerusalem" (13:22). Later we find the phrase once more, "On the way to Jerusalem Jesus was going through the region between Samaria and Galilee" (17:11). Finally we read, "After he had said this, he went on ahead, going up to Jerusalem. . . . As he came near and saw the city, he wept over it" (19:28, 41). Through this progression, marked by the literary signposts, Luke develops his messianic theme of salvation through identity with the poor, the sick and the outcasts, calling his own disciples into the power of God revealed through redemptive suffering.

When we remember that Luke was Paul's occasional missionary companion, we are not surprised to see this emphasis on the power of God made manifest through weakness. The eschatological signs and wonders that both Jesus and Paul performed were not the primary manifestations of God's power. Rather for Paul the power of God is revealed in the conversion of the Gentiles to God in fulfillment of the messianic promise through Christ Jesus and the Holy Spirit. As to his own personal life and ministry, Paul learned that the "power of Christ" is made perfect in his weakness (2 Cor 9—10). We continue to look for a more biblical treatment of power in the theological reflection of the Third Wave.

Clearly alert to the charge that power evangelism neglects the larger and more complex issues of human life, Wagner suggests that the ministry of the kingdom of God ought to include concern for the poor and oppressed. "We should provide food for the hungry here in our own nation and around the world. We should seek to change social structures that create degrading conditions for fellow human beings, such as apartheid in South Africa or the caste system in India."[10] Yet he does not apply "power" to these situations, though he earlier listed the poor, war and oppressed people among six areas of the kingdom of God that were contained within the gospel of Christ. Only the demon possessed, the sick and the lost are taken up as themes for power evangelism.[11] And only the sick and the demonized attract the attention of his book in the main.

More recently Wagner and others in the Third Wave movement have addressed more directly the need for transformation of social structures and the meeting of human social needs. Here we begin to see a concern for the more wholistic agenda of the kingdom of God as outlined in Wagner's earlier book. At the same time this approach continues to stress the supernatural aspect of social transformation through various forms of power encounters.[12]

Many theologians tend to dismiss the Third Wave movement as partial in its approach to the kingdom of God, superficial in its Christology, unscientific in its documentation as to "signs and wonders" and marginal to orthodoxy in its preoccupation with experience over doctrine. This is unfortunate, for the movement deserves better than that.

Christopraxis is the continuing Pentecost event that takes place through the growth of the church in the world. Even mere numerical church growth, if it is the growth of those who participate in God's mission through Christopraxis, is a pentecostal mission theology event. The church growth movement, which tends to rely overly much on sociological principles and strategies for its success, could well find in the praxis of Pentecost its theological mandate as well as its spiritual muscle. The Third Wave movement, with its focus on the supernatural, could well find in mission theology a Christopraxis that includes the power of God manifest in weakness as well as the miraculous.

Implicit to the mission theology of the church as construed above is the theology of church growth that is *numerically commissioned*—"make disciples of all nations" (Mt 28:19)—*geographically mandated*—"to the ends of the earth" (Acts 1:8)—*pentecostally empowered*—"you will receive power when the Holy Spirit has come upon you" (Acts 1:8), and *ecclesially multiplied*—"and day by day the Lord added to their number those who were being saved" (Acts 2:47). Church growth as a movement must become part of church growth as mission, with mission theology once more becoming the basis for the theology and praxis of the church as the missionary people of God.

Toward an Authentic Charismatic Theology

The authentic charism that liberates is not the spirit of power but the Spirit of Christ. An authentic charismatic theology empowers blacks in South Africa to participate in the franchise of full membership in the human race as defined socially, politically and spiritually. It is a theology that empowers women to have full parity in every structure of society, especially the church and its ministry. It is a theology that empowers the poor, the marginalized, the weak and the homeless to live meaningful and comfortable lives as human beings created in God's image. An authentic charismatic theology disarms the church of its pride and privilege, causing it to repent and to enact repentance toward God through responsible service toward the world that God loves. Thomas Smail has said it well:

> The charismatic Christian with his world-affirming approach and his awareness of both the demonic and the prophetic should be among those who can catch the vision. God wants to give in local churches structures of relationship that have their roots in the central relationship to himself, but that express themselves horizontally and practically in such a way as to challenge the oppressive structures of society in which the church lives.[13]

Charismatic Christians, Smail continues, should be as much concerned for the socially demonic in the form of oppressive structures as for the personally demonic. Exactly! The incarnation is not only a supernatural phenomenon, but also a truly human occurrence of the natural in the sphere of the human, which occurs in place, power and time.[14]

The incarnational basis for mission theology is not grounded in the humanity of those who possess the Spirit in the same way that the humanity of Jesus of Nazareth did. Rather, the humanity of men and women who exist in their specific time and place under conditions of powerlessness constitutes the incarnational praxis of Christ. James Torrance helps us to see this when he says: "Christ does not heal us by standing over against us. . . . He is the true Priest, bone of our bone, flesh of our flesh." As such, he bears upon his divine heart our sins and injustices and effects our reconciliation in his vicarious humanity.[15]

Todd Speidell reinforces this when he adds:

Christ presents himself in the depths of human need—the hungry, the thirsty, the naked, the sick, the imprisoned (Mt. 25:31ff). The stranger among us, the homeless and psychologically debilitated, may be the place of Christ's presence among us. The Gospel of Matthew does not exhort us simply to be like Christ—ministering to the needy "as Jesus would" (which implies that he is not actively present but merely serves as a model for our social action)—but attests that Christ discloses himself through the stranger. We must be where Christ is, and act where he acts.[16]

"Is Pentecost only an experience and evangelical only a theology?" I am still stung by that question! If that is the perception of the situation today in our schools and our churches (and I am afraid that it is), we need theological as well as personal repentance. From the very first chapter of this book I have attempted to correct this perception by arguing that the praxis of Pentecost is Christopraxis. The Christ of Pentecost is the charism of the Spirit. Without the charism of the Spirit there can be no theological insight into the praxis of Christ. And without the praxis of Christ, the charism of the Spirit disintegrates into the many spirits of human and even demonic distortion.

There can be no authentic charismatic ministry without a charismatic theology. Charismatic theology has its roots in mission theology. Mission theology is guided in its theological instincts as much by orthopraxy (right actions) as by orthodoxy (right thinking). What connects orthodoxy to orthopraxy is orthopathy—authentic concern. Jesus Christ continues to be the "way, the truth and the life." We cannot go wrong when we follow Christ's concerns and life in order to discover Christ's truth. This is how the Spirit leads us into all truth (Jn 16:13).

PART 3

ORTHOPRAXIS

10

A CONCERN FOR TRUTHFUL LIFE

What is truth?" asked Pilate of Jesus, who answered not a word. It was not meant to be a question, and there was no need to wait for an answer. Jesus had already said, "Everyone who belongs to the truth listens to my voice" (Jn 18:37-38). Pilate was not listening, at least not to Jesus. He heard the crowd clearly enough—their charge that Jesus attempted to be a king and their insinuations that failure to put him to death would not be viewed kindly by the emperor (Jn 19:12). Truth is what you embrace to preserve your own life, and the name you give to your right to destroy others.

One of the largest Protestant denominations in America, perceived by many to be conservative in theology, is undergoing a painful and tragic internal upheaval over the issue of biblical inerrancy. At stake, many argue, is the very truth of the Bible and therefore of the orthodoxy of the theology taught in the denomination's seminaries.

A pastor from this denomination recently discussed his dilemma with me. "The seminary from which I graduated has been torn apart by this issue," he told me. "The faculty has been split apart, persons attacked, and pastors challenged to take sides in the debate. I have refused to become involved, and to have my orthodoxy called into question. I don't understand how people can be so sure that their own view of truth is the only one. Am I wrong to think that Jesus was more concerned for doing the truth than for claiming the truth?"

"Doing the truth"—it does sound like what Jesus meant! "If you know these things, you are blessed if you do them" (Jn 13:17). "Anyone who resolves to do the will of God will know whether the teaching is from God or whether I am speaking on my own" (Jn 7:17).

There is a form of right thinking, called orthodoxy. And there is a form of right action, called orthopraxy. Are these two incompatible? Does the truth lie only with orthodoxy, and is orthopraxy only a humanistic or political strategy? In this chapter I intend to answer these questions and to point the way toward the truthful life that issues out of the person and life of Jesus as the "way, and the truth, and the life" (Jn 14:6).

A historical perspective will help us place the discussion in context, followed by some contemporary responses.

The Roots of Orthodoxy

To be orthodox means to "conform in one's thinking to the approved doctrines or ideas." The formulation of approved doctrines by the early church led to the canons of orthodoxy—the theological confessions and creeds of Christian faith from which deviation was considered heretical.

Orthodoxy as a theological criterion emerged out of the first five centuries of the church's struggle to interpret the incarnation of God in Jesus Christ in ways that attempted to preserve his true deity and his true humanity. The cosmological approach to Christology on the part of some early theologians, such as Arius, was an attempt to answer the question of how the eternal and unchanging deity could be contained within a finite and created humanity. This approach tended toward a highly speculative and philosophical search for a "logos Christology" that preserved the unique quality of Jesus as the incarnation of the divine Logos, existing before creation as a "firstborn" deity, now having become flesh.

In response, Athanasius along with the three Cappadocian theologians argued, from the perspective of soteriology, that it must be the very being of God, not a created logos, who died upon the cross. One could say that this approach was concerned more with the praxis of God as redeemer of humankind (soteriology) than with the question of how infinite being could be contained with finite creaturely being (cosmology). Athanasian theology won the day at the Council of Nicea (A.D. 325) and was further confirmed at the Council of Chalcedon (A.D. 451). In this way the mainstream of orthodox theology was rooted in the christological confession that Jesus is one person with two natures, "very God and very man."

The soteriological question as to God's work of salvation in Christ pointed toward a praxis theology of God's action through Christ for the salvation of humankind. Even so the christological debates, concerned primarily with abstract questions regarding Christ's true nature, tended to subordinate the praxis of Christ's redemption to the semantics of true faith. The concern for christological orthodoxy as a criterion turned theology in the direction of apologetics. Apologetics is the attempt to defend the true faith against heresy and to argue the case for the truth of Christianity in the court of other worldviews. A further shift occurred when theology sought to ground the praxis of the Spirit in the ecclesial office, with episcopal continuity as its apostolic authority. This, as I see it, was the beginning of a theology of the church that subordinated Pentecost to incarnation by subordinating the praxis of the Spirit to the teaching office of the church.

In becoming a formal ecclesial theology, orthodoxy lost its connection to the continuing praxis of God's action through the Spirit. Already by the end of the first century Ignatius, bishop of Antioch, stated that the priestly *episcopos,* or bishop, is the central point around which the church is built. Irenaeus (bishop of Lyons, A.D. 178-200), argued that the guarantors of the tradition are the bishops, and Cyprian (bishop of Carthage, A.D. 248-258), stated that the Holy Spirit is bound up with the office; therefore, that church cannot err which is episcopally organized and guaranteed by the continuity of transmission of office. Very early in the development of the church there was a strong tradition of fusing "orthodoxy with office."[1]

While one strand of theological orthodoxy continued to develop along the lines of institutional and doctrinal continuity with the incarnation, the Greek Orthodox theologian John Zizioulas points to another tradition of orthodoxy that was centered in the praxis of Eucharist as the contemporary and eschatological form of Christ's identity in the community. The logos theologians of the first three centuries, Zizioulas tells us, were caught up in abstract questions of truth as revelation of being. At the same time other bishops were more concerned with truth as life, as opposed to the theoretical concept of truth as impersonal being. This, says Zizioulas, was closer to the Old Testament idea of truth as praxis.[2]

In other words, despite their association of the Spirit with the ecclesial office, some of these early bishops had a dynamic as opposed to a static concept of truth. This, says Zizioulas, was quite different from the prevailing Greek idea of truth as abstract principle or "being" (ontology). This continues to be a distinctive that is more true of the orthodox theology of the Eastern church than of the Western church. The Western church, which was influenced more by the Roman concept of truth as authority transmitted through office, defined orthodoxy in terms of more static and abstract concepts.

My own tradition is that of the Western church represented by both the Roman Catholic and Protestant version of orthodox theology as contained in creedal formulations that preserve truth as doctrine. This tradition has a tendency to become a theology of the church without praxis as its mode of life and truth. Charles Davis refers to this kind of orthodoxy when he says:

> Religion when maintained as an orthodoxy claims a permanent self-identity, remaining unscathed by social and practical changes. It involves some purely theoretical center of reference to serve in an abstract way as a norm of identity. . . . The presupposition of orthodoxy is the contemplative conception of knowledge, according to which knowledge is the result of disinterested viewing of reality by individuals.[3]

This is a severe criticism, but not unwarranted in many cases. Orthodox theology becomes dull and deadly and no longer relevant when it fails to show concern for the truthful existence of persons in their own human and historical context. When theology becomes irrelevant it is no longer threatening to the oppressive and dehumanizing effects of sin upon humankind.

Theology loses contact with the praxis of God when it seeks to ground its existence in some kind of continuity with a natural right or law, even when these natural laws become supportive of its religion. There is nothing so destructive to the humanity of persons as a theology of the church that fuses race, religion and political theory. At the same time there is nothing so contemporary, compelling and downright dangerous to such deadly orthodoxy as the humanity of God unleashed as the mission of Christ in the world. The humanity of God in Jesus Christ, his birth, life, death and resurrection, is both the "personalising of persons" and the "humanising of man," as T. F. Torrance once put it.[4]

The criterion by which orthodox theology must be measured is not its own possession of the truth but its existence for the sake of restoring humanity to truthful life both in this world and in the world to come. When the church claims divine providence and historical priority for its prerogatives and power of self-preservation, it dehumanizes both Christ and those he came to save.[5]

The Shift from Orthodoxy to Orthopraxis

A theology grounded in an orthodoxy that tends to value true dogma over truthful living has caused some to call for orthopraxis as an alternative. If orthodoxy's concern is primarily for "right thinking" as a form of truth, orthopraxy is offered as an alternative of "right action" for the sake of truth. Some who have rejected orthodoxy suggest an orthopraxy by which the criterion for the ministry of the church is more contemporary and contextual than are the doctrines of orthodoxy. Indeed, some have even suggested that orthopraxy should replace orthodoxy as a criterion for the ministry of the church today. Orthopraxy, it is argued, takes seriously the condition of oppressed humanity and makes liberation a test of theological method as well as a hermeneutical approach to Scripture. It is in liberation as praxis that the Word and work of God is revealed, they say, not in the confession of orthodox doctrines.[6]

Having criticized orthodoxy so severely, Charles Davis is equally critical of orthopraxy as a conceptual alternative to orthodoxy. He argues that it is a "half-hearted compromise" that merely transfers sacral authority from doctrines to social and political strategies. The dialectic between theory and praxis, he contends, represents the best approach.

Davis's criticism of orthopraxy is insightful. In the dominant strain of Latin American liberation theology, the institutional theology of the Roman Catholic tradition with its Aristotelian and Thomistic basis in natural theology finds a congenial home for some liberation theologians in the sociohistorical process. This can result in an attempt to develop mission praxis on the basis of natural theology rather than a praxis of Christ through continuity between the Holy Spirit, Christ Jesus and the mission of God in Israel. The exodus event in the Old Testament is politicized and used as a metaphor for liberation as salvation in history.

Some theologians are attempting to find a middle ground in the debate by envisioning a dialectic between orthodoxy and orthopraxy. One such theologian, Clodovis Boff, suggests that the dual responsibility of theology is that of establishing internal consistency for theological statements (epistemological validation) and correlation between theology and experience (pistic verification). In this dialectic he suggests that praxis constitutes the indirect norm for theology.[7] Boff wishes to preserve the epistemological content of theology as a criterion for its truthfulness as set over and against the experiential content of faith.

It seems to me that this sunders faith as experience of truth from truth as an object of theological reflection. This dichotomy has plagued theology from the beginning. In the Protestant tradition of mission theology, rightly understood, faith is more than intellectual assent to propositional truth. Faith, for mission theology, is a lived-out set of convictions based on the living truth of God as revealed through Christ in the power and presence of the Holy Spirit. Normative biblical truth is found in holding the faith of the church accountable to its mission of life and obedience to Jesus Christ in his continuing mission to the world.

Toward an Orthopathic Orthodoxy

As Ernst Bloch has said, what we have now "in the West is a patronizing, pluralistic boredom. . . . It looks like a partial eclipse of the sun. Everything is remarkably grey and either the birds do not sing or they sing differently. Something is wrong in any case. The transcending being is weak." Or else the dangerous memory has been extinguished and the eschatological memory has become exhausted.[8]

Without passion, Christian faith is pathetic. Without a praxis in which the presence of Christ takes hold of our faith, compelling us with a convicting sense of mission, our memory becomes sentimental and superficial. Christianity was once dangerous and subversive! For many it is now dull and deadly. Where did orthodoxy lose its passion?

Johann Metz, somewhat like Boff, suggests a "praxis of imitation" whereby praxis itself is not considered to be the primary criterion. He suggests instead that "imitation of Christ" as a praxis of solidarity in suffering be considered as an apocalyptic form of action for the sake of liberation. As an alternative and opposition to the apathetic structures of human society (including orthodoxy), Metz suggests a "pathic structure" for Christian presence in the world as a form of social praxis. This, he argues, retains the distinctive element of Christian praxis in a theology of liberation.[9]

Metz attempts to qualify orthodoxy by adding the quality of pathos in the form of shared suffering with the oppressed. This offers a kind of "orthopathic" dimension to orthodox theology. In addition to right thinking as a form of preserving the truth, one should also practice genuine concern about those who suffer. Praxis becomes the ethical dimension of orthodoxy, but as such, places ethics outside of or alongside of the life of the church as a gathered community. I am troubled by this, for it appears to separate questions of truth (orthodoxy) from questions of moral concern (orthopathy). The church would still be free to define heresy solely in terms of orthodoxy, not lack of orthopathic attitudes and actions!

Dennis McCann and Charles Strain, in a critical approach to a practical theology, reject Metz's formulation as "too orthodox" and call for a "religious praxis" that is less christologically and apocalyptically oriented. Nor are they persuaded by the claims of orthopraxy, which they find no more acceptable than orthodoxy. Instead they propose a praxis orientation that is guided by a transcending vision for religious values that are intrinsic to human experience itself.[10] This, however, seems to throw humanity back upon itself as a continuum on which Christ is placed as the exemplar of religious praxis.

Christopraxis carries orthodox theology into the arena of God's ministry in the world, where emancipation of persons under the bondage of sin takes place. Orthodoxy as faithful witness to the truth of Jesus Christ is tested by its power to effect the transforming work of redemption actualized in human lives. I use the word *emancipation* cautiously in this context, for it carries ideological overtones that could easily mislead us. In his penetrating analysis of emancipation and redemption, Johann Metz suggests that

> any emancipation cast as a universal historical totality is dangerously abstract and contradictory. A universal theory of emancipation without a soteriology remains caught under an irrational mechanism of exoneration or guilt-repression. A history of emancipation without a history of redemption, faced with the concrete history of suffering, subjugates the historical subject to new irrational constraints and either man is forced into a transcendental suspension of his own historical responsibility or he is forced into irreconcilable enmity or finally to negate himself as a subject.[11]

Metz is concerned for a praxis of Christian presence in the world that takes seriously the history of suffering of the past generations as well as of the present and future generations. He will not surrender the redemptive reality of Christ to mere spiritual expressions of faith and so turn away from solidarity with and redemption of actual human situations. Nonetheless, he fears that a praxis of emancipation that has as its primary gospel a historically realizable goal will ultimately fail humanity. This promise of emancipation does not issue out of the eschatological reality of the new heaven and new earth that is anticipated in the signs of liberation wrought in the present age. At the same time an orthodoxy that is blind to historical realities will also fail by abandoning those who are oppressed and hopeless in the present age.

There must be an "apocalyptic sting" to this imitation of Christ, Metz suggests, thus preserving the eschatological dimension.[12] In this way he seeks to overcome the ambivalence between orthodoxy and orthopraxy. The history of redemption cannot be a history of freedom, Metz argues, without also being a history of suffering.

We can agree with much of what Metz offers by way of Christian praxis. His suggestion that we view a praxis of imitation of Christ as the appropriate Christian presence in the world through solidarity in its pathic structures offers a helpful correction to an orthodoxy without concern for humanity. Metz points us in the right direction when he speaks of a praxis that "tries to keep the Christian memory of redemption alive in narrative form as a dangerous and liberating memory of redeemed freedom."[13]

At the same time I would want to insist upon Christopraxis as a ministry of empowerment rather than as mere imitation. I am reminded here of what Bonhoeffer called "participating in the sufferings of God in a godless world." There is something here as well of what the apostle called "completing what is lacking in Christ's afflictions for the sake of his body" (Col 1:24). Empowerment for sharing in Christ's presence and ministry among those who are suffering is the right kind of praxis!

The Praxis of the Living Christ

This brief survey of contemporary options in a praxis orientation toward the role of church in society demonstrates the ambivalence that pervades the thinking of theologians concerned for authentic praxis alongside of authentic faith. Defenders of orthodoxy are deeply committed to the normative criterion of truth as revealed through a divine Logos and expressed as a propositional theological formulation. At the same time they are uneasy over the ease with which these orthodox formulas can be held in abstraction from human suffering.

On the other hand proponents of orthopraxy are radically committed to the normative criterion of human suffering under oppressive social and political structures, quite certain that God's truth is revealed through actions that are salvific rather than through creedal confessions that are sanctified through dogma. At the same time they realize that ideology alone has no eschatological confirmation, though it promises a historical future, and that liberation without transformation contains the seeds of its own destruction.

Orthodoxy, it is true, can lose touch with humanity through abandonment of the concrete situation for the sake of the eternal verities of theology. On the other hand orthopraxy may fail precisely at the point where it expects more from human action than it can deliver. Where human actions undergirded by the agenda of liberation become the praxiological criteria for a theology of ministry, humanity will inevitably betray its own cause. We continue to witness dehumanizing and destructive social consequences where liberation from oppressive political structures has occurred. The restoration of the social fabric of human life does not occur as a result of liberation alone. Redemption must accompany liberation for it to become truly human.

The praxis of Christ redeems humanity from the social, political and institutional forms of power that dehumanize. But here too we must realize, as Metz has warned, that total emancipation can become a utopian vision, not an eschatological reality fulfilled in history. If there are manifestations of this eschatological reality of liberation, they may serve as signs that evil has already been encountered through the presence of the Redeemer in world history.

Mary Magdalene experienced the praxis of liberation through the power encounter between Jesus and the demonic spirits. Yet her story is one of empowerment to be a faithful and loving witness to Jesus, ministering to him and to others as part of the "communion of saints" (Lk 8:2; Mt 28:1-10). In the dramatic story of the healing of the man possessed by a legion of demons who fled into the swine, Mark tells us that this deranged and dangerous man was found with Jesus, "clothed and in his right mind" (Mk 5:15). One wonders who provided the clothes! It is one thing to cast out the demons of a tormented man. It is quite another to receive him back into the community and treat him as one who belongs rather than as an outcast.

The man experienced not only liberation but sanctification through the act of his community, which clothed him. Jesus then empowered him to be his witness: " 'Go home to your friends, and tell them how much the Lord has done for you, and what mercy he has shown to you.' And he went away and began to proclaim in the Decapolis how much

Jesus had done for him; and everyone was amazed" (Mk 5:19-20).

Liberation of persons from alien spirits or powers that bind and oppress them is impoverished when it fails to empower those same persons to be the missionary people of God, participants in Christ's mission through his church. Power encounters can quickly be reduced to magic where competition between the "powers" is misunderstood and loses its authenticity in the struggle for liberation and empowerment.

Moses' power encounter with the magicians of Pharaoh's court is not the central paradigm of the mission theology of the exodus event. Rather, God's empowering of the people to become a "missionary people" and enter into the land of promise through the power of the Spirit of Jahweh is the core paradigm of the Old Testament. In this liberation event, people were called out of their own hardness of heart and stubborn disobedience into a covenant community of love and justice.

The empowerment of Christ gives persons strength and faith to suffer under contradictions to our status as children of God as "humanly" as he himself does. No warrant should be assumed, however, for justification of that which opposes the purpose of Christ to uphold the humanity of those who are oppressed. Those structures which fail to recognize the humanity of others are opposed to Christ (God) himself.

This empowerment might take the form of mental, emotional and physical therapy wherein the goal is the humanization of persons through restoration to fellowship with God and the human community. Or it might take the form of advocacy for social justice where there is injustice. *Diakonia* is empowered service for creaturely well-being and comfort, as well as the breaking down of racial and sexual discrimination, which "disempowers" persons.

If on occasion there is the need for "extraordinary exorcism" in order to break the hold that evil forces and structures have over human beings, there are other, less dramatic forms than demonic exorcism. Focusing on such phenomena, ambiguous as they are, tends to attract attention to supernatural displays of divine power over evil. At the same time there is often little consideration or concern for the empowerment of the humanity of the persons from whom the demons have been exorcised. I think that it would be fair to say that one can drive out the demons and yet not produce a "holiness that humanizes."

Christopraxis as a ministry of Christ in the world does not shrink from such power encounters, but values empowerment of persons as a more valid criterion of the ministry of Christ than simply power over evil itself. Christopraxis is not unfamiliar with the phenomenon of exorcism, in the broad sense of the word. There is an "ordinary exorcism" by which dehumanizing forces, both personal and impersonal, are challenged and disarmed of their power.

Paul points to love as the "more excellent way" because it is a "power which empowers" and a gift that brings all other gifts of the Spirit into harmony and wholeness (1 Cor 13). "If God is *for us*," writes Paul, "who is against us?" (Rom 8:31). If God is *for us*, we are empowered to turn toward the good and away from evil.

Christopraxis is the critical intersection of the new humanity of Christ with the structures of humanity in this world. What ideological praxis sees as primarily a struggle between an inhuman social order and a human social order is understood through Christopraxis to be a power encounter between the old, unredeemed human order and the new, redeemed order, with Christ himself the authority *(exousia)*. This ordinary exorcism has as its criterion not humanity as a general principle but the person of Christ, who, in his own redeemed humanity, pledges himself to human beings who suffer under the old order.

The goal of Christopraxis is not merely deliverance from evil nor emancipation from structures that bind, but empowerment to be truly human even under circumstances and situations that are not yet redeemed. This is an unacceptable idea for liberation theology, as it appears to compromise the very nature of liberation itself. This ideological form of praxis grants the entitlement to be considered truly human only through the attainment of liberation as historical actuality. Christopraxis, however, understands entitlement as acheived through Christ's own praxis of advocacy and empowerment. Liberation is thus the goal of that which is authentically human. But it is the humanity of God in Christ that defines this goal.

The church finds its true ministry in the upholding, healing and transformation of the humanity of others as already grasped and reconciled to God through the humanity and ministry of Jesus Christ. The humanity of Christ serves as a vicarious basis for the ministry of the church as well as for the salvation of sinners and their reconciliation to God.

The incarnation of God in Christ is itself a praxis that constitutes the criterion for both orthodoxy and orthopraxis. The vicarious humanity of Christ is thus considered not only to be a theological construct for establishing a true doctrine of salvation but a contemporary praxis of ministry revealed in the historical form and practice of the church as a continuation of the humanity and ministry of Jesus Christ for the world.

Through the manifesting of the Spirit of Christ in the world through Pentecost, the vital link between the experience and power of the Spirit and the mission of God in Christ is preserved. This grounds the praxis of the Spirit in the incarnation of God in Jesus Christ and at the same time liberates the mission of Christ from the church's institutional and organizational structure to flow into the world through the missionary people of God.

Mission theology is the praxis of Jesus Christ through the presence of the Holy Spirit, reaching out to the church through the arms of those whose humanity needs healing and whose hearts need hope. Christopraxis goes beyond liberation theology; it is a theology of the liberating Christ and of persons reconciled to God.

Todd Speidell has reminded us that the risen Jesus Christ provides the basis for an ongoing reality of liberation in which we participate, instead of relying upon our own resources to "imitate Jesus." He argues that the incarnation provides a christological criterion as a corrective to liberation as praxis:

> The incarnation as the concrete reality of God's liberating presence from above to below provides a hermeneutical correction to liberation Christology. The hermeneutical criterion is Christ as the Son of God, who in the presence and power of the Spirit assumes and heals human existence. This Christological criterion may provide a corrective to liberation Christology, which places Jesus on a continuum with us [on] a common pathway to the Father. A Christological

critique, however, points the way forward to a liberating praxis based on Christ's praxis, which is not a function of liberation that we must imitate, but the reality of liberation in which God summons us to participate.[14]

Speidell has helpfully reoriented us back to the incarnation of God in Jesus Christ as "liberating presence." I would add that this liberating presence must be understood within the context of the church as the missionary people of God—the ecclesia. This helps to avoid the identification of Christ's presence with contemporary agendas that are derived out of sociological and political analysis rather than out of mission praxis. In order for this not to become an institutional theology of the church, with incarnation as the historical and ontological basis for the church's own existence, what Speidell calls "Christ's praxis" must be developed in the form of a mission theology where Pentecost becomes the criterion rather than the need for liberation itself as praxis.

In all of the contemporary concern for action as opposed to theory, forms of praxis end up driven by ideological agendas. If this happens, praxis will disintegrate into aimless and inarticulate spasms of revolutionary and radical activity. Praxis that becomes an expression of a theory of human life and therefore the right life can be as relentless and ruthless as any doctrine, when pursued for the sake of itself. "Ideas exist for the sake of life, not life for the sake of ideas," Dietrich Bonhoeffer once wrote. "Where life itself is made into an idea, real life (created and redeemed life) is more thoroughly destroyed than by an other idea. . . . Only the life from God is purposeful and fulfilling, overcoming the contradiction between what is and what ought to be."[15]

The task of mission theology is not only to find a modern agenda for the church to define its missionary programs but to reflect back upon the mission of God through the centuries of historical theology as well. Mission theology thus provides an integrative basis for a theology of the church in its mission praxis.

For mission theology to be a praxis theology it must be grounded in the praxis of the living God who has attended his creation from the beginning, and who has entered humanity through Jesus Christ to take hold of the world of fallen humanity from below. This he did through incarnation, bearing in his own life the death that had become the fate of humanity fallen away from God. Being raised from the dead, for death could not contain him, Christ continues to be the source of life through the life-giving Spirit released through Pentecost and spread throughout the world by those who bear his light and life.

Only the life from God is purposeful and fulfilling. But this life "was the light of men," and this light is the "true light that enlightens every man," wrote the apostle John (Jn 1:4, 9 RSV). Life from God issues from the Word of God who became flesh, and who "was in the world" and who "came to his own home" (1:10-11). Grace and truth came though him, and his name is Jesus Christ. This is the praxis of God. It is the act of God's own self, becoming human; and being human, he recognized and affirmed what is human through actions as well as words. Both grace and truth have their source from above and their effect from below; both are revealed simultaneously in the human and historical life of Jesus Christ as the act, or praxis, of God.

Pentecost means the formation of the church as the missionary people of God—finding its being in "being for the world." This is the praxis of God in its full trinitarian sense. God the Father is the Creator, who is the eternal source of grace and freedom for all human life; God the Son is the Reconciler, whose resurrection life is pledged to all who are under sentence of death; and God the Spirit is the Redeemer, who actualizes this life in individuals and baptizes them into the body of Christ, the church.

Christ is not only the truth but also the way. He is the way into the lives of those who are lost, who are oppressed, who suffer indignity and loss of humanity in the very midst of our society.

11

THE CHRIST OF THE CITY

In the riots that turned the inner city of Los Angeles into a flaming inferno in April of 1992, there was an outbreak of ethnic and racial anger as well as an outcry against economic and legal perceptions of injustice. This was an outbreak of a "charismatic spirit" quite different from the Pentecost event, and a phenomenon for which the churches, evangelical and pentecostal alike, were largely unprepared to understand, and with which they were certainly ill equipped to deal. When asked to respond with a theological critique, I chose the theme "The Humanity of God and the Soul of a City."[1]

The humanity of God is the particular, concrete humanity of Jesus of Nazareth. The humanity of this person, this circumcised Jew, this member of a particular family and particular culture, exists as the real form of humanity. Yet this person also recognized and affirmed the humanity of the non-Jew, the uncircumcised, the despised Samaritan, the lowly slave, the invisible woman, the foreigner with his Greek language and culture, and even the hated Roman soldier, who represented the oppressive power of the quasi-divine claim of Caesar. Jesus penetrated through these social and cultural forms of humanity and addressed the true humanity of each person, revealing his own humanity as the touchstone of divine grace.

For the Korean-American, the Asian-American, the Mexican-American and the African-American, the connecting tissue is not "American" but human. When one's ethnic identity serves only as the adjective and not the noun, there is already a loss of personhood at the human level. When the noun that defines our identity is the impersonal and imperious ideal of a state or nation, demagoguery fuels political rhetoric to the fever point. Such ideology is the disease, not the cure.

Through Jesus Christ we see that real humanity occurs as a particular form of humanity, never as abstract and ideal humanity. The "flesh" that the divine Logos assumed (Jn 1:14) was Jewish flesh, stamped with both the promise and judgment of the divine Word. The death and resurrection of Jesus put an end to all claims that racial, sexual, social or cultural identity and status have a claim upon the grace and righteousness of God. Now it is revealed that the Spirit of God is poured out upon "all flesh," as Joel prophesied and as was revealed at Pentecost (Acts 2). Racial, sexual and cultural distinctives are not obliterated. Instead, real humanity is now to be experienced in and through these distinctives.

The humanity of God in the person of Jesus Christ seeks incarnation in the soul of the city before taking up residence in the sanctuary of religion.

In drawing persons around him, Jesus re-created humanity in the form of a community of shared life and common identity. Even this narrower circle, defined by the specific calling of the twelve, was structurally open to the unclean leper, the tormented demoniac, the self-righteous Pharisee and the woman of ambiguous reputation. In contact with Jesus, humanity was liberated from the blind and capricious powers of nature and disease, as well as from the cruel and inhuman practices of the social and religious tyranny of the strong over the weak. In the real humanity of Jesus we see the humanization as well as the socialization of humanity.

Being human means living as this specific person belonging to these particular people who speak the same language and participate in the same rituals of community life. All human self-perception is thus culturally conditioned and socially determined. Not to have the social approval of one's own people is to suffer estrangement, if not derangement. Jesus himself experienced this powerful social judgment when he was thought to have an "unclean spirit" as judged by the standard of the self-perception of the Pharisees (Mk 3:30). Even his mother, brothers and sisters sought to intercept his ministry and remove him from public exposure because they concluded that "he is beside himself" (Mk 3:21 RSV).

The effects of sin as inhumanity are not overcome through a more rigorous form of spirituality, but through a renewed structure of sociality. Love is defined as living peaceably in a domestic setting, as clothing the naked, feeding the hungry and loving the neighbor as oneself. The ethical criterion is exhausted by the command of love, as Paul makes clear in his letter to the Roman church: "Owe no one anything, except to love one another; for he who loves his neighbor has fulfilled the law. . . . Love does no wrong to a neighbor; therefore love is the fulfilling of the law" (13:8-10 RSV).

The effect of sin on self-perception is not to be identified primarily with cultural forms but with social relations. It is in the structure of core social relations of human life that false self-perceptions arise. Although self-perception acquires cultural forms, it is rooted in one's core social identity. No true knowledge of oneself or of one's own humanity can occur apart from a true knowledge of the other with whom one is bound in social relationship. The continuity of real humanity by definition cannot be grounded in self-perception, but rather must be discovered through repentance toward both God and the neighbor.

Authentic repentance seeks the restoration of right relationships. This is not achieved by an immersion in guilt but through responsible actions and commitment to the preservation and sustaining of life. The core identity of true humanity is thus bound up with this shifting of the criterion for self-perception to the other person. Ethnic self-identity as the sole criterion leads to the ghetto of ethnic self-perception. This is where repentance must begin, not in renouncing ethnic identity but in allowing ethnic self-perception to be judged by the criterion of the other as essential to one's own humanity. In the parable of the good Samaritan, the Samaritan remains a Samaritan in becoming good. His goodness is in his perception of the other and in being a neighbor to him (Lk 10).

The single commandment of love—to love God and to love the neighbor as oneself—is grounded in social humanity, not merely in individual humanity. Any attempt to define humanity on our own terms incorporates the fallacy of self-perception into our social constructs. Social revolution alone cannot lead to the recovery and true form of humanity. The constant factor through social and cultural changes in self-perception is the structure of humanity as a social reality of love experienced as a reciprocity of relations in which Jesus Christ is present as the objective reality of grace, freedom and responsibility.

It was in Ephesus, we remember, that Paul created something of an uproar and even a riot when it was discovered that the profitable business of those who practiced the magical arts was threatened by their conversion to Christ (Acts 19). In his letter to the Ephesian Christians Paul drew out the implications of the gospel of Christ in such a way that the basic structures of that society were to be "humanized" through the activation of the Spirit and law of Christ. Paul did not seek to replace their culture with a concept of "Christian culture." Rather, he called for the liberation of authentic human life within the culture as a freedom from the magical as well as from the mythical, from the demonic as well as from the delusional.

The norm for determining what is the good is consistent with the "humanization of humanity" through Christ. No longer are human beings under the power and spell of their natural passions and natural religion. No longer are they "strangers and foreigners" one to another. No longer are they "tossed to and fro and carried about with every wind of doctrine" (Eph 4:14 RSV). No longer are they subjected to the inhumanity of personal egos bent on destructive and malicious behavior; no longer are they caught in the humiliating and demeaning roles that are defined by economic, sexual or political status.

In the same way Paul deals with our concern for the conservation of the essential order and stability of foundational human structures. With the breakdown of traditional orders, and with the secularizing of sacred myths and concepts that were used to provide stability for the Gentile world, Paul provides a criterion of Christian community that is grounded in the identification of Christ himself with those in whom his Holy Spirit dwells. Here too both Jew and Gentile must learn to shift their obedience and loyalty from traditional concepts of authority by which they sought stability and order to the structure of social life as regulated by the community as the body of Christ (Eph 2:11-22). The foundational social structures of family, marriage, parents and children, as well as the existing political and economic structures, are basically affirmed as good and necessary. Yet all of these structures are radically qualified by the "humanization of humanity" that occurred through Jesus Christ (see Eph 5—6).

Ethical norms remain constant when grounded in the true humanity of the other person rather than in culturally conditioned self-perceptions of individuals or in the collective cultural mass. When understood in this way, the meaning of that which is good is not first of all an abstract principle mediated through one's own perception of the good, but is first of all an ethical event that takes place between persons as the command of God.

When Jesus healed on the sabbath, ate with publicans and sinners, and asked a Samaritan women to minister to his thirst, he penetrated through all racial, sexual, social and cultural barriers to restore true humanity to others. Indeed, his own humanity could hardly have been the true humanity that it was if he had drawn back from the real humanity of others. Nor did Jesus institute some new ethical concept of the good as a kind of Christian ethic. Instead, he reinstated the criterion of goodness that belongs to true humanity as the ethical foundation for all of the laws and commandments. This same criterion was quite clear to the prophet Micah: "He has showed you, O man, what is good; and what does the LORD require of you but to do justice, and to love kindness, and to walk humbly with your God" (6:8 RSV).

The power struggle is not between the gospel and culture, but between the gospel and the "powers" within any culture that dehumanize and enslave persons. Paul sought the renewal of the social structures and the humanization of culture, not the replacing of these structures and culture with a kind of freedom that destroys them. The continuity of order and stability through social change and cultural pluralism is thus grounded in the nature of the human itself as that which produces and lives by culture. In this respect, only when culture is open to change is it able to remain in continuity with the development of true humanity and those social structures that uphold humanity.

The "soul of a city" has become a metaphor that speaks of the humanity of a people who share a common destiny and whose lives impinge upon one another in a struggle for survival and sustenance. In biblical times Moses established "cities of refuge" for those who sought protection from violence and as a haven for the homeless (Num 35:9-15). These cities constituted the "soul of the people" and the guarantee of human and civil rights.

Viewed from this perspective, the United States appears to have lost its soul. Our urban societies have become national disposal centers for the homeless and chemical-dispensing outlets for drug traffickers. Social anonymity without communal identity breeds autonomy and finally anarchy. The badge of belonging for the unemployed and disenfranchised youth comes with gang colors, graphic graffiti and spilled blood. Ethnic diversity without an infrastructure of social humanity produces ethnic rage. Economic materialism without an underlying core of spiritual humanism creates cultural hedonism.

Perhaps this is what Jesus prophetically saw when he paused before entering Jerusalem and wept over it, saying, "If you, even you, had only recognized on this day the things that make for peace! But now they are hidden from your eyes" (Lk 19:41-42).

The church's flight from the cities is a retreat from the struggle for the soul of a society. Not every church has abandoned the city, it is true. But by and large the church has failed when it has tried, and fled when it has found greener pastures. The disciples of Christ may have to give ground, wrote Dietrich Bonhoeffer, "provided they do so with the Word, provided their weakness is the weakness of the Word, and provided they do not leave the Word in the lurch in their flight."[2] In the abandonment of the city the church may well be leaving Jesus "in the lurch." Christians cannot turn away from any form of inhumanity without separating themselves from the humanity of God.

Most Christians would be scandalized to be told that abandoning the homeless, overlooking the deep injustice of poverty and systematically excluding the socially unacceptable is the moral and spiritual equivalent of apartheid. But it is so.

In an attack upon the practice of apartheid in South Africa, Johannes Verkuyl speaks to the various forms of separation of peoples practiced in other Western societies. His words are highly relevant for the church in every society.

> It is far easier to believe in a god who is less than love and who does not require a discipleship of love. But if God is love, separation is the ultimately opposite force to God. The will to be separate is the most complete refusal of the truth. Apartheid is a view of life and a view of man which insists that we find our identity in dissociation from each other. A policy of separate development which is based on this concept therefore involves a rejection of the central beliefs of the Christian Gospel. It reinforces divisions which the Holy Spirit is calling the people of God to overcome. This policy is, therefore, a form of resistance to the Holy Spirit.[3]

The church finds its true humanity in the relation between Jesus Christ and all humanity. The church finds its true ministry in the upholding, healing and transformation of the humanity of others as already grasped and reconciled to God through the incarnation, atoning life, death and resurrection of Jesus Christ. This is the authentic praxis of Christ's ministry through his humanity; this is Christopraxis. The church cannot be truly human when it denies and dehumanizes the humanity of others.[4]

A Call to Repentance and Responsibility

I often tell my students, "Only the church which is willing to repent of being the church can truly be the church of Jesus Christ." They always want me to say more!

First of all, I must explain that repentance is itself a positive and creative turning toward the source of life and renewal in God. As such repentance is not a "once and for all" act of renouncing the world, but a continuing act of transformation of a worldly mind. The transformed mind seeks to be conformed to the mind of Christ. One of the New Testament words used for this process is *metanoia,* which means having a new or different mind. John warned those who came out to be baptized by him, "Bear fruits worthy of repentance" (Lk 3:8). Jesus used the example of the people of Nineveh, who repented at the preaching of Jonah as a witness against his own generation. In this case an entire city was spared destruction through corporate repentance and spiritual renewal (Lk 11:32).

"Do not to be conformed to this world," wrote Paul, "but be transformed by the renewing of your minds" (Rom 12:2). To the Philippian church Paul wrote: "Let the same mind be in you that was in Christ Jesus, who, though he was in the form of God, did not regard equality with God as something to be exploited, but emptied himself, taking the form of a slave, being born in human likeness, he humbled himself and became obedient to the point of death—even death on a cross" (Phil 2:5-8).

Repentance is the spiritual gift of having the "mind of Christ." This mind runs contrary to the mind of the world, which is set on self-preservation and self-justification. Christ assumed the form of humanity in its rebellion against God and bent that mind back into conformity and obedience to God through the empowerment of the love of the Son for the Father and the Father for the Son. The mind of Christ is thus a mind that has already been "transformed" from death to life and from self-serving to self-giving through his own positive obedience.

"But why should the church need to repent of being the church?" my students persist. I explain further.

The church exists in the world and for the world, though it does not "belong to the world" (Jn 17:16). At the same time Jesus prayed that the Father might send the church into the world "as you have sent me into the world" (17:18). The church, as the body of Christ, can exist in the world only by means of worldly forms, even as Jesus ate the same food, used the same boats and followed the same customs of his day. The church must be in the world, says Karl Barth, "on the same level and footing, in the same boat and with the same limits as any or all of them." This must be done "willingly and with a good conscience," Barth added.[5]

But the church will also have the same temptation as other organizations and institutions in the world. The church will always have the temptation to make a name for itself, and to build its towers to reach up to the heavens. This is why the church must repent of being the church in order truly to be the church of Christ.

The sin of the people who built the tower at Babel was not their common life and language, but their technological presumption to "make a name for ourselves" and to reach up into the very heavens (Gen 11). The Holy Spirit, given at Pentecost, releases the Spirit of Christ into the world, reversing the confusion and division of humanity at Babel, enacting the ecclesial reality of liberation and reconciliation accomplished through the life, death and resurrection of Jesus.

The early church experienced a form of repentance in the breakdown of ethnic, religious and language barriers. There were conflicts and struggle, to be sure, as evidenced in the controversy between the Greek-speaking and Jewish widows (Acts 6). But the apostles insisted upon the full assimilation of each group into the life of the community. Where the Spirit of Christ prevails, there can no longer be discrimination based on race, gender or economic status (Gal 3:28). There can be no "acts of favoritism," writes James, where the "royal law of liberty" prevails through Christ. To show partiality is to commit sin (Jas 2:1-9). The ministry of God as Redeemer in the particular work of the Holy Spirit commands and enables us to restore the true humanity of every person through the praxis of Pentecost.

Through the resurrection of Jesus Christ and the coming of the Holy Spirit at Pentecost, the very structures of human social and political existence are opened up for redemption. Where there is emphasis on individual repentance alone, there is a tendency to concentrate on the means by which persons enter the church through personal repentance and faith. This is important, to be sure, but such an individualistic understanding of repentance can fail to call the church and social structures into repentance for the sake of healing, liberation and hope. Both individual repentance and social repentance reveal a praxis of empowerment and the reality of the kingdom of God as the eschatological and transforming power of the Holy Spirit.

Mission theology begins by calling the church itself into a radical conformity with the Spirit of Christ as the formative reality of new humanity. Mission theology becomes the hermeneutical criterion and spiritual conscience of the life and mission of the church.

"But *how* does a church repent?" my students ask. Theologically, spiritually and socially, I respond.

Theological repentance is demanded of the church when it offers flavored water to those who come expecting the new wine, and stale bread to those expecting a nourishing meal. The church repents through engaging in theological reflection on the work of God's Spirit under the mandate of God's Word. Theological repentance begins with the confession that the church has exchanged its theological birthright for the fast food of cultural relevance. When the church confesses with the church at Laodicea that its theology is "wretched, pitiable, poor, blind, and naked," the Christ who stands at the door knocking will find a welcome. "Who do you say that I am?" asks this Christ. When the church has answered that question fully and forthrightly, it will have rediscovered its theological heritage.

Spiritual repentance is demanded of the church when it is found opposing the mission of God for the sake of preserving its own institutional and traditional forms. The church repents when it brings out new wineskins of worship and weaves new patterns of communal life out of the "unshrunk" cloth of the next generation.

After several years of ministry as the pastor of a church, I stood before the congregation and announced, "It is my intention to take this church away from you and give it to your children!" When the members concluded that this was more than a statement intended to shock, it brought a mixture of reactions. Some were delighted, while others were offended and defensive. Spiritual repentance for the church involves the labor pains of giving birth and the joyful welcome of unexpected twins! The wind of the Spirit "blows where it chooses," said Jesus (Jn 3:8). When the church opens its windows to the world and feels the fresh breeze of the Holy Spirit blowing in its face from across the street, it has begun the process of repentance. "Do not quench the Spirit," urged Paul (1 Thess 5:19). But we have! And we repent of it.

Social repentance is demanded of the church when its institutional life demands a privileged space in the world for God's grace without expressed concern for those without benefit of food, shelter and justice. Christological repentance is demanded of the church when it binds Christ solely to its rituals at the altar, abandoning the Christ who is naked and in prison.

As the mediator who stands with humanity as advocate, healer and transformer, Jesus Christ is not primarily a principle by which ministry is defined but, as James Torrance has reminded us, is present with and among us as the ministering One:

> Christ does not heal us by standing over against us, diagnosing our sickness, prescribing medicine for us to take, and then going away, to leave us to get better by obeying his instructions—as an ordinary doctor might. No, he becomes the patient! He assumes that very humanity which is in need of redemption, and by being anointed by the Spirit in our humanity, by a life of perfect obedience, by dying and rising again, for us, our humanity is healed *in him*. We are not just healed "through Christ" because of the work of Christ but "in and through Christ."[6]

The authentic praxis of Christ's ministry through his humanity is *objectively completed* through his own vicarious life in solidarity with all humanity; *eschatologically confirmed* through his resurrection to be a living and faithful paraclete ever-present alongside of and on behalf of all humanity; and *historically manifested* as a healing and transforming presence in the life and ministry of the church. If the church is found to be in resistance to the praxis of Christ, it must search out a contemporary mission theology that renews the vision of Pentecost and traces out the contours of Christ's ministry in the midst of and on behalf of the peoples of the world.

A Call to Celebration and Renewal

From Pentecost the church views its origins in the crucified and risen Messiah of Israel and envisions its destiny as the "holy city, the new Jerusalem, coming down out of heaven from God, prepared as a bride adorned for her husband" (Rev 21:2). The city over which Jesus stands weeping is a metaphor that gathers up the tragedy of human pain and suffering. The city that John sees descending from heaven is one with foundations, whose architect and builder is God (Heb 11:10).

The one city will pass away, along with the heavens and the earth.

"Death will be no more; mourning and crying and pain will be no more, for the first things have passed away" (Rev 21:4). The holy city, the new Jerusalem, is the dwelling place of God. "He will dwell with them as their God; they will be his peoples, and God himself will be with them; he will wipe every tear from their eyes" (Rev 21:3).

The church in the world not only stands with the weeping Jesus over the city, it celebrates the victorious and glorious Jesus as the coming One whose manifestation breaks through the broken clouds like the bright rays of the dawning sun. The church is called not only to repentance and responsibility but to celebration and renewal of this vision of Christ.

The church not only points to the future that is yet to come; it is the advent of the glorious kingdom of God that is even now coming. These two concepts of the future are represented by the Latin words *futurum* and *adventus.* Our English word *future* is derived from the Latin *futurum,* which means what will be, or what may be. The *futurum* arises out of the present and has its possibilities in what does not yet exist.

In contrast, the English word *advent,* derived from *adventus,* points to that which is coming into the present and which already is manifest in the present. The New Testament concept of the future in terms of the advent of the Day of the Lord at Christ's coming is quite different from that of the ancient Greeks. Hesiod described the eternal being of Zeus by saying, "Zeus was and Zeus is and Zeus will be." John, in the prologue to his vision of the new Jerusalem writes, "peace from him who is and who was and who is to come" (Rev 1:4). Instead of using the future tense of the verb *einai,* "to be," for the third phrase, John uses the future tense of *erchesthai,* "to come." God's future is not in "what comes to be," but in him "who comes."[7]

When John baptized Jesus he announced: "Here is the Lamb of God who takes away the sin of the world" (Jn 1:29). John did not point away from his own ministry toward an invisible personage. He pointed to the one already present and announced his mission. The baptism of John was a call to both repentance and celebration of the one who "baptizes with the Holy Spirit."

In the same way the church of Jesus Christ experienced the baptism of the Spirit at Pentecost and through repentance and renewal celebrates the advent of the risen and coming Christ. In becoming the church through repentance and renewal, the church makes visible its reality as the dwelling place of God's Spirit on earth. Where the Spirit of Christ is there will be celebration of life.

The vision of John was not that of an ideal church that will never be. Rather, the vision is that of the real church that has its provisional and partial manifestation in its temporal and institutional form.

I meet far too many Christians who say that they are disillusioned by the institutional church and want no part of it. "Jesus yes, the church no!" is their credo. I understand their frustration and even cynicism concerning the church. At the same time I question their alternative. One does not baptize oneself into Christ.

The reality of Christ in the world is his body, the community of believers indwelt by the Holy Spirit. Christ seeks to gather Christians into fellowship and communion. The world isolates persons and then gathers them into anonymous crowds, only to exploit them for its own gain. Christ personalizes and humanizes persons, creating new families of fellowship where each one is a brother and sister to the other.

The praxis of Pentecost does not seek to replace the church with private and individual experiences of Christ. The Christ of Pentecost is not a lone ranger, riding into town with silver bullets and leaving without a forwarding address. The Christ of Pentecost is not a rancher, branding his sheep and then turning them loose without a name. He is the great shepherd; he knows his sheep by name and, while he has other sheep, "they will listen to my voice. So there will be one flock, one shepherd" (Jn 10:16).

Pentecost occurs wherever and whenever the kingdom of God appears with the power of the Spirit manifesting the eschatological signs of healing, forgiveness of sins and restoration to emotional and spiritual wholeness in community. Pentecost promises a paraclete to everyone who stumbles and falls, to everyone who is weak and powerless, to everyone who is tormented and torn by the demons of doubt, discouragement and despair. Jesus is the Christ of the wounded city.

Pentecost occurs wherever and whenever the church as the body of Christ celebrates the presence of the glory of Christ in its worship and life in community. Pentecost delivers the promise of the resurrected

Christ to return and light up the lives of those who dwell in darkness. He is the bright and morning star already appearing in the new heavens and earth. Jesus is the Christ of the heavenly city descending to earth.

It must be that Christ is involved if there is reality of change into the good. If, instead of the righteousness of Christ as a mental substitute for my own reality as a person, I acknowledge the existence of God in the inner movements of my own awareness, and this I claim with assurance in that Christ did send the Holy Spirit, his own Spirit into my life, so that the estrangement of myself from myself and from God could be bridged; if then I acknowledge the presence of God in my movements, those who become part of me through that perilous exchange of selves involved with genuine relationship, cannot escape being involved in the reality of God in a redemptive way.[8]

The presence and reality of Christ in the world must take place through our own presence and in our relationships with others. We have no alternative. If the church is to be the redemptive presence and power in the world that God intends, it will be where the Spirit of Christ crosses the boundary and breaks through the wall that separates us from each other, and where the world and the church live separate lives. Even so, come Lord Jesus!

Epilogue:
Memo to Theological Educators

This book has been written for men and women who are preparing for Christian ministry in its manifold forms. I have also had in mind those participating in the mission of Christ in the world as pastors and leaders of the church as well as those involved in the ministries of the people of God in every place and by whatever means.

Now I want to address myself to those responsible for providing the theological education for these ministries. I am well known by my own theological faculty and administrators for writing provocative and, I am afraid, sometimes pretentious memos.

I do not claim either the honest perception or the naive courage of the boy who cried out, "But the Emperor has no clothes!" On the other hand, I have sometimes been known to say out loud what others have been thinking. Because I think that this may be one of those times, I write this memo with the hope that it will be read with some degree of seriousness by those to whom it is directed, and that all others may look over my shoulders as I write it.

To My Colleagues in Theological Education for Ministry
Do you sometimes feel, as I do, that we serve two masters? On the one hand, our academic and professional status as members of theological

faculties is rigorously defined and reviewed by criteria that carry the threat "publish or perish." At the same time we are held accountable to the mission statements of our respective schools, which set high standards and goals that have to do with spiritual formation, personal mentoring of students and building of community.

As academicians, we are fitted for the iron collar of scholarship forged in the dungeons of the universities and led through the promotional ranks with the whips and goads of scholarly footnotes and literary fetishes. At the same time we are reminded that we are accountable to the church to provide men and women who are spiritually mature, biblically astute and skilled practitioners of a dozen crafts that are needed for successful ministry.

Here is the immediate problem as I see it.

The captivity of the church's theological agenda by the guild of so-called professional scholars in academic theological education is a charge often raised by pastors as they look back upon their theological education. Some have likened it to the alliance that Israel created with the Assyrians for the sake of gaining political power and to compensate for its own weakness! I am afraid that I must agree.

The church as an institutional structure has too often become an accomplice in the seduction and captivity of its theological nerve center by the professional academic academy. Intimidated by the claims of biblical scholars and theologians whose own professional careers are evaluated and affirmed by other scholars, the church acquiesces by surrendering its role in determining its own theological agenda. Seldom permitted access to the halls of scholarship or to the helm of theological education, the church receives its theology through a "trickle-down" process. The filter, unfortunately, is so constructed that most theology as well as the tools of critical biblical study are thrown out with the "coffee grounds" when the students return to take up their posts on the frontline of ministry. There, under the pressure of being successful leaders of the organizational church, they are easily attracted to pragmatic strategies for church growth, conflict management and effective pastoral counseling.[1]

This is not a new problem; its historical antecedents go back to the first century.

I see two traditions directing the task of theological education, emerging out of the New Testament period itself. One is based on a theology of the nature of the church as an institutional embodiment of Christ, and the other follows the trajectory of Pentecost as providing a paradigm for the mission and ministry of the church.

One can see the antecedents of these two traditions in the way in which the formulation of the first-century church emerged. Peter, James and John were the "pillars" in the Jerusalem church to whom Paul refers in his sarcastic aside when writing to the Galatians (2:9). Peter, though he thought of himself as God's choice to preach the gospel to the Gentiles (Acts 15:7), and though he defended Paul at the Jerusalem Council, never seemed to get very far away from Jerusalem! During this entire period there is no indication that Peter ever planted a Gentile church, nor did he contribute any substantive theology to this movement, even taking into consideration the two epistles that bear his name. Peter had a profound eschatological vision of salvation through Jesus Christ, which provided both a source of confidence through suffering as well as encouragement for witness to the world (1 Pet 1—2, 4). But there is little hint of Pentecost in his appeal for steadfastness and in his mission strategy.

James, the brother of Jesus and apparently titular head of the Jerusalem church due to this relationship, was viewed by Paul as the source of a good deal of the trouble that the Judaizers contributed to his own efforts. He charges Peter with being intimidated by this tradition; "until certain people came from James, he used to eat with the Gentiles. But after they came, he drew back" (Gal 2:12). James contributed an apparently early and very practical epistle, but again there is no evidence of a substantive theological contribution to the issue of the church and its mission and ministry. The Jerusalem church may have been influenced more by a "traditional-hierarchical" leadership model in its organization than an "entrepreneurial-situational" leadership style, as we would put it today.

My point is that the Jerusalem community sought to extend its own life as the church of Jesus Christ through continuity with the historical transmission of authority in the "tradition of the twelve" rather than through the new event of Pentecost. This approach tended to subordinate the charismatic order of the church to the traditional order as represented by those who had historical continuity with Jesus and the disciples. This is what I mean by an institutional embodiment of Christ as contrasted with a charismatic, pentecostal presence of Christ through the Spirit.

Paul's theology and mission were directed more by the Pentecost event, which unleashed the Spirit of Christ through apostolic witness rather than through apostolic office. This praxis of Pentecost became for Paul the "school" for theological reflection. In Paul's theology the nature of the church was revealed through a theology of its mission and ministry as related to Pentecost. From Pentecost as a praxis of the Spirit, Paul then reflected back upon the resurrection, and beyond to the historical significance of Jesus Christ as the incarnation of God, the Messiah promised to Israel. Indeed, one might argue that this was the way in which the theology of the church in the first century took its initial shape and form.

At the same time one must agree with Brunner when he suggests that the Pauline vision of the community of Christ as the charismatic fellowship *(ekklēsia)* gave way to the institutional and sacramental structure of the church by the end of the first century.[2] Though Brunner may have overstated his case, a strong argument can be made for the fact that, very quickly, the early church moved toward a centralized and highly organized concept of the church's teaching and sacramental authority. Within this tradition the mission theology of Paul became subordinate to an official "ecclesial theology," with the result that the praxis of the Spirit became subordinate to the ecclesial office and teaching.

I do not despise the contributions made to our present theological task through an understanding of history and appreciation of tradition. It is not as though tradition itself is to be cast aside and ignored. All theology is practiced within a context of tradition, which gives it continuity with past theological reflection and enables it to enter into dialogue with others who share common theological and ecclesial roots. But a tradition can become closed and turned in on itself. Christian tradition is misunderstood and misused if it becomes institutionalized and loses its cumulative and liberating function within the praxis of the Spirit.[3]

Theology is in danger of losing contact with its object of study when it is no longer open to the critical interaction of spiritual praxis and revealed truth. A mission theology is not neglectful of tradition but practices theological reflection in the context of mission. Mission theology begins with Pentecost as the formative event of the church in its relation to the incarnate Son of God on the one hand, and the world as the object of God's mission on the other hand.

The development of an official ecclesial theology along the lines of continuity with the incarnation led gradually to the theological and institutional marginalization of a pentecostal experience where the ministry of the Holy Spirit appeared in the form of supernatural phenomena of ecstatic utterance, miracles of healing and dramatic "power encounters" with demonic spirits. Left without a strong theological tradition of its own, pentecostal experience tended to develop its own criteria for the ordering and empowering of ministry. "Evidences" of the Spirit's manifestation were given the status of authority and even infallibility with regard to what is personally real, as opposed to what is only formally true.

When the mainstream theological tradition set out to define its task primarily as abstract reflection on the nature of God, Christ and the church, the pentecostal experience saw little value in theological dogmatics of this nature. First, pentecostal experience itself was not susceptible to this kind of theological examination because the Spirit was not considered capable of definition in the abstract categories that theologians tended to use. Second, for many pentecostals most such theological works were at best uninteresting and at worst deadly. The charge that the pentecostal experience lacked "theological integrity" was taken by many pentecostals as assurance that their experience and movement had spiritual vitality!

With the marginalization of Pentecost as a phenomenon of experience, the incarnational theology of the church took up issues that had more to do with its own origin and nature than with its mission. Pentecost as a praxis of the Spirit and a means of access into theological reflection on the incarnational mission of the church lost its place in the theological curriculum.

The triumph of orthodoxy over orthopraxis in the church left mission theology without a christological center. The mission of God was left without theological content; missiology replaced mission theology, with cultural anthropology as its core curriculum. Some schools have even gone so far in this direction as to separate theology from missions altogether, with missionaries teaching missions and academic theologians teaching future pastors for the church! The school of missions was considered an adjunct to the central task of the seminary. The school of theology was placed at the center, making it accountable to the theological academy rather than to the mission of God and to the church.

The theological task that properly belongs to the church as a means of determining its own origin, nature and mission has been handed over to the scholars, so that church theology has become academic theology. While the church continues to ordain its ministers, the theological academy, usually in the context of the university, prepares its theologians. These theologians then train students in their respective disciplines of study for the church to ordain to ministry. Even the freestanding theological seminaries, while serving the church in the main, look to professional academic accrediting associations for certification of their degrees. This means that faculty members are, for the most part, university trained with little or no experience and expertise in leading the mission of the church.[4]

Despite the monumental efforts of Karl Barth to recover an authentic theology of the church, the theological momentum tends to remain with the academy. Barth's own christological instincts led him toward a theology of the proclaimed Word, and thus the event of proclamation became for him the locus of evangelical theology. At the same time Barth's theological agenda was dominated by the same issues that had preoccupied the older theological tradition, namely, the origin and nature of the church's existence and confession. He rightly saw that the incarnation of God in Jesus Christ is the theological basis for the reconciliation of the world to God as an act of God's freedom and grace. From this perspective he critically reviewed all of the loci of theology, grounding each doctrine in the completed ministry of God's reconciliation through Christ. In the end his magnum opus stands "outside the camp" of the theological mainstream for his radical refusal to bind theology to the critical mind of the scholar/theologian. At the same time his attempt to do a "theology of the Word" left him tantalizingly near but strangely remote from the context where the mission of the church is actually taking place.[5]

Let me now become more specific.

By and large the theological academies to which the church sends its members to be taught and equipped for ministry are staffed by faculties that tend to isolate biblical studies and theology from the Holy Spirit's ministry in the context of the church's interface with the world. This generalization allows for plenty of exceptions while still being true. The teachers in these theological schools often earn their doctoral degrees and receive their academic promotions by practicing research and scholarship that center primarily on the citation of each other's work in copious footnotes. One becomes a scholar when one's own thought is cited in the footnotes of other scholars! This is a form of scholarship appropriate to the mastery of knowledge in a particular discipline of study. As such it is a criterion of excellence in matters that relate to disciplined thinking, writing and the guidance of others in this process.

What I question here is not the striving for excellence in knowledge but the omission of competence in discerning God's Spirit in the revealing of truth through God's ministry in the world. There is no need to denigrate the academic profession in its striving for excellence in things of the mind. Saul of Tarsus sat at the feet of the renowned scholar Gamaliel (Acts 22:1), and later says of himself, "I advanced in Judaism beyond many among my people of the same age" (Gal 1:14). Yet after his own private Pentecost on the Damascas road where the Spirit of Christ encountered him, Paul counts all of these credentials as nothing for the sake of knowing Christ (Phil 3:7-8). The degree of knowledge that one has is not a measurement of the degree of truth that one possesses when it has to do with the things of God. Paul's interpretation and teaching of the Old Testament Scriptures changed radically after he had encountered Christ and experienced the manifestation of the Holy Spirit through his preaching of Christ.

In many theological seminaries those who teach the art of biblical preaching are not ordinarily permitted to teach the Bible to those who are preparing to be preachers. In many cases only those with earned doctoral degrees in the science of biblical and textual criticism are allowed to teach the Bible. Many of these professors of Bible have never subjected their own teaching to the critical test of effective preaching and teaching.

It seems to me that the truth of Scripture is discovered in its effect— that is, in the context of its effective preaching and teaching, as well as in its source. The prophet speaks for God when he says: "So shall my word be that goes out from my mouth; it shall not return to me empty, but it shall accomplish that which I purpose, and succeed in the thing for which I sent it" (Is 55:11). Are there not truths of Scripture that can be known only through preaching and teaching the Word? It is not unusual for graduates from university divinity schools to move directly into teaching positions in theological seminaries without having demonstrated competence in the ministry of the gospel. Many become teachers of those who are preparing for ministry without themselves having served as ministry interns under supervision and in a network of accountability.

A Modest Proposal

It would not be fair of me to raise such serious questions and make such radical criticisms without offering some suggestions for consideration as a means of integrating mission theology with a theology of the church in the task of theological education.

1. *Introduce a praxis-based curriculum.*

In a praxis mode of theological education the goal, or telos, is located beyond the issuing of the diploma in divinity. Those who complete the degree and enter into the ministry for which they have been prepared become critical points of validation of the curriculum in the context of their lives and ministry. One could say that in a praxis-based curriculum designed to prepare women and men for Christ's ministry, those who teach are accountable to the effectiveness of those who are taught rather than primarily to their academic colleagues. In a praxis-based curriculum one teaches toward competence in ministry rather than merely toward a discipline of study.

Those who have earned doctoral degrees in theology write theological manuals and dissertations that are reviewed by other theologians. Seldom are they evaluated by pastors, missionaries or therapists who experience regularly in their work the power of God in the burning bush and tongues of fire. In my seventeen years of teaching in a theological seminary I have yet to experience a debriefing by the theological faculty in which those who are attempting to carry out the teaching and strategy received in school return to discuss the effectiveness of this theology with their teachers.

In my parable of firefighters and theologians (see the opening section of this book), the firefighting manuals are revised following a debriefing with the firefighters and the members of the command center. Research into the cause and nature of fires and firefighting is often field research, where those who study the science of fires team up with those who fight fires.

In the theological academies it is usually quite the opposite. Research is done in the catacombs of the library, not among the smoldering embers of the latest firestorm. Even where the "tongues of fire" creep into the seminary constituency, such manifestations of the Spirit's presence are sometimes viewed with suspicion, if not alarm.

Therefore I propose the creation of some kind of feedback loop where those involved in the praxis of ministry provide critical insight into the assumptions and methods by which the theological curriculum is constructed and delivered by the schools. Without abandoning commitment to excellence in rigor of critical thought and study, a more rigorous demand upon the curriculum needs to be made from the context of its outcome as measured by the effectiveness of those who are *doing* the ministry of Christ in the world.

2. *Establish parity between mission theology and academic theology.*

Too long have we relegated mission theology to the back benches in establishing the theological core of the curriculum. Systematic theology need no longer have exclusive franchise rights over the teaching of theology. This deprives those doing academic theology of a mission context and so diminishes and distorts theology itself. This also tends to allow the praxis of mission to avoid critical theological reflection on its methods and practices.

I suggest that the theological mandate to develop an authentic mission theology be placed upon those who are experiencing the praxis of Pentecost. Like Paul, those who attribute to the work of the Spirit a revelation of the inner relation between Holy Spirit, Spirit of Jesus Christ and Spirit of God should be expected to practice theological reflection. This theological mandate begins with the praxis of mission and reflects back through the church to the gospel.

We have no right to expect theological credibility of those who practice the theology of Pentecost without enabling them to occupy some of the chairs of theology in the mainstream theological schools. In this way a creative and fruitful interchange could result between academic theology and mission theology.

The problem is as much a structural problem in the formation of a theological faculty as it is a problem between theology and mission. When the mission of the church becomes separated from the institutional theology of the church and takes up its task under the discipline of missiology, both suffer from this structural dichotomy. When theologians have no praxis context from which to do theological reflection, academic theology and mission theology find it difficult to coexist, much less have fruitful dialogue.

3. *Restructure the academic units of the faculty around mission outcomes rather than disciplines of study.*

It is time to approach the problem creatively by suggesting a new configuration for theological training for the whole of God's missionary people throughout Christ's body. This includes ordained ministers and missionaries as well as laypersons.

The traditional separation of biblical studies, church history, theology and ministry (practical theology) into separate academic divisions follows too closely the modern university model. It tends to reinforce the separation of theological study from the task of ministry and lends support to the idea that ministry, or practical theology, is primarily a matter of acquiring pastoral, pedagogical, homiletical or liturgical skills and techniques. It further reinforces the approach to biblical study as a discipline involving matters of source criticism, problems of authorship and literary construction. This approach allows biblical studies to become a discipline or field of study alongside other academic disciplines, in which one can earn a doctoral degree by mastering the literature in the field and making a small contribution to that literature.

Without discounting the value of the scholarly work that has contributed much to our modern understanding of the Bible in its rich context and tradition along with the historical development of the church and its theology, we can surely find more creative ways of structuring the faculty and curriculum. If mission theology as defined in this book were taken as a guide, one could first of all integrate more clearly the missiological and the theological curriculum and faculty. The various degrees granted by a theological seminary or college could each be defined in terms of ministry or vocational outcomes as appropriate, drawing upon a faculty that is rich in the interdisciplinary fields relating to the total mission of God in the world through his people.

Where the content of the Bible is taught, the faculty should be experts in teaching the Bible, preaching from the Bible and using the Bible in addressing social and spiritual needs of persons as well as in the critical study of the text and its sources. Here there would be a creative dialogue within the faculty as well as a rich resource for students who come to study the Bible for degree purposes relevant to their own life and ministry in the church and the world.

In a similar way, where formal academic theology is taught, the faculty should be experts in evangelism and church growth, equipping members of the church for ministry, leading and managing the church organization, and pastoral care and counseling as well as in the history of the church's life and theology.

This proposal would lead to the displacing of systematic and historical theology as the theological core and creating a multiplex theological faculty with mission theology as the integrating force. For some schools this may require another "Jerusalem conference" such as Paul experienced (Acts 15). There will be those who will remain at Jerusalem. But if Paul had not won his right to be the primary theologian of Pentecost, Christian theology might very well have become a subheading under Jewish theology!

This is a proposal for the recovery of an authentic mission theology alongside of historical theology, both for the sake of preparing men and women for church ministry and for the ministry of the people of God in the world. This proposal calls into question the structure of the traditional theological curriculum, where biblical studies tends to be preoccupied with critical textual concerns, and where theological reflection in the context of the mission of the church in the world is dominated by critical historical theology.

The theological mandate can best be fulfilled from the perspective of those who are responsible to answer the question: How do you account for what you are doing in the name of Jesus Christ? This is not to say that systematic and historical theology are unimportant. Theological reflection as mission theology must be informed by historical theology. Those who are to take leadership in the mission of the gospel as well as in the church, however, must have a mission theology, not merely a foundation of systematic and historical theology.

A Call for Repentance and Renewal

The church as an organization finds its real continuity by always being open to theological repentance in order to manifest the power and presence of the kingdom of God. Theological repentance was at the very heart of Peter's sermon on that first Pentecost when he said, "This Jesus . . . you crucified and killed. . . . But God raised him up" (Acts 2:23-24). Mission theology places the church in its institutional life at the foot of the cross for the sake of its participation in the pentecostal life given to it through the life of the resurrected Lord Jesus.

In social repentance the church confesses its sin of neglecting the humanity of the world as the object of God's loving grace while it is preoccupied with its own institutional life. In theological repentance the church submits its doctrinal formulations to the praxis of mission informed by theological reflection upon the mission of God through Christ as an eschatological and apostolic form of its sending into the world.

This is also a call for institutional repentance whereby the educational institutions that serve the church in its mission can subject their teaching curriculum and faculty orientation to the critique of Christopraxis as competence in the training of the members of the church for ministry.[6]

Educational institutions charged with the mandate of serving the church in its total mission will be called to repentance for separating mission theology from academic theology, and bowing before the false gods of academic scholarship on the one hand while sacrificing to the contemporary gods of pragmatism and secularism on the other hand. The mandate of equipping and preparing the total people of God through the church will be the first step toward recovering an authentic mission theology and the reformation of the theology of the church in its life and mission.

The theological mandate of Christopraxis will lead to the emancipation and liberation of the church from captivity to the philosophy and structures of its own creation. This calls for a renewal and reorientation of the church from the side of its mission of being sent into the world as well as new theological reflection back upon the mission of God as delivered through the gospel of Christ through the empowerment of Pentecost.

All of this will mean a radical revisioning of the comfortable dichotomy between clergy and lay categories of ministerial service and preparation. Mission theology is first of all the task of the entire missionary people of God. As the people of God determine the various orders of ministry, persons can be set aside (ordained) and prepared to exercise this ministry in specific vocational forms. However, the baptism into Christ constitutes the calling of every Christian into the ministry of Christ.

Through the praxis of Pentecost, a revisioning of ministry can take place, with the old wineskins giving way to new and creative forms of ministry.

Notes

Chapter 1: The Christ of Pentecost

[1]Aristotle, *The Nichomachean Ethics,* trans. J. E. C. Welldon (New York: Prometheus Books, 1987), p. 192 (bk. 6, chap. 5). The use of the term *praxis* in contemporary theology has been greatly influenced by the quasi-Marxist connotation given to it by some Latin American liberation theologians. My own attempt in using the word is to recover the authentically biblical connotation of God's actions, which reveal his purpose and truth. I appreciate the concept of praxis as used by Orlando Costas; see *The Church and Its Mission: A Shattering Critique from the Third World* (Wheaton, Ill.: Tyndale House, 1974). I have discussed this further in my essay "Christopraxis: Competence as a Criterion for Theological Education," in *Theological Students Fellowship (TSF) Bulletin,* January-February 1984.

[2]James Will offers a helpful comment when he says, "If incomplete and ideologically distorted persons nevertheless have the dignity of participation with their Creator in the preservation and completion of the creation, then praxis is a necessary dimension of theology. But praxis must not be misunderstood as practice. Practice has come to mean the use of external means to attain a theoretically defined end. It suggests that finite and sinful persons may so understand the meaning of God's peace as to be able to devise economic, political, diplomatic, and even military means to attain it. The end of peace is thought to be a transcendent value that appropriate external means may effect. Praxis, on the other hand, is a dialectical process of internally related events from which a result dynamically emerges. Given the finite and ideological character of our preconceptions of peace, they cannot be treated as sufficient definitions of an eternal value to guide our practice. Rather, we need a praxis; that is, peace must be allowed to emerge from a dialogical and dialectical process that may continuously correct our ideolog-

ical tendencies. Praxis is thus a process of struggle, negotiation, and dialogue toward a genuinely voluntary consensus" (*A Christology of Peace* [Louisville, Ky.: Westminster/John Knox, 1989], pp. 24-25).

[3]Harry R. Boer, *Pentecost and Missions* (Grand Rapids, Mich.: Eerdmans, 1961), p. 98.

[4]Karl Barth, *Church Dogmatics,* vol. 4 pt. 2, trans. Geoffrey Bromiley and Thomas Torrance (Edinburgh: T. & T. Clark, 1962), p. 563.

[5]Among those who have questioned this mechanistic view of nature, Fritjof Capra argues persuasively that modern physics has overcome the mechanistic view in favor of a holistic and dynamic conception of matter. See *The Turning Point: Science, Society and the Rising Culture* (London: Collins/Fontana, 1963), p. 89. Capra's latest book extends his thinking on the relation of nature, God and human knowledge: Fritjof Capra and David Steindl-Rast, *Belonging to the Universe: Explorations on the Frontiers of Science and Spirituality* (San Francisco: Harper, 1991). See also Thomas F. Torrance, *The Christian Frame of Mind: Reason, Order, and Oneness in Theology and Natural Science* (Colorado Springs, Colo.: Helmers and Howard, 1989).

[6]Christoph Schwöbel, "The Creature of the Word: Recovering the Ecclesiology of the Reformers," in *On Being the Church: Essays on the Christian Community,* ed. Colin E. Gunton and Daniel W. Hardy (Edinburgh: T. & T. Clark, 1989), p. 117.

[7]Douglas John Hall, *Thinking the Faith: Christian Theology in a North American Context* (Minneapolis: Augsburg, 1989), p. 105.

Chapter 2: A Vision of Healing and Hope

[1]Jürgen Moltmann has made a convincing argument that the theological axis is laid in the praxis of the resurrected Christ experienced in the praxis of discipleship: "Christopraxis in the narrower sense must be understood as the life of the community of Christians in the discipleship of Jesus. . . . To know Jesus does not simply mean learning the facts of christological dogma. It means learning to know him in the praxis of discipleship. Theological christology remains related to this christopraxis, and has to absorb its experiences, and open people for again new experiences along this way. Christology emerges from Christian living and leads to Christian living" (*The Way of Jesus Christ: Christology in Messianic Dimensions* [San Francisco: Harper & Row, 1990], pp. 42-43).

[2]My use of the term *Christopraxis* began with my published article "Christopraxis: Competence as a Criterion for Education for Ministry," *TSF Bulletin,* January-February 1984. Fredrick Herzog has since used the term *Christo-Praxis* in his book *God Walk: Liberation Shaping Dogmatics* (Maryknoll, N.Y.: Orbis, 1988). Herzog uses the term to include a historical encounter with the corporate self of the Messiah Jesus represented in the universal cry

for justice among the oppressed. He thus seeks to preserve the uniqueness of the Christ of history with the contemporary encounter with Christ in history as a form of the continuing messianic summons to justice and reconciliation (p. 106). Herzog's attempt to preserve a trinitarian theology within a theology of liberation leads him to speak of Theo-Praxis and finally of Spirit-Praxis. Spirit-Praxis, says Herzog, "is that activity of God through which, in a 'networking' of spirit, God draws all human beings together in the corporate self of Messiah Jesus and expresses special solidarity with all those who are suffering and oppressed" (p. 170). If I understand Herzog correctly, he has used the theme of liberation and the dynamic of praxis to provide a new approach to dogmatic theology, not from above, nor from below, but from within the praxis encounter of God's working through the threefold mold of Creator, Messiah Jesus and Spirit. As it will be made clear, my own use of the term *Christopraxis* seeks to preserve a more radical disjunction between the praxis of Christ through the Spirit and the praxis of the human spirit in its struggle against oppression for the sake of liberation.

[3]James Dunn has argued convincingly that the doctrine of the preexistence of the Logos and the doctrine of Incarnation are not found in the Synoptic Gospels, but only in the later Gospel of John. See *Christology in the Making* (Philadelphia: Westminster Press, 1980). He also suggests that the text "No one knows the Son except the Father, and no one knows the Father except the Son" (Mt 11:27) may be the source of John's Christology rather than a later insertion.

[4]The designation *Spirit Christology* has both a broad and narrower sense. In the broad sense, a Spirit Christology holds that Jesus became the Christ (Anointed One) at the time of his own "inspiration" by the Spirit of God. Thus, instead of Jesus being the incarnation of divine Logos, he was "inspired" by the Spirit of God in a unique and complete way so as to become a Son of God. This Christology attempts to substitute inspiration for incarnation. See G. W. H. Lampe, *God as Spirit* (Oxford, U.K.: Clarendon Press, 1977), especially pp. 96ff., 196ff. Lampe does not clearly differentiate between the Spirit that inspired Jesus and the spirit that is universal in all humanity. It appears to be quantitative rather than qualitative, and thus tends toward unitarianism, as pointed out by Colin Brown, *Miracles and the Critical Mind* (Grand Rapids, Mich.: Eerdmans, 1984), p. 299. Brown himself inclines toward a Spirit Christology in the narrower sense by focusing attention on the miracles of Jesus as performed only through his humanity as inspired by the Spirit of God. This does not rule out a Word Christology, Brown argues, but directs our attention to the title *Christ* as determinative of Jesus' ministry under the power of the Spirit in the fullness of his humanity. See his *That You May Believe: Miracles and Faith Then and Now* (Grand Rapids, Mich.: Eerdmans, 1985), pp. 121-22, 145-46.

[5]For a discussion of baptism as ordination into Christian ministry, see "Christ's Ministry Through His Whole Church," a contribution of the Department on the Laity, Fourth World Conference on Faith and Order, July 1963, in *Theological Foundations for Ministry*, ed. Ray S. Anderson (Grand Rapids, Mich.: Eerdmans, 1979), pp. 430-57.

[6]Dietrich Ritschl's comment is apropos: "The goal of *diaconia* is not the attuning of those who receive the *diaconia* to the faith of those who perform it. The basis of *diaconia* should not be confused with its goal: *diaconia* in solidarity with the poor and those without rights can be practised without the secret aim of convincing the recipients of the basis of the *diaconia*. The conversion of the recipients of works of *diaconia* to the faith of those providing it is a particular and additional miracle of the presence of the Spirit of God. It is not the goal of the diaconal activity" (*The Logic of Theology*, trans. John Bowden [Philadelphia: Fortress, 1987], pp. 270-71).

Chapter 3: A Vision of Forgiveness and Freedom

[1]Henrik Ibsen, *Four Plays of Ibsen*, trans. R. V. Forslund (New York: Chilton, 1968), pp. 130-32.

[2]R. E. Hudson, "At the Cross," copyright 1916, in *Church Service Hymnal* (Winona Lake, Ind.: Rodeheaver Hall-Mack, 1948).

[3]I have drawn upon the work of Jacob Firet for the substance of this paragraph. See his *Dynamics in Pastoring*, trans. John Vriend (Grand Rapids, Mich.: Eerdmans, 1986), p. 70.

[4]I am indebted to my colleague Charles Van Engen for the concept of the church as the "Missionary People of God." See his *God's Missionary People: Rethinking the Purpose of the Local Church* (Grand Rapids, Mich.: Baker Book House, 1991).

[5]Thomas F. Torrance, "Service in Jesus Christ," in *Theological Foundations for Ministry*, ed. Ray S. Anderson (Grand Rapids, Mich.: Eerdmans, 1979), p. 724.

[6]Ronald M. Enroth, *Churches That Abuse* (Grand Rapids, Mich.: Zondervan, 1991).

[7]See Dietrich Bonhoeffer, *Letters and Papers From Prison*, enlarged ed. (New York: Macmillan, 1972), pp. 300, 344, 362.

[8]Karl Barth, *Church Dogmatics*, vol. 4 pt. 3, trans. Geoffrey Bromiley and Thomas Torrance (Edinburgh: T. & T. Clark, 1962), p. 780.

Chapter 4: A Vision of Emancipation and Consecration

[1]John de Gruchy defends a version of liberation theology as essential to the gospel of Christ: "There is no other gospel. Liberation theology does not reduce salvation to something we can achieve by our effort or merit. On the contrary, the gospel of God's saving grace in Jesus Christ is proclaimed as that power which liberates men and women from sin and enables them to

serve others in the struggle for justice in the world" ("No Other Gospel: Is Liberation Theology a Reduction of the Gospel?" in *Incarnational Ministry: The Presence of Christ in Church, Society and Family*, ed. Christian D. Kettler and Todd H. Speidell [Colorado Springs, Colo.: Helmers and Howard, 1990], p. 187).

[2]For a discussion of addiction and perspectives on overcoming it, see William Lenters, *The Freedom We Crave: Addiction as a Human Condition* (Grand Rapids, Mich.: Eerdmans, 1985); Archibald Hart, *Healing Life's Addictions* (Ann Arbor, Mich.: Servant, 1990); G. May, *Addiction and Grace* (San Francisco: Harper & Row, 1988); J. VanVonderen, *Good News for the Chemically Dependent: How a Healthy Family Can Help Free a Loved One from the Bonds of Addiction* (New York: Nelson, 1985).

Chapter 5: A Vision of Entitlement and Empowerment

[1]I have discussed the issue of the maleness of Jesus with respect to the incarnation in "The Incarnation of God in Feminist Christology: A Theological Critique," in *Speaking the Christian God*, ed. Alvin F. Kimmel (Grand Rapids, Mich.: Eerdmans, 1992).

[2]Werner Jeanrond, "Community and Authority," in *On Being the Church: Essays on the Christian Community,* ed. Colin E. Gunton and Daniel W. Hardy (Edinburgh: T. & T. Clark, 1989), p. 96. He goes on to say, "That the Christian community needs some form of leadership nobody doubts. That the Christian community needs an ordained ministry, however, cannot be taken for granted, but needs to be discussed with reference to both the theological demands of the Christian faith and the organisational demands of a contemporary human association. Given these requirements it seems rather odd that in some Churches the particular understanding of the ordained ministry is still focused on the now obsolete metaphysical understanding of past times and on the organisational needs of medieval congregations. Most urgently needed is a reassessment of the relationship between the ordained minister and the ordained community" (p. 98).

[3]For a helpful discussion of the situation at Ephesus, which sheds light on the meaning of Paul's injunction to Timothy, see Richard Kroeger and Catherine C. Kroeger, *I Suffer Not a Woman: Rethinking 1 Timothy 2:11-15 in Light of Ancient Evidence* (Grand Rapids, Mich.: Baker Book House, 1992). The Kroegers produce evidence that a Gnostic sect existed at Ephesus that taught that Eve was spiritually superior to Adam and, as a female, offered more direct access to deity than did a male. Paul's statement to Timothy could then be read: "I do not permit the teaching that women have authority over men."

[4]This is Paul Jewett's position in *Man as Male and Female* (Grand Rapids, Mich.: Eerdmans, 1975).

[5]"The history of creation is a great cosmic prelude and example of that history

of Israel which is the proper theme of the Old Testament. Creation is the outward basis of the Covenant (Genesis 1) and the covenant is the inward basis of creation (Genesis 2)" (Karl Barth, *Church Dogmatics*, vol. 4 pt. 1, trans. Geoffrey Bromiley and Thomas Torrance [Edinburgh: T. & T. Clark, 1959], p. 27). See also *Church Dogmatics*, vol. 3 pt. 1, pp. 94ff., 288ff. and especially pp. 231-32; Otto Weber, *Foundation of Dogmatics* (Grand Rapids, Mich.: Eerdmans, 1983), 1:494, 496, 500.

[6]See John Stott, *Issues Facing Christians Today* (London: Marshall, Morgan and Scott, 1984; Old Tappan, N.J.: Revell, 1985), pp. 249-54.

[7]This is the position taken by C. E. B. Cranfield, "*Diakonia* in the New Testament," in *Service in Christ*, ed. James McCord and T. H. L. Parker (Grand Rapids, Mich.: Eerdmans, 1966).

[8]Edward Schillebeeckx, *The Church with a Human Face: A New and Expanded Theology of Ministry* (New York: Crossroad, 1985), pp. 38-39.

[9]See my essay "The Resurrection of Jesus as Hermeneutical Criterion: A Case for Sexual Parity in Pastoral Ministry," *TSF Bulletin*, March-April 1986.

[10]Jürgen Moltmann, *The Way of Jesus Christ: Christology in Messianic Dimensions* (San Francisco: Harper & Row, 1990), pp. 43-44. This follows closely my own suggestion that Christopraxis has hermeneutical significance in relating the effects of Christ's contemporary work with the inspired Word of Christ in Scripture.

Chapter 6: A Pauline Perspective

[1]For a discussion of the emergence of the concept of the incarnation of a preexistent Logos in the Synoptic Gospels and in Paul's writings, see James D. G. Dunn, *Christology in the Making* (Philadelphia: Westminster Press, 1980). According to Dunn, Paul viewed Jesus as the "embodiment of God's wisdom." Commenting on Paul's use of wisdom in his first letter to the Corinthians, Dunn says: "In other words, *Christ is being identified here not with a pre-existent being but with the creative power and action of God.* And the thought is not of Christ as pre-existent but of the creative act and power of God now embodied in a final and complete way in Christ" (p. 182; emphasis in the original). At the same time Dunn concludes by saying, "Herein we see the origin of the doctrine of the incarnation" (p. 212).

[2]David F. Ford. "Faith in the Cities: Corinth and the Modern City," in *On Being the Church: Essays on the Christian Community*. ed. Colin E. Gunton and Daniel W. Hardy (Edinburgh: T. & T. Clark, 1989), p. 248. Because Paul's concept of authority was grounded in the eschatological as well as the historical Christ, Ford says: "Perhaps on no other area are Churches so subject to legalisms, bondage to the past, entanglement with distorting interests and idolatries than in that of authority. Paul's clarity about his ministry as helping to realise God's future and his refusal to absolutise past or present is a principle of

liberation with wide relevance. At its heart is the great symbol of authority, the glory of God, enabling freedom and confidence, inspiring a whole community in energetic mutuality and glorifying of God, while recognising that the full transformation into the glory is to come (2 Cor. 3). And incarnating the glory of God is the fact of Christ, the ultimate embodiment of a persuasive, vulnerable authority, freely distributed through his Spirit" (p. 253).

[3] See my essay "The Resurrection of Jesus as Hermeneutical Criterion," *TSF Bulletin,* January-February 1986.

[4] Edward Schillebeeckx, *The Church with a Human Face: A New and Expanded Theology of Ministry* (New York: Crossroad, 1985), p. 206.

[5] John Zizioulas, *Being as Communion: Studies in Personhood and the Church* (Crestwood, N.Y.: St. Vladimir's Press, 1985). In particular, he says, "Now if *becoming* history is the particularity of the Son in the economy, what is the contribution of the Spirit? Well, precisely the opposite: it is to liberate the Son and the economy from the bondage of history. If the Son dies on the cross, thus succumbing to the bondage of historical existence, it is the Spirit which raises him from the dead. The Spirit is the *beyond* history, and when he acts in history he does so in order to bring into history the last days, the *eschaton*" (p. 130).

[6] Colin E. Gunton, "The Church on Earth: The Roots of Community," in *On Being the Church: Essays on the Christian Community,* ed. Colin E. Gunton and Daniel W. Hardy (Edinburgh: T. & T. Clark, 1989). In particular, he says, "What is required, therefore, is a reconsideration of the relation of pneumatology and christology, with a consequent reduction of stress on the Church's institution by Christ and a greater emphasis on its constitution by the Spirit. In such a way we may create fewer self-justifying and historicising links with the past and give more stress to the necessity for the present particularities of our churchly arrangements to be constituted by the Spirit. . . . What is needed is, rather, a greater emphasis on the action of the Holy Spirit towards Jesus as the source of the *particularity* and so historicity of his humanity" (pp. 62-63).

Chapter 7: An Apostolic Mandate

[1] Karl Barth restates the traditional case for the Protestant view of apostolic authority when he says, "The apostolic community means concretely the community which hears the apostolic witness of the New Testament, which implies that of the Old, and recognises and puts this witness into effect as the source and norm of its existence. The apostolic Church is the Church which accepts and reads the Scriptures in their specific character as the direct attestation of Jesus Christ alive yesterday and today. . . . The Church is apostolic and therefore catholic when it exists on the basis of Scripture and

in conformity with it" (*Church Dogmatics,* vol. 4 pt.1, trans. Geoffrey Bromiley and Thomas Torrance [Edinburgh: T. & T. Clark, 1959], p. 722). See also C. K. Barrett, *The Signs of an Apostle* (New York: Harper & Row, 1970); K. H. Rengstorf, *Apostleship and Ministry* (St. Louis: Concordia, 1969).

[2]Jürgen Moltmann, *The Church in the Power of the Spirit* (New York: Harper & Row, 1977), pp. 83, 80, 199, 204-5.

[3]Wolfhart Pannenberg, *The Church* (Philadelphia: Westminster Press, 1983), pp. 56-57.

[4]Ibid.

[5]Hans Küng, *Truthfulness: The Future of the Church* (London: Sheed and Ward, 1968), pp. 126, 51, 215.

Chapter 8: An Emerging Church

[1]"We must understand that God is the measure of all reality and propriety, understand that eternity exists first and then time, and therefore the future first and then the present, as surely as the Creator exists first and then the creature. He who understands that need take no offense here." Karl Barth, *Church Dogmatics,* vol. 1 pt. 1, trans. G. W. Bromiley, 2nd ed. (Edinburgh: T. & T. Clark, 1975), p. 531.

[2]Emil Brunner has argued the thesis that the earlier Pauline ecclesiology based on the ecclesial community under the direction of the Spirit stands opposed in the New Testament to the Jerusalem form of the "church." He also argues that by the end of the New Testament period, the Pauline community had given way to the hierarchical and institutional form of the church. See *Dogmatics,* vol. 3, *The Christian Doctrine of the Church, Faith and the Consummation* (London: Lutterworth, 1962). He presented this thesis earlier in *The Misunderstanding of the Church* (London: Lutterworth, 1952). Karl Barth's response and criticism of Brunner's thesis is found in *Church Dogmatics,* vol. 4 pt. 2, trans. Geoffrey Bromiley and Thomas Torrance (Edinburgh: T. & T. Clark, 1962), pp. 683-87. Otto Weber, while not following Brunner's argument to its conclusion, also suggests that the New Testament "always conceives of the *Eklesia* as the 'eschatological community of salvation,'" and that this is based on the fact that the coming Christ is the present Christ in the community. *Foundations of Dogmatics,* trans. Darrell Guder (Grand Rapids, Mich.: Eerdmans, 1983), 2:514-15.

[3]Even the Roman Catholic theologian Hans Küng suggests that traditional ecclesiology has given priority to the Pastoral Epistles as well as the Acts of the Apostles, which tend to locate the authority and order of the church in the office and the transmission of authority through the laying on of hands, and neglects the pneumatological and charismatic order of the church. "The rediscovery of the charisms is a rediscovery of specifically Pauline ecclesiology, the importance of which for the problems of Cathol-

icism and ecumenism cannot be overstated." Hans Küng, *The Church* (New York: Sheed and Ward, 1967), pp. 180-81.

Chapter 9: A Charismatic Dynamic

[1]Annie Dillard, *Holy the Firm* (New York: Harper & Row, 1977), p. 59.

[2]For report and subsequent discussion of this issue, see *Ministry and the Miraculous,* ed. Lewis Smedes (Grand Rapids, Mich.: Eerdmans, 1987).

[3]An important contribution to a mission theology from the perspective of a charismatic Anglican is the book by Thomas S. Smail, *The Forgotten Father* (Grand Rapids, Mich.: Eerdmans, 1980). Smail argues that the charismatic experience of the Holy Spirit leads directly into the inner relation between the Son and the Father. The neglect of this theological grounding in the Trinity, suggests Smail, can lead the pentecostal experience into a renewal experience as a spiritual end in itself without producing the renewal of all of the structures of life as grounded in the Creator and renewing Father through the reconciliation of the world achieved by Christ as the Son of the Father. This supports my contention that a theology of Pentecost leads directly to a trinitarian theology, while a church theology of the Trinity may not produce a theology and experience of Pentecost.

[4]C. Peter Wagner, *How to Have a Healing Ministry Without Making Your Church Sick* (Ventura, Calif.: Regal Books, 1988), pp. 16-17.

[5]Ibid., pp. 23ff.

[6]See John Wimber with Kevin Springer, *Power Evangelism* (San Francisco: Harper & Row, 1986). Critical appraisals of this movement can be found in *Wonders and the Word: An Examination of Issues Raised by John Wimber and the Vineyard Movement,* ed. James R. Coggins and Paul G. Hiebert (Hillsboro, Kans.: Kindred, 1989); and John White, *When the Spirit Comes with Power: Signs and Wonders Among God's People* (Downers Grove, Ill.: InterVarsity Press, 1988).

[7]Wagner, *How to Have a Healing Ministry,* pp. 113ff.

[8]Dietrich Bonhoeffer in *Christ the Center* (San Francisco: Harper & Row, 1978) suggests that the first question that must be asked concerning Jesus Christ is "Who?" not "What?" or "How?" This approach sets aside metaphysical speculation concerning the natures of Christ and goes directly to the essential issue of his person as the very being and revelation of God in the form of Jesus of Nazareth.

[9]The issue of the relation of an evangelism that is directed toward individual salvation as contrasted with a gospel of the kingdom that seeks social justice and transformation of society has been a continuing debate within the Lausanne Conference movement, with John Stott as a primary spokesperson. See *Evangelism and Social Responsibility: An Evangelical Commitment* (London: Paternoster, 1982). A more recent discussion between John Stott and David Edwards can be found in *Evangelical Essentials: A Liberal-Evangelical Dialogue*

(Downers Grove, Ill.: InterVarsity Press, 1988), pp. 273-331. The prevailing theology of the church growth movement tends to divide social responsibility from evangelism, giving priority to evangelism, but also attempting to include social responsibility as indispensable to the mission of the church though not a primary form of the church's mission. See, for example, George W. Peters, *A Theology of Church Growth* (Grand Rapids, Mich.: Zondervan, 1981). The apostles, Peters writes, "put spiritual ministries before social and material services, . . . combined prayer with preaching without allowing either to usurp the place of the other . . . [and] put evangelism before all other ministries" (p. 125).

[10]Wagner, *How to Have a Healing Ministry,* p. 106.

[11]Ibid., pp. 100-101.

[12]C. Peter Wagner, *Warfare Prayer* (Ventura, Calif.: Regal Books, 1992). Wagner also deals with the issue of social transformation in *Breaking the Strongholds in Your City* (Ventura, Calif.: Regal, 1993).

[13]Smail, *Forgotten Father,* p. 179.

[14]Dietrich Ritschl makes this point well: "The natural affects human existence by limiting it in three ways, in place, power, and time. These are more fundamental anthropological constants than the human drives and desires to which so much attention is paid in classical theology" *(The Logic of Theology,* trans. John Bowden [Philadelphia: Fortress, 1987], p. 232).

[15]James B. Torrance, "The Vicarious Humanity of Jesus Christ," in *The Incarnation: Ecumenical Studies in the Nicene-Constantinopolitan Creed, A.D. 381,* ed. Thomas F. Torrance (Edinburgh: Handsel, 1981), p. 130.

[16]Todd Speidell, "Incarnational Social Ethics," in *Incarnational Ministry: The Presence of Christ in Church, Society and Family,* ed. Christian D. Kettler and Todd H. Speidell (Colorado Springs, Colo.: Helmers and Howard, 1990), p. 146.

Chapter 10: A Concern for Truthful Life

[1]See Emil Brunner, *Dogmatics,* vol. 3, *The Christian Doctrine of the Church, Faith and the Consummation* (London: Lutterworth, 1962); *The Misunderstanding of the Church* (London: Lutterworth, 1952).

[2]John D. Zizioulas, *Being as Communion: Studies in Personhood and the Church* (Crestwood, N.Y.: St. Vladimir's Press, 1985), p. 78.

[3]Charles Davis, *Theology and Political Society: The Hulsean Lectures in the University of Cambridge, 1978* (Cambridge, U.K.: Cambridge University Press, 1980), p. 130.

[4]Thomas F. Torrance, *The Mediation of Christ* (Exeter, U.K.: Paternoster, 1983; new ed. Colorado Springs, Colo.: Helmers and Howard, 1992), pp. 78-79.

[5]A contemporary example of a church that cloaked itself in theological orthodoxy and yet claimed divine providence in its doctrine of apartheid is the Dutch Reformed Church in South Africa. The Afrikaner church defended its position by pointing to its largely successful mission work and the

resulting formation of churches among the blacks. At the same time, the practice of separating black Christians from white Christians in the body of Christ reverses the reconciliation and redemption of humanity that Christ came to accomplish. Under the banner of orthodoxy the Dutch Reformed Church undergirded apartheid as public policy and insisted on the separation of people of color from the whites as a fundamental pillar in its own theology of the church. See my essay "Toward a Post-Apartheid Theology in South Africa," *The Journal of Theology for South Africa,* June 1988.

[6]The rejection of orthodoxy as an epistemological and hermeneutical criterion is a well-known theme in liberation theology, with varying degrees of emphasis. The seminal work in liberation theology written by Gustavo Gutiérrez sets the agenda for this position; see *A Theology of Liberation: History, Politics and Salvation,* trans. and ed. Sister Caridad Inda and John Eagleson (Maryknoll, N.Y.: Orbis, 1973). See also Leonardo Boff, *Jesus Christ Liberator: A Critical Christology for Our Time,* trans. Patrick Hughes (Maryknoll, N.Y.: Orbis, 1978); and Jon Sobrino, *Christology at the Crossroads: A Latin American Approach,* trans. John Drury (Maryknoll, N.Y.: Orbis, 1978). A more recent and more critical view of orthopraxis as a substitute for orthodoxy can be found in the comprehensive work by Clodovis Boff, *Theology and Praxis: Epistemological Foundations* (Maryknoll, N.Y.: Orbis, 1987). While sympathetic to the concerns expressed in the move toward orthopraxy, Boff suggests that praxis is "not what explains" but "what must be explained" (p. 200).

[7]Ibid., pp. 199-200.

[8]Johann B. Metz, *Faith in History and Society: Toward a Practical Fundamental Theology,* trans. David Smith (New York: Seabury, 1980), p. 92. The "dangerous memory" to which Metz refers is the radical and eschatological contemporaneity of Jesus Christ breaking into our history: "This definite memory breaks through the magic circle of the prevailing consciousness. It regards history as something more than a screen for contemporary interests. It mobilizes tradition as a dangerous tradition and therefore as a liberating force in respect of the one-dimensional character and certainty of the one whose 'hour is always there' (Jn 7.6). It gives rise again and again to the suspicion that the plausible structures of a society may be relationships aimed to delude. . . . Christian faith can and must, in my opinion, be seen in this way as a subversive memory. . . . The criterion of its authentic Christianity is the liberating and redeeming danger with which it introduces the remembered freedom of Jesus into modern society and the forms of consciousness and praxis in that society" (p. 90).

[9]Metz, *Faith in History and Society,* p. 57-58. Later he says, "In faith, Christians accomplish the *memoria passionis, mortis et resurrectionis Jesu Christi.* In faith, they remember the testament of Christ's love, in which the kingdom of God

appeared among men by initially establishing that kingdom between men, by Jesus' confession of himself as the one who was on the side of the oppressed and rejected and by his proclamation of the coming kingdom of God as the liberating power of unconditional love. This *memoria Jesu Christi* is not a memory which deceptively dispenses Christians from the risks involved in the future. It is not a middle-class counter-figure to hope. On the contrary, it anticipates the future as a future of those who are oppressed, without hope and doomed to fail. It is therefore a dangerous and at the same time liberating memory that oppresses and questions the present because it reminds us not of some open future, but precisely this future and because it compels Christians constantly to change themselves so that they are able to take this future into account" (p. 90).

[10]Dennis McCann and Charles Strain, *Polity and Praxis: A Program for American Practical Theology* (New York: Seabury, 1985), pp. 40, 45, 142.

[11]Metz, *Faith in History and Society,* p. 127.

[12]Ibid., pp. 73ff.

[13]Ibid., p. 133.

[14]Todd Speidell, "The Incarnation as the Hermeneutical Criterion for Liberation and Reconciliation," *Scottish Journal of Theology* 40 (1987): 253. See also his essay "Incarnational Social Ethics," in *Incarnational Ministry: The Presence of Christ in Church, Society and Family,* ed. Christian D. Kettler and Todd H. Speidell (Colorado Springs, Colo.: Helmers and Howard, 1990), pp. 140-52.

[15]Dietrich Bonhoeffer, *Meditating on the Word,* trans. and ed. David McI. Gracie (Cambridge, Mass.: Cowley, 1986), p. 135.

Chapter 11: The Christ of the City

[1]For some of what follows I have drawn upon my essay "The Humanity of God and the Soul of a City," *Theology, News and Notes* (Fuller Theological Seminary), June 1992.

[2]Dietrich Bonhoeffer, *The Cost of Discipleship,* trans. R. H. Fuller et al. (New York: Macmillan, 1963), p. 207.

[3]Johannes Verkuyl, *Break Down the Walls: A Cry for Racial Justice,* ed. and trans. Lewis Smedes (Grand Rapids, Mich.: Eerdmans, 1973), p. 144.

[4]Adrio König, a member of the Dutch Reformed Church in South Africa and professor of systematic theology and ethics at the University of South Africa, writes: "What makes the separation of apartheid so bad is that it is enforced, and that it benefits one group and harms the other group. It is actually not separation, but a marginalization of the blacks away from the center of the country. Thus apartheid is essentially the exploitation, humiliation, and oppression of certain people over against the inclusion and advantage of the other group, who knowing or unknowingly plays the role of the oppressor"

("Covenant and Image: Theological Anthropology, Human Interrelatedness and Apartheid," in *Incarnational Ministry: The Presence of Christ in Church, Society and Family*, ed. Christian D. Kettler and Todd H. Speidell [Colorado Springs, Colo.: Helmers and Howard, 1990], p. 163).

[5]Barth goes on to say, "Solidarity with the world means full commitment to it, unreserved participation in its situation, in the promise given it by creation, in its responsibility for the arrogance, sloth and falsehood which reign within it, in its suffering under the resultant distress, but primarily and supremely in the free grace of God demonstrated and addressed to it in Jesus Christ, and therefore in its hope. . . . Solidarity with the world means that those who are genuinely pious approach the children of the world as such, that those who are genuinely righteous are not ashamed to sit down with the unrighteous as friends, that those who are genuinely wise do not hesitate to seem to be fools among fools, and that those who are genuinely holy are not too good or irreproachable to go down into 'hell' in a very secular fashion. . . . Since Jesus Christ is the Savior of the world, [the church] can exist in worldly fashion, not unwillingly nor with a bad conscience, but willingly and with a good conscience. It consists in the recognition that its members also bear in themselves and in some way actualise all human possibilities" (*Church Dogmatics*, vol. 4 pt. 3, trans. Geoffrey Bromiley and Thomas Torrance [Edinburgh: T. & T. Clark, 1962], pp. 773-74).

[6]James B. Torrance, "The Vicarious Humanity of Christ," in *The Incarnation: Ecumenical Studies in the Nicene-Constantinopolitan Creed A.D. 381*, ed. Thomas F. Torrance (Edinburgh: Handsel, 1981), p. 141.

[7]For this discussion of *adventus* and *futurum* I am indebted to the essay by Jürgen Moltmann, "Theological Perspectives on the Future," paper presented at the Lutheran Brotherhood Colloquium, Houston, Texas, January 29, 1979.

[8]Ray S. Anderson, unpublished journal notes, December 1, 1964.

Epilogue

[1]For a discussion of the contemporary situation with regard to theological education, see *Shifting Boundaries: Contextual Approaches to the Structure of Theological Education*, ed. Barbara G. Wheeler and Edward Farley (Louisville, Ky.: Westminster/John Knox, 1991).

[2]Emil Brunner, *The Misunderstanding of the Church* (London: Lutterworth, 1952).

[3]Writing from within the context of the South African theological tradition, John de Gruchy says, "Theological reflection within the community of faith has, then, the task of being critical of the tradition in which it stands. . . . The practical theologian, at that moment of theological reflection in the pastoral-hermeneutical circle, draws on the insights and symbols of the tradition

in order to help the community of faith find its way. In particular, the practical theologian reappropriates those symbols in the tradition which communicate the liberating and transforming power of the gospel of the Kingdom of God in Jesus Christ" (*Theology and Ministry in Context and Crisis: A South African Perspective* [Grand Rapids, Mich.: Eerdmans, 1987], pp. 153-54).

[4]Edward Farley has made a trenchant and provocative critique of this trend in *Theologia: The Fragmentation and Unity of Theological Education* (Philadelphia: Fortress, 1983): "Theology as a personal quality continues (though not usually under the term *theology*), not as a salvation-disposed wisdom, but as the practical know-how necessary to ministerial work. Theology as a discipline continues, not as the unitary enterprise of theological study, but as one technical and specialised scholarly undertaking among others; in other words, as systematic theology" (p. 39).

Wolfhart Pannenberg argues for the unity of the theological disciplines from the perspective of the historical integrity of theology as a science, alongside of the other disciplines in the university curriculum. See *Theology and the Philosophy of Science* (Philadelphia: Westminister Press, 1976). For a critique of both Farley and Pannenberg, see Richard Muller, *The Study of Theology: From Biblical Interpretation to Contemporary Formulation* (Grand Rapids, Mich.: Zondervan, 1991), pp. 45-60. Muller's own approach leans closer to Pannenberg's search for objectivity through the discipline of historical methodology and, as such, is a textbook example of what I have called an "institutional church theology." One looks in vain for any mention of the Holy Spirit in his depiction of the theological task, either as part of the hermeneutical circle or as the praxis of Christ in the mission of the people of God.

[5]I would argue, though this is not the time or place, that Karl Barth offers more encouragement for the development of a mission theology than does any other modern theologian. His fascination with the Blumhardts, who took Pentecost seriously and who saw the manifestation of the "signs and wonders" of the kingdom of God, caused him to lean ever so slightly in the direction of a praxis of the Spirit as a theological hermeneutic. His emphasis on the present and historical reality of the Holy Spirit as the ontological connection with the inner relation of the Father and the Son provides a beginning point for a mission theology that is both incarnational and trinitarian. His emphasis on the nature of the church as "proclamation event" produced a dialectic that prevented nature from encapsulating grace. What remained elusive for him, however, was the dynamic of Pentecost as related to the formation of the church through the Spirit's ministry in the world *extra ecclesia*. In the end he retreated from the kingdom theology of the Blumhardts and produced a church theology with the world already encompassed by the eschatological

reality of the incarnate Word of God. We can learn from Barth, but must go beyond him for the sake of integrating Pentecost with incarnation and the mission of the church with the nature of the church.

[6]See my essay "Christopraxis: Competence as a Criterion for Theological Education," *Theological Students Fellowship (TSF) Bulletin,* January-February 1984.

Bibliography

Anderson, Ray S. "Christopraxis: Competence as a Criterion for Theological Education." *Theological Students Fellowship (TSF) Bulletin*, January-February 1984.

———. "The Humanity of God and the Soul of a City." *Theology, News and Notes* (Fuller Theological Seminary), June 1992.

———. "The Incarnation of God in Feminist Christology: A Theological Critique." In *Speaking the Christian God*, ed. Alvin F. Kimmel. Grand Rapids, Mich.: Eerdmans, 1992.

———. "The Resurrection of Jesus as Hermeneutical Criterion," Part One. *TSF Bulletin*, January-February 1986.

———. "The Resurrection of Jesus as Hermeneutical Criterion—A Case for Sexual Parity in Pastoral Ministry," Part Two. *TSF Bulletin* March-April 1986.

———. "Toward a Post-Apartheid Theology in South Africa." *The Journal of Theology for South Africa*, June 1988.

———, ed. *Theological Foundations for Ministry*. Grand Rapids, Mich.: Eerdmans, 1979.

Aristotle. *The Nichomachean Ethics*. Trans. J. E. C. Welldon. New York: Prometheus Books, 1987.

Barrett, C. K. *The Signs of an Apostle*. New York: Harper & Row, 1970.

Barth, Karl. *Church Dogmatics* 1/1. 2nd ed. Trans. G. W. Bromiley. Edinburgh: T. & T. Clark, 1975.

———. *Church Dogmatics* 4/1-3. Trans. Geoffrey Bromiley and Thomas Torrance. Edinburgh: T. & T. Clark, 1959-62.

Boer, Harry R. *Pentecost and Missions*. Grand Rapids, Mich.: Eerdmans, 1961.

Boff, Clodovis. *Theology and Praxis: Epistemological Foundations*. Maryknoll, N.Y.: Orbis, 1987.

Boff, Leonardo. *Jesus Christ Liberator: A Critical Christology for Our Time*. Trans. Patrick Hughes. Maryknoll, N.Y.: Orbis, 1978.

Bonhoeffer, Dietrich. *Christ the Center*. San Francisco: Harper & Row, 1978.

_____. *The Cost of Discipleship.* Trans. R. H. Fuller et al. New York: Macmillan, 1963.

_____. *Letters and Papers From Prison.* New and enl. ed. New York: Macmillan, 1972.

_____. *Meditating on the Word.* Trans. and ed. David McI. Gracie. Cambridge, Mass.: Cowley, 1986.

Brown, Colin. *Miracles and the Critical Mind.* Grand Rapids, Mich.: Eerdmans, 1984.

_____. *That You May Believe: Miracles and Faith Then and Now.* Grand Rapids, Mich.: Eerdmans, 1985.

Brunner, Emil. *Dogmatics.* Vol. 3, *The Christian Doctrine of the Church, Faith and the Consummation.* London: Lutterworth, 1962.

_____. *The Misunderstanding of the Church.* London: Lutterworth, 1952.

Capra, Fritjof. *The Turning Point: Science, Society and the Rising Culture.* London: Collins/Fontana, 1963.

Capra, Fritjof, and David Steindle-Rast. *Belonging to the Universe: Explorations on the Frontiers of Science and Spirituality.* San Francisco: Harper, 1991.

Coggins, James R., and Paul G. Hiebert, eds. *Wonders and the Word: An Examination of Issues Raised by John Wimber and the Vineyard Movement.* Hillsboro, Kans.: Kindred, 1989.

Costas, Orlando. *The Church and Its Mission: A Shattering Critique from the Third World.* Wheaton, Ill.: Tyndale House/Philadelphia: Westminster Press, 1980.

Davis, Charles. *Theology and Political Society: The Hulsean Lectures in the University of Cambridge, 1978.* Cambridge, U.K.: Cambridge University Press, 1980.

De Gruchy, John. "No Other Gospel: Is Liberation Theology a Reduction of the Gospel?" In *Incarnational Ministry: The Presence of Christ in Church, Society and Family,* ed. Christian D. Kettler and Todd H. Speidell. Colorado Springs, Colo.: Helmers and Howard, 1990.

_____. *Theology and Ministry in Context and Crisis: A South African Perspective.* Grand Rapids, Mich.: Eerdmans, 1987.

Dillard, Annie. *Holy the Firm.* New York: Harper & Row, 1977.

Dunn, J. D. G. *Christology in the Making.* Philadelphia: Westminster Press, 1980.

Edwards, David, and John Stott. *Evangelical Essentials: A Liberal-Evangelical Dialogue.* Downers Grove, Ill.: InterVarsity Press, 1988.

Enroth, Ronald M. *Churches That Abuse.* Grand Rapids, Mich.: Zondervan, 1991.

Farley, Edward. *Theologia: The Fragmentation and Unity of Theological Education.* Philadelphia: Fortress, 1983.

Firet, Jacob. *Dynamics in Pastoring.* Trans. John Vriend. Grand Rapids, Mich.: Eerdmans, 1986.

Ford, David F. "Faith in the Cities: Corinth and the Modern City." In *On Being the Church: Essays on the Christian Community,* ed. Colin E. Gunton and Daniel

W. Hardy. Edinburgh: T. & T. Clark, 1989.

Gunton, Colin E. "The Church on Earth: The Roots of Community." In *On Being the Church: Essays on the Christian Community,* ed. Colin E. Gunton and Daniel W. Hardy. Edinburgh: T. & T. Clark, 1989.

Gutiérrez, Gustavo. *A Theology of Liberation: History, Politics and Salvation.* Trans. and ed. Caridad Inda and John Eagleson. Maryknoll, N.Y.: Orbis, 1973.

Hall, Douglas John. *Thinking the Faith: Christian Theology in a North American Context.* Minneapolis: Augsburg, 1989.

Hart, Archibald. *Healing Life's Addictions.* Ann Arbor, Mich.: Servant, 1990.

Herzog, Fredrick. *God Walk: Liberation Shaping Dogmatics.* Maryknoll, N.Y.: Orbis, 1988.

Ibsen, Henrik. *Four Plays of Ibsen.* Trans. R. V. Forslund. New York: Chilton, 1968.

Jeanrond, Werner. "Community and Authority." In *On Being the Church: Essays on the Christian Community,* ed. Colin E. Gunton and Daniel W. Hardy. Edinburgh: T. & T. Clark, 1989.

Jewett, Paul. *Man As Male and Female.* Grand Rapids, Mich.: Eerdmans, 1975.

König, Adrio. "Covenant and Image: Theological Anthropology, Human Interrelatedness and Apartheid." In *Incarnational Ministry: The Presence of Christ in Church, Society and Family,* ed. Christian D. Kettler and Todd H. Speidell. Colorado Springs, Colo.: Helmers and Howard, 1990.

Kroeger, Richard, and Catherine Kroeger. *I Suffer Not a Woman: Rethinking 1 Timothy 2:11-15 in Light of Ancient Evidence.* Grand Rapids, Mich.: Baker Book House, 1992.

Küng, Hans. *The Church.* London: Sheed and Ward, 1967.

_____. *Truthfulness: The Future of the Church.* London: Sheed and Ward, 1968.

Lampe, G. W. H. *God as Spirit.* Oxford, U.K.: Clarendon, 1977.

Lenters, William. *The Freedom We Crave: Addiction as a Human Condition.* Grand Rapids, Mich.: Eerdmans, 1984.

May, G. *Addiction and Grace.* San Francisco: Harper & Row, 1988.

McCann, Dennis, and Charles Strain. *Polity and Praxis: A Program for American Practical Theology.* New York: Seabury, 1985.

Metz, Johann B. *Faith in History: Toward a Practical Fundamental Theology.* Trans. David Smith. New York: Seabury, 1980.

Moltmann, Jürgen. *The Church in the Power of the Spirit.* New York: Harper & Row, 1977.

_____. *The Way of Jesus Christ: Christology in Messianic Dimensions.* San Francisco: Harper & Row, 1990.

Muller, Richard. *The Study of Theology: From Biblical Interpretation to Contemporary Formulation.* Grand Rapids, Mich.: Zondervan, 1991.

Pannenberg, Wolfhart. *The Church.* Philadelphia: Westminster Press, 1983.

_____. *Theology and the Philosophy of Science.* Philadelphia: Westminster Press,

1976.

Peters, George W. *A Theology of Church Growth.* Grand Rapids, Mich.: Zondervan, 1981.

Rengstorf, K. H. *Apostleship and Ministry.* St. Louis: Concordia, 1969.

Ritschl, Dietrich. *The Logic of Theology.* Trans. John Bowden. Philadelphia: Fortress, 1987.

Schillebeeckx, Edward. *The Church with a Human Face: A New and Expanded Theology of Ministry.* New York: Crossroad, 1985.

Schwöbel, Christoph. "The Creation of the World: Recovering the Ecclesiology of the Reformers." In *On Being the Church: Essays on the Christian Community,* ed. Colin E. Gunton and Daniel W. Hardy. Edinburgh: T. & T. Clark, 1989.

Smail, Thomas S. *The Forgotten Father.* Grand Rapids, Mich.: Eerdmans, 1980.

Smedes, Lewis, ed. *Ministry and the Miraculous.* Grand Rapids, Mich.: Eerdmans, 1987.

Sobrino, Jon. *Christology at the Crossroads: A Latin American Approach.* Trans. John Drury. Maryknoll, N.Y.: Orbis, 1978.

Speidell, Todd. "The Incarnation as the Hermeneutical Criterion for Liberation and Reconciliation." *Scottish Journal of Theology* 40, no. 2 (1987).

_____. "Incarnational Social Ethics." In *Incarnational Ministry: The Presence of Christ in Church, Society and Family,* ed. Christian Ketter and Todd Speidell. Colorado Springs, Colo.: Helmers and Howard, 1990.

Stott, John. *Evangelism and Social Responsibility: An Evangelical Commitment.* London: Paternoster, 1982.

_____. *Issues Facing Christians Today.* London: Marshall, Morgan and Scott, 1984; Old Tappan, N.J.: Revell, 1985.

Torrance, James B. "The Vicarious Humanity of Jesus Christ." In *The Incarnation: Ecumenical Studies in the Nicene-Constantinopolitan Creed, A.D. 381,* ed. Thomas F. Torrance. Edinburgh: Handsel, 1981.

Torrance, Thomas. *The Christian Frame of Mind: Reason, Order and Openness in Theology and Natural Science.* Colorado Springs, Colo.: Helmers and Howard, 1989.

_____. *The Mediation of Christ.* Exeter, U.K.: Paternoster, 1983. New ed. Colorado Springs, Colo.: Helmers and Howard, 1992.

_____. "Service in Jesus Christ." In *Theological Foundations for Ministry,* ed. Ray S. Anderson. Grand Rapids, Mich.: Eerdmans, 1979.

VanVonderen, J. *Good News For the Chemically Dependent: How a Healthy Family Can Help Free a Loved One from the Bonds of Addiction.* New York: Thomas Nelson, 1985.

Verkuyl, Johannes. *Break Down the Walls: A Cry for Racial Justice.* Ed. and trans. Lewis Smedes. Grand Rapids, Mich.: Eerdmans, 1973.

Van Engen, Charles. *God's Missionary People: Rethinking the Purpose of the Local*

Church. Grand Rapids, Mich.: Baker Book House, 1991.

Wagner, C. Peter. *How to Have a Healing Ministry Without Making Your Church Sick.* Ventura, Calif.: Regal, 1988.

———. *Warfare Prayer.* Ventura, Calif.: Regal Books, 1992.

———, ed. *Breaking the Strongholds in Your City.* Ventura, Calif.: Regal, 1993.

Weber, Otto. *Foundations of Dogmatics.* Vol. 2. Grand Rapids, Mich.: Eerdmans, 1983.

Wheeler, Barbara G., and Edward Farley, eds. *Shifting Boundaries: Contextual Approaches to the Structure of Theological Education.* Louisville, Ky.: Westminster/John Knox, 1991.

White, John. *When the Spirit Comes with Power: Signs and Wonders Among God's People.* Downers Grove, Ill.: InterVarsity Press, 1988.

Will, James. *A Christology of Peace.* Louisville, Ky.: Westminster/John Knox, 1989.

Wimber, John, with Kevin Springer. *Power Evangelism.* San Francisco: Harper & Row, 1986.

Zizioulas, John. *Being as Communion: Studies in Personhood and the Church.* Crestwood, N.Y.: St. Vladimir's Press, 1985.

Index